# POMMIES

## England cricket through an Australian lens

William Buckland

# POMMIES

## England cricket through an Australian lens

Matador
9 De Montfort Mews
Leicester LE1 7FW, UK
Tel: (+44) 116 255 9311 / 9312
Email: books@troubador.co.uk
Web: www.troubador.co.uk/matador


ISBN 978 1906510 329


Typeset in 12pt Bembo by Troubador Publishing Ltd, Leicester, UK
Printed in the UK by TJ International Ltd, Padstow, Cornwall

**Matador** is an imprint of Troubador Publishing Ltd

*For Don Tandy, actor and raconteur,*
*who opened my eyes to the magic of the game.*

# CONTENTS

# PREFACE

This book is an investigation into England professional cricket addressed to all those who follow it in the UK. Written from a fan's perspective and with the interests of fans in mind, it covers both cricketing and commercial aspects of the game in the form of three chronological stories.

The first of these, Chapters 1 and 2, tracks my increasing curiosity about the way this game is run. It explains the need for an investigation and sets out the questions that need answering. The second section, Chapters 3 to 5, starts the investigation with a brief history of England and Australia cricket between 1972 and 2002. The last section, Chapters 6 and 7, completes the investigation with an examination of the years 2002 to 2007. The book concludes with a discussion of possible futures for the professional game in England.

Necessarily, there is some financial analysis and other detail, but most of this is relegated to an extensive notes section at the end. The notes explain which of the financial figures are estimates and which are exact, and how estimates were calculated. Cricket is stuffed to the gills with proper nouns and I have to assume some familiarity with the major cricket personalities. All statistics are correct as of 31 December 2007.

I would like to thank nine current or recent officials who gave me their time and insights. I refer to them in the text as *officials*. In response to a request for access to its documents archive and to key executives, the England & Wales Cricket Board (ECB) informed me that it had a policy regarding books about the game. This policy, it said, was to co-operate only if granted editorial control. Having just read the ECB's testimony to a House of Commons Select Committee inquiry into its television deal with British Sky Broadcasting (BSkyB), I declined to go along with this peculiar, and possibly quite new, policy.

Thanks to David Willis, David Brook and Richard Bevan for their time and help, and to staff at the British Library, Cambridge University Library, Companies House and the Financial Services Agency. I am grateful to my friend and editor, Robert Franklin, and to my brother James Buckland, my wife Tania November and friends Joe Ireland, Paul Ford, Mark Alban, Gerry Slora, Tim Hardman, John Adedoyin, Pete Flatt and Steve Davies for commenting on drafts of the manuscript.

I have no pecuniary interest in any of the proposals contained herein except as an ordinary cricket fan.


                                                    William Buckland
                                                           London
                                                     January 2008

# PROLOGUE

At about 6pm on 12 September 2005, two men strolled across the green turf of the Oval, London SE11. One, a tall, burly man, glanced gravely every few seconds at the other, an elderly gent in a suit. This gent looked as if he was being escorted to his own funeral.

Inside the pavilion, Kevin Pietersen was recounting his heroic deeds to the cameras, describing them, the occasion and everything else as 'fantastic'. Up above, the England team was cavorting in the changing room, players emerging sporadically to acknowledge the last-day crowd of real cricket fans. Many waved England flags. Others sang. All of them exulted at the best day in England cricket certainly since 1981 and quite possibly for a lot longer than that. Nobody was going anywhere.

As the two men ambled by, some fans applauded the gent as they had earlier in the day. Few seemed to pay any attention to the burly man, which was strange because statistically he was the second-best England all-rounder since World War Two.

While Channel 4's cameras followed Richie Benaud and Tony Greig across the turf, I tore myself away from the television and dug out a dusty copy of *Wisden* 1978. On page 123, it says:

> *G. Boycott was invited to take part in the scheme but declined. Richie Benaud and his Sports Consultancy Company were engaged in the management of the series. Many of the signings were carried out during the Centenary Test match in Melbourne, and the New Zealand-Australia series.*

Then, a quick search of the BBC archives revealed the following:

> *Over the coming weeks, Greig personally oversaw the recruitment of the World XI team that he was to captain. John Snow, Greig's*

*Sussex team-mate, and Kent's Alan Knott and Derek Underwood were both told to meet at London's Churchill hotel where 'something big' would be discussed. And with the help of representatives from JP Sport, the company Packer had assigned to orchestrate the project, and a 45-minute video from Ian Chappell, the Australia XI captain, attesting the legitimacy of the offer, Greig flew to Port-of-Spain, Trinidad, where Pakistan and West Indies were about to start a Test match.*

*'I signed eight players in two days,' Greig recalls, 'And I can tell you that it wasn't difficult. My problem was who to leave out.'*

After 42 years, Richie Benaud had completed his last commentary stint in Britain, his valedictory statement rudely interrupted by a wicked ball from Glenn McGrath that bowled Pietersen for 158. Benaud was the voice of cricket in England for more than a generation and gently initiated millions of novice fans into the game.

Not so Tony Greig. Although he commentates every season in Australia, he is rarely heard in the country whose cricket team he captained 14 times. He has long been an un-person in England, only receiving the honorary MCC life membership customarily given to ex-captains 21 years after his last Test. If his voice is known at all here, it is because of *The Twelfth Man*.

For about the last thousand years, with a few exceptions, the English have preferred to fight wars for control behind closed doors, using the dark arts of back-scratching and back-stabbing. We call it evolution: the accommodation of state and society to the forces of history without resort to the guillotine.

Greig's crime was to fight a war against the Establishment from the outside, in alliance with a man who had five things wrong with him from the traditional English perspective. Kerry Packer was a businessman. His God (apparently) was money. He was not Establishment. He did not mince his words. And he was an Australian.

Greig then committed an even greater sin. Together with Packer, Benaud, Ian Chappell, over 50 other international cricketers and a few top Australian business executives, he won. In the process, the International Cricket Council, the Marylebone Cricket Club and the Test and County Cricket Board were all made to look, as Benaud might have said, very stupid indeed.

# SECTION 1

# Effects

## CHAPTER 1

# INSPIRATION

*Under the Southern Cross I stand*
*A spring of wattle in my hand*
*A native of my native land*
*Australia, you fucking beauty!*

Rod Marsh at the Oval, 16 August 1972

Everybody remembers the first day they went to a Test match.

They remember the trip to the ground, where they sat and who they were with. They remember the weather and the crowd, the shape of the ground and the contents of their picnic box. And if, years later, they see the scorecard or a commentator mentions it, the whole day magically reconstitutes itself and they are instantly transported back 10, 30 or 60 years.

Some first-timers are lucky. Their first day is the Oval 2005 or Lord's 1990. Others are unlucky. Their first day is the Oval 1999 or a Headingley drizzler, with England 100–4 after seven rain interruptions. Most people see an average day: a few runs, a few wickets, nothing special. But everybody remembers.

I was one of the lucky ones. Mine was 12 August 1976, the first day of the Fifth Test between England and the West Indies at the Oval. I was ten. This day and the whole game are among the best-remembered since World War Two.

## West Indian ball

A month before, I switched on the family television set to see that England were fielding at Old Trafford and Mike Selvey was doing some damage to the West Indies, although Gordon Greenidge was still in. Tony Greig was our captain and Richie Benaud was commentating.

A few days later there was a family get-together and my uncle, an actor named Don Tandy, popped the question: would you like to go? On the television I had seen one West Indian throw the ball in flat from the boundary with an underarm flick, another help it over midwicket for six with a wave of the bat, and a third propel it past a hapless English batsman, over the keeper's head and into the boundary board. Whenever the West Indians came into contact with the ball, it went farther and faster than when our lot did. The umpires may have been English, but the ball was definitely West Indian.

For this boy switching on to the game, the West Indian team's talent was a feast. I knew nothing of Brixton, of C.L.R. James, or of how Africans got to the West Indies in the first place. Nor did I know that Greig had said on BBC *Sportsnight* at the beginning of the series that he would make the West Indians grovel.[1]

And so, in August 1976, I sat on the 64 bus in a state of uncontainable excitement. Don was born in 1918 and lived the early part of his life in Lambeth, a few hundred yards south of Waterloo station. On the way to the game he told me how he had gone down Harleyford Road one morning in 1934 on the upper deck of a tram and looked over the stand at the Oval to see Bill Ponsford and Don Bradman batting. Several hours later, on the way home, he peered over the stand again. Ponsford and Bradman were still batting. This was their stand of 451 for the second wicket, to this day the highest partnership in Ashes history. Then he told me that he had also been there in 1948 when Bradman was bowled by Eric Hollies for nought and received two standing ovations in five minutes: one out, one back.

Our seats were on the gasometer side, next to the old scoreboard. The Caribbean section[2] was directly in front of us and, like me, they could not keep still. Above them, the upper half of Bob Willis sprinted in from the Vauxhall End, his trademark right-arm motion making him look like he was pumping the handle of a railway trolley. Suddenly, there was a small thud, followed by a low shout, and then an almighty roar surrounded me like a crashing tidal wave. In the distance, Greenidge looked up to see the umpire's finger raised. He turned and trudged back towards the pavilion at a snail's pace. I decided to be a bowler.

The crowd settled back as Viv Richards marched in. A couple of early boundaries got the Caribbean section going. Then a crack reverberated across the ground as Richards square-cut the ball one bounce into the hands of a huge man right in front of me. The man flung the ball back and performed a madcap dance which meant: take that, Whitey. The rest of the day was Richards. The West Indies reached 373–3, Richards exactly 200 not out, Clive Lloyd about 70 not out. I decided to be a batsman.

Despite my pleas that we go again, Don went to work at the telephone exchange the next day. His big break—a run in *EastEnders*—lay in the future. On the television, I saw nine England players bowl as the West Indies accumulated 687 for eight.

On the evening of the second day, I joined my family holiday on the South Coast. The 1976 drought was at its peak and the New Forest was on fire. I saw Dennis Amiss reach his double century in our first innings with huge columns of smoke in the distance and the smell of smoke in my nostrils.

The rest of the game consisted of Michael Holding jogging in from the Vauxhall End and with his blur of an action pinging the batsman so fast as to shrink the pitch to half its size. He took 14 wickets for 149 in what Benaud was later to call 'one of the greatest pace bowling exhibitions it's ever been my pleasure to watch'. England reached 435 and the West Indies slogged 182–0 in 32 overs to set a target of 435. On the fifth day, England scratched out 203 and lost by 231 runs.

The little black-and-white television on which I saw Holding barely worked, so I had to lie on my stomach in front of it and twist the aerial constantly. It was in this position that I saw Greig's wicket splattered by a Holding yorker[3]. I decided to be a bowler.

The next summer, I tried to do Willis but my arm nearly flew out of its socket. In athletics I was a middle-distance runner, more like Holding than the sprinting Willis, so I lengthened my run-up and cultivated the fast jog and the blur release. So far, I have played about 750 games of recreational cricket, although I never played for a county. I have splattered one stump on a few occasions, but never two.

Two other boys saw Holding bowl at this Test, though. One was Jonathan Agnew, aged 16. The other was David 'Syd' Lawrence, aged 12.[4]

## Two for Two Hundred and Two

In the mid-nineties, a new phraseology entered recreational cricket in the UK. One would turn up at a ground, sit down on the bench in the front of the pavilion and within a few minutes some wag would incant 'We all know the Bill and Tony niggling aggro thing's working its arse off' or 'Tony Greig jammed another bunch of those fucking keys of his into the pitch'. Bill Lawry could be heard saying in his excited, high-pitched voice: 'Jesus, you're fucked in the head sometimes, Tony.' I once heard two players who had never previously met run through a competitive five-minute rendition of *The Twelfth Man*.

Slowly but surely, the Aussies took over from the West Indians in international cricket. In the recreational game, the big Caribbean bowler from the eighties was supplanted by the upright Aussie batter with his thunderous drives through the arc and slog-sweeps into the trees at midwicket. For England, the age of David Gower and Ian Botham wound down from the late eighties, leading to a miserable decade for the national team.

In the early 2000s, England got going again as attractive new players like Michael Vaughan and Andrew Flintoff arrived. In 2002, I played in a pro-am tournament where a South African Test player was the guest professional. I batted with him for half an hour and then asked him about his favourite grounds. He replied that Lord's is Lord's, Eden Gardens is India at its most raw and the Melbourne Cricket Ground (MCG) is a huge bowl. His favourite? The MCG.

So, in November 2002, I went to play some grade cricket, see the Australian cricketing machine in action and get a look at this place they call the MCG.

## The chat

When I arrived we were already down one-nil in the Test series. The tour started with the first three Tests, switched to one-day mode for December, then back to the Boxing Day and New Year's Tests, finally finishing with more one-day cricket in January. I was hoping to see four good Tests but England quickly slumped to a 0–3 defeat with only Michael Vaughan left standing.

The Channel Nine commentary was outstanding, though. There were four Australian captains in Benaud, Lawry, Mark Taylor and Ian Chappell, then Tony Greig and the chirpy Ian Healy, rounded off with new English commentator Mike Atherton. This team, especially Lawry, evinced the same excitable and boyish love of the game that makes BBC Radio Four's *Test Match Special* so popular.

On the field, I was quickly apprised of my position in the Australian pyramid. A single hierarchy in each city integrates park, grade and district cricket, with the state second and first teams at the top. Above that sit Australia A and then Australia. An elder statesman in my team told me, 'There's state pyramids plus the national pyramid above them. Makes one single pyramid, smooth and simple.' Apparently, I was fourth grade, with potential for third if I put in the effort.

In the bar after games, if I wasn't being evaluated myself, the England team was. I found myself expected to be an ambassador for my country. Many England cricketers and fans had experienced this, but even though I was warned in advance I was still unprepared.

'Mate, who on earth is this Irani bloke? Some kind of comedian?'

Many Aussies wanted to know more about Ronnie Irani of Essex, who became a celebrated mediocrity among Australians during the 2002/03 tour. Where did he come from? Did I realise he would struggle to play first grade? How can he follow in the footsteps of Len Hutton, Fred Trueman, Frank Tyson, John Snow, Geoff Boycott, Ian Botham, David Gower and Chris Broad?

I told them Irani was a bits-and-pieces merchant whose job was to bowl 10 overs for 40 and nurdle 30 at number seven. That argument foundered when Irani started going in at number three. Then I took to dressing up bits-and-pieces as a clever concept beyond the one-dimensional thinking of the unsophisticated Aussies.

To them, a bits-and-pieces player is a cricketer designed by committee. One snorted, 'You mean he can't bat and can't bowl? So he's a specialist fielder then. Mate, my dog could field better than him.'

I explained that Irani was a notable county cricketer, one of the best on the circuit, and that he had come up through the ranks and earned his chance with England. That drew a similar set of ripostes:

'County cricket? That's shithouse.'

'Last time we were over there I went to Lord's to see a county game. Couldn't believe they pay those blokes to muck about like that. No wonder your mob is losing three nothing'

'Mate, Hussey scores triple centuries in county cricket and can't even get a game for Australia.'

Another favourite was the assertion that not one England player would make a combined XI. When I mentioned Vaughan, they asked who I would drop. If Michael Slater, Michael Bevan, Mike Hussey and Mark Waugh were not in their team, then how could Vaughan possibly be?

My line was that Vaughan had scored two centuries in the first three games against their bowling attack, one of the best in history, and that this qualified him for any side in the world. I would therefore drop any of the Australian players to make room for him. Ha!

I had no success there either. All their players were just too good.

The Aussies were worried about the future for England. Where are the good players, they demanded, tell us their names. Why is county cricket so shit? Why are all your blokes injured?

I had no answer to any of these questions. I could only praise Shane Warne and Glenn McGrath, as so many others had done, and repeat that their team was exceptional. But even that didn't shut them up.

'Have you heard of Stuart MacGill?

Although I had heard of the second Aussie leg-spinner I didn't know that over the years he had accumulated over 80 Test wickets at 25 apiece.

'Mate, let me tell you something. MacGill has got more wickets than all of your blokes except Caddick, and he's a bloody Kiwi.'

## New South Wales

The first professional match I saw live in Australia was a one-day game between England and New South Wales at the Sydney Cricket Ground in early December. This was a warm-up game for England, and I expected a weak state team to get thumped in front of a small crowd like the counties do at home against the tourists.

I bought the match programme and sat in a crowded section behind the bowler's arm next to a middle-aged man with binoculars. I asked him if NSW usually put out a strong side against touring sides. Absolutely, he said, licking his lips.

Around the ground the crowd was gathering, 10,000 at least. Then, a familiar figure appeared on the turf. It was McGrath. And then another. Brett Lee. And Steve Waugh.

14,000 people turned up to watch an NSW bowling attack of McGrath, Lee, Nathan Bracken and MacGill. Their batting featured Steve Waugh, Slater, Bevan, Michael Clarke and Simon Katich, for a total of nine current or future Australian players. We batted first and Irani went in at three, facing 140 balls for 81. It was much too slow, but there was nothing else he could do. England laboriously eked out 206.

Thumbing through the programme during the half-way break, I came across the fixtures list[5] for professional cricket in Australia during the 2002/03 season. The first part was arranged in a two-page spread. Most of the fixtures seemed to involve national teams – Australia, England and the other visiting team that season, Sri Lanka. So I turned the page to read the rest.

There was no rest. I waved the programme at my neighbour.

'That's the entire list of fixtures in Australia this summer?'

'Used to be smaller before Tasmania came along. Back in the old days we had fewer one-dayers too. You could get the whole thing on one page.'

'It's incredibly small. The England one is miles bigger. It takes up a whole page of a broadsheet paper in small print. '

'I know. It's a real advantage for you guys. We're thinking of adding teams so we can give you a game.'

There were no one-match teams, no MCC, no Oxford and Cambridge or UCCE-type outfits, and no one-day competitions dangling off the side. Only eight home teams featured, of which two were national sides and the other six were the states. It was spare and uncluttered, a model of elegance and simplicity.

My neighbour and I watched New South Wales get the runs in 42 overs for two wickets, with Slater making a popular century in what turned out to be his last game against England. Waugh came in at the end for a cameo 24 not out off 12 balls, with three sixes, in front of an adoring crowd. Clarke and Katich did not bat.

I left the ground wondering how England were going to compete in their remaining fixtures, because Team Australia clearly meant to pummel the English until they were compelled by sheer embarrassment to stop being a useless, whimpering shambles. It was perfectly obvious they were going to lose all four VB games against Australia, and they did. By beating Sri Lanka three games to one, though, they went through to the best-of-three finals against Australia at the end of January. It was equally obvious that only two of these matches would be required, and they were.

## The Home Of Cricket

Three weeks later, I went to the Melbourne Cricket Ground to see the Fourth Test between England and Australia, which began on Boxing Day. I flew down from Sydney on the second morning, dumped my bags at a hotel and made my way over to the ground. About a kilometre away, the taxi driver told me he wouldn't go any closer. So I got out and walked.

I was half an hour late for the start of play and was increasingly keen to get there. I crossed over a railway line and there, looming above me, was the ground. It was vast beyond belief, the first real cricket stadium I had ever seen. One of the stands was under redevelopment and through the hole I could see the players.

There was a deep, rumbling roar which surfaced my memory of Willis getting Greenidge LBW for five at the Oval in 1976. I felt a force acting on me which I recognised from childhood, and I started to run. As I ran, I remembered the South African Test player:

'You must go to the MCG, man. It is the cathedral of cricket.'

Fifteen minutes later, I was thirty metres up in the Great Southern Stand looking straight down the wicket. To my left was another taxi driver, this one taking the day off. To my right was a couple, who introduced themselves. All around me were real cricket fans: posh fans, poor fans, youths, ancients, couples, families, men with sons, groups of women, the hard core with radio earpieces and the casuals chattering away over drinks. There were seats left over, and someone said it hadn't been full for decades. A man mentioned 1960/61 and told me that the first Test match and One-Day International had been played there. I realised that I was the only Pommy in the block.

I asked the taxi driver how this stadium came to be so huge, and he told me that in 1956 it was the venue for the Olympic Games. The ground used to have a slope, like Lord's, but it had to be levelled out for the running track.

For three days, I enjoyed a view which had everything the television had and more. From high up, I could see the ball against the grass background, which was a treat. I could gauge the length as Lee bounced England's batsmen. I could see MacGill turning the ball this way and that. And so could tens of thousands of others, looking down the wicket or sitting high up at the sides. I was transfixed. Sunburns developed on my legs and I barely noticed them.

## Landscape

The series long gone, England spent the second day collecting the ball from the distant corners of the ground as Australia rattled up 500 against a dispirited bowling attack. Justin Langer reached his double-century with a big straight six and the Aussies relentlessly accumulated runs.

Midway through the afternoon came a point almost as low as at the NSW game.

Out of options and in charge of a team that had nothing left to give, Nasser Hussain decided to bring Mark Butcher on to bowl. His insipid medium pace had virtually no chance of capturing a wicket, and all we could do was concede four an over while the main bowlers rested.

There was a lull in the crowd and my Aussie neighbours wondered when England were going to start competing again. The taxi driver said he felt sorry for Martin Love, on his debut, because any runs he scored against this rubbish would count for nothing. That turned out to be correct.

Just at that moment, about 6,000 people started singing:

*God save your gracious Queen*
*Long live your noble Queen*
*God save your Queen (you're a convict)*
*Send her victorious*
*Happy and glorious*
*Long to reign over you*
*God save your queen*

The Australians around me looked crestfallen and sheepish. Yes, they had voted for the Queen as their Head of State. Or, in truth, they had chosen not to vote for any of the less-good alternatives they had been given by their Prime Minister. But it wasn't the words of the song that was bothering them.

I looked over at the Barmy Army. There they were, waving, shouting and cheering in the bright sunlight.

They were definitely the better fans. Livelier, wittier, louder, keener people, easily out-singing 10 times as many Australians even though England were being drubbed once again. Fans who had travelled halfway across the world to support an awful team bereft of Graham Thorpe, Darren Gough and Andrew Flintoff. Fans from the North and South of England, squaddies and public schoolboys and lots of women. Fans who sang long, sledging songs which made the Aussies feel bourgeois, suburban and positively English.

I sat among the Aussies and listened some more. They seemed to see in the Barmy Army a romantic version of themselves: larrikins who call each other 'mate' and don't take life in this desert country—essentially a large mine with good sports facilities—too seriously. Then, as Butcher served up his dross in the boiling sun, I began to feel that the Aussies somehow feared these fans. How many more of these are there back home, someone asked. Are they like this at Lord's? Can they play cricket?

As I discussed matters with my neighbours, the question hung in the air: what would the England team be like if the spirit and organisation of the Barmy Army were transferred from the stands and on to the playing arena and the management of our game? For a minute or two, a landscape of almost infinite possibility opened up.

One man mentioned Douglas Jardine and Bodyline as a possible consequence. Another said that we would hammer the Aussies every time. But I didn't think so. From 12,000 miles, I looked back at the Mother Country with the nostalgic eye of George Orwell,[6] who remembered:

> ... the railway-cuttings smothered in wild flowers, the deep meadows where the great shining horses browse and meditate, the slow-moving streams bordered by willows, the green bosoms of the elms, the larkspurs in the cottage gardens; and then the huge peaceful wilderness of outer London, the barges on the miry river, the familiar streets, the posters telling of cricket matches and Royal weddings, the men in bowler hats, the pigeons in Trafalgar Square, the red buses, the blue policemen – all sleeping the deep, deep sleep of England, from which I sometimes fear that we shall never wake till we are jerked out of it by the roar of bombs.

It seemed to me that the spirit of the Barmy Army would remain bottled up at home and only released every fourth year in Australia. The transference that these Aussies feared could never happen because the sleeping giant of world cricket would remain semi-conscious for the rest of eternity.

Australia declared at 551–6 and got to work on England's batting. During a break some time on the third or fourth day, I went to a café in the concrete corridor that runs through the middle of the Great Southern Stand. As I waited in the queue I watched Channel Nine on a monitor.

Mike Atherton was commentating. Irritated by the prospect of another England defeat on top of its 0–3 position in the series, he launched into a diatribe against Robert Key, who had just come in. Key, said Atherton, had learned his cricket with Kent, and county cricket is soft: soft bowling, soft batting, soft cricketers, soft everything. Atherton seemed to think that Key was hopelessly unprepared and incapable of rising to the challenge.

I thought he was being needlessly cruel to a fellow England player. But the next over Key was out and Atherton was vindicated. He said nothing further, and I got my food and went back to my seat.

Atherton's spiel sounded exactly like what Australians were saying to me almost every day. Was this vestigial bitterness from years of Aussie humiliations in his own career? Had he turned into a Pommy-basher? Or did he have a point?

## Sydney

The third and last game I attended was the Fifth Test at the Sydney Cricket Ground in early January. On the last day, I saw Andy Caddick bowl out the Australians on a disintegrating wicket and England turn a likely 5–0 whitewash into a mere 4–1 kicking.

Afterwards, the Australian team did a circuit around the edge of the field to thank the fans for coming. Any male could shake hands with the players and any female could kiss them. I watched with mounting amazement as this all-star side snaked round to where I had been sitting. Perhaps two thousand people drifted to the front row and waited their turn, many of them Barmy Army. Another load of Barmy Army stayed where they were and carried on singing.

As the Aussies got closer I noticed that they were extremely fit. They looked like a squad of middle-distance runners with no meat on any of them. Ricky Ponting was so slight he looked like he had been shrunk in the wash. Brett Lee resembled an Action Man from a seventies cereal packet.

Some of the Barmy Army, using the advanced queue-avoiding techniques that all Britons learn in the womb, had moved round to my bit where the crowd had been thinner. Many were thrilled and incredulous, and I was getting pretty excited myself as it dawned on me that I was actually going to shake hands with a half-dozen of the Aussie players.

An Englishwoman about 10 people along from me kissed Lee and then went headlong into a swoon of the type described in Mills and Boon novels. Her boyfriend shook Lee's hand and jabbered at him nervously. This was repeated a couple of times, and then Lee got to me. As I shook his hand I tried to understand how that arm and the body to which it was attached could propel a ball at 95 mph. By focusing on this more technical aspect of Lee's physical presence, I managed to avoid the embarrassment of swooning myself. But by the time the Aussies had passed me I was in a daze.

A couple of weeks later I got back to a mate's house after a long day at the beach and switched on the TV to watch a VB Series one-day game between England and Australia. The Aussies had done some heavy squad rotation, presumably to rest the main bowlers before the 2003 World Cup and the West Indies tour following that. Their attack consisted of Lee and four bowlers I had never heard of.

We batted first and made heavy weather of their second-string attack. My host returned, and we opened a couple of beers. Midway through our innings I fell into a beach-induced slumber.

The noise of a wicket falling woke me up, and I focused in again. A left-armer jogged up to the wicket and delivered a ball from the back of his hand which spun sharply away from the right-handed batsman. I thought I was hallucinating, and it took me half a minute to work out what was going on.

'Wasn't that a Chinaman googly?'

'Oh, that's Brad Hogg. He's been around for ages.'

I had thought that Chinaman bowlers were extinct. In fact, I had never heard of one in international cricket at all. For England, who had no right-handed wrist-spinners, a left-handed one was like a five-limbed Martian shifting the ball through the fourth dimension. For the Australians, this made three wrist-spinners good enough to play for the national side.

I told my friend that every way I looked at it they were far, far ahead of us.

'We're OK, it's more that you Poms are a rabble.'

I had heard this term a few times and was confused about its origin. 'Isn't a Pommy a Prisoner Of Her Majesty? If so, doesn't that mean that it's the Aussies that are Pommies?'

'You got that one wrong. Legend says it's the name given to the new arrivals by the survivors. Same reason – the lettering on the shirts. The Poms were the new ones off the ship. I don't believe the shirt thing anyway, it's all bullshit. But that's what a Pom is – muddled and all at sea.'

'You mean, pre-Aussie?'

In the previous week vast clouds of smoke from huge forest fires around Sydney had wafted over the city. The smell of burning was everywhere and the news programmes were full of stories about evacuation and other emergency preparations. A storm welled up too, and giant waves smacked against the beaches all along the Eastern shores. It wasn't too hard to imagine what life was like for the first European settlers.

'Yeah, Poms still have the characteristics that are wiped out by being here a while. We've evolved, mate. You're still a coterie of clowns.'

'Is there anything else?'

Another English wicket fell, and we laughed. I waited for my mate to say 'batting, bowling and fielding', but he didn't.

'We like to think we're a modern, simple, plain-speaking people. Whatever we think we are, the Poms are by definition the opposite. That means they're traditional, sophisticated and political. Say one thing, mean another thing and actually do a third thing. That's according to myth and stereotypes, of course.'

Muddled, all at sea, traditional, sophisticated and political. This was too much hack social anthropology for one night. If you ask an Aussie a direct question, brace yourself for the answer.

## Startling

On the way home, I reflected on the many startling elements of the Australian cricketing package. The most remarkable feature was the strength of their reserves: the Australia Second XI would have beaten this England side without much ado. The batting was stronger than ours and, with two wrist spinners and the likes of Andy Bichel, Bracken and Michael Kasprowicz, their bowling had the edge too.

It seemed that the strength of the Australian team was a direct result of the quality of their Second XI. This had allowed the selectors to force Mark Waugh out of the Australian side as part of a long-term succession management strategy. Not only would Waugh have easily made our side, but this brutal move also showed that Aussie management practices were far in advance of ours.

Access for fans to the national side was astounding. Channel Nine, unlike Channel 4 in the UK, provided uninterrupted coverage, and also employed a far superior commentary team. The grounds were huge, the views excellent and ticket availability nearly 100% at prices that were virtually negligible. The only blemish was the policy of not broadcasting the game in the host city if the ground was not full. This mildly irritating arrangement disadvantaged those who could only watch for an hour or two.

Commerce and money played no visible role in the game. I watched five days in person and about another 10 days on the TV and, ignoring travel and accommodation costs, the total effect on my pocket of those 15 days was under $100, or about £35.

The overall package was stunningly attractive. From a management point of view, it was obvious that the simple pyramid structure of the recreational game allied with a strong emphasis on developing cricketers to their potential formed a conveyor belt that produced talent in abundance.

Finally, I also saw that I had been recruited as a fan and a player twice, in 1976 and 2002/03, by the combination of a great team, good television and excellent experiences at cricket grounds. Recruitment by this *Inspiration Effect* is achieved through ready access to the national team, for all fans, whatever the sport. It is part of a greater virtuous circle that attracts fans and produces a good national side: success and access generate money, and money produces success and access. This means that success and access are self-perpetuating so long as the money generated from the audience is used to good effect.

Australia had mastered this virtuous circle and England hadn't, and the gulf between the two countries in the three areas appeared, in early 2003, to be unbridgeable. In the event, however, England did bridge the success gap a couple of years later. But not for long.

That, and my trip to Australia in 2002/03, inspired me to look further at the questions of access and money in England cricket.

# CHAPTER 2

# INVESTIGATION

*The MCG is the people's ground … for crowd involvement and
as an arena, a coliseum, the MCG was my favourite … It was
absolutely inspirational … How could you not be affected by
60,000 or 70,000 people willing you on? And I'm sure it was
daunting for the opposition.*

Dennis Lillee, 2006

Before the first section of the high-speed Channel Tunnel Rail Link
joining London with the mouth of the Channel Tunnel opened in
2003, those riding Eurostar could enjoy an experience that
epitomised the muddle of UK public infrastructure investment.

After leaving Waterloo, the train used to thread its way along the
Victorian railway network through south-eastern London for about
half an hour. As it broke out into the fields and low hills of the
Kentish Weald, the Eurostar accelerated to 80 mph for the straight
stretch through Tonbridge and Ashford. In the tunnel itself, the train
would speed up to 100 mph.

On surfacing at Calais, the train would usually dawdle for a bit
while it got its bearings. Then came a low humming noise which to
the French meant that they had arrived. To Britons it presaged the
twenty-first century. The sound was that of the Eurostar powering
up to 186 mph. At this speed the countryside zooms by and the
traveller can only gawp as the church spires shift backwards. Lille
comes and goes and, before one knows it, the *Gare du Nord* has
arrived.

On the return journey the train decelerated to 80 mph on exit from
the Channel Tunnel. Two minutes later, passengers looked up when

they realised that they hadn't accelerated. With their tut-tuts, their why-oh-whys and sardonic sighs, middle-class Britons registered that they were back in silly old Blighty. What did the French think? A spot of *hauteur*? Or maybe they thought that a swift dose of 1789 would not go amiss.

Arriving like this in crusty old England is a common experience. At airports, for instance, one can usually spot a piece of inoperative machinery within two minutes of disembarkation. But feeling bad about one's home country makes one feel bad about oneself: second-best, powerless and small, miserable and complaining. We can blame the politicians, the unions, the managers, the City, or whomever. But, in the end, our country's failures are our own.

## The Lord's Effect

This sense was exactly what I registered when I walked into Lord's in 2004 for my first visit to an England Test ground since returning from Australia.

Like the Kent countryside, the ground is beautiful in the extreme. The architecture is top-notch, with the Media Centre both complimenting and complementing the pavilion. The tented roofs of the Grand Stand and the Mound Stand add a festive eccentricity that reminds us that a cricket match is, after all, a party. But Lord's is far from being a coliseum and is distinctly Victorian in look and feel. In all, it was 80 mph and Steam Age in comparison to the 186 mph, TGV feeling of the Melbourne Cricket Ground.

On big days at Lord's, the MCC takes the pavilion end of the ground for its members. Debenture holders get most of the upper deck of the Grand Stand and the top of the Mound Stand, so the hoi polloi get the Edrich and Compton Stands straddling the Media Centre, the lower decks of the Mound and Grand Stands, and the lower Tavern Stand. This is about 16,000–18,000 seats, or 55–60% of its 29,300 capacity.

The top deck of the Edrich and Compton are the best public seats because they are in the open air and they give a view straight down the wicket. The next-best seats are in the Mound Stand, followed by the Tavern and the lower Grand Stand. All of those are sideways-on and low-down, and the spectator cannot see the ball against the human background on the other side. But at least they are in the open air. The lower deck of the Compton and Edrich is cold, miserable and dark. For anyone with an appropriately-tuned television these seats are out of the question.

I had applied for the top of the Edrich and Compton but got the Tavern Stand. With my cricket-trained eyes, I could follow the ball up to 70 mph, but my companion, a non-cricketer, could not and there was no point in her going. Because our tickets costs nearly £50 each—40% more than my five days in Australia combined—we went anyway and sat out the day.

There was no atmosphere whatsoever. Most of the crowd was white, male, upper middle-class and well-behaved, and the Barmy Army was not represented at all. There were no taxi drivers, few couples, fewer children and no groups of women. Anglo-Caribbeans were few and far between. MCC members and their ilk dominated and, like a fir plantation in Scotland, the place was a sterile monoculture.

Half the fun of going to a game is leaving real life outside and concentrating on the operatic fantasy unfolding inside the white line. It is a childish, quasi-religious pleasure that requires a submissive concentration. At Lord's, the tickets were expensive and the food and drink over-priced, and I felt I was trapped inside someone else's private club having my pockets picked clean. The game became a sideshow.

The following year, I was unable to get tickets to the Ashes game because the ground was heavily over-subscribed. Instead, I went to see Bangladesh play England in their first Test here. The ground was half-empty but Bangladeshis were as rare as at the Viceroy's garden party. As far as I could tell, nobody from the MCC had been down to Tower Hamlets and flogged tickets at £10 a go.

Many of the upper Compton and Edrich seats are now allocated to the Associate Members of the MCC, reducing the chances of the hoi polloi yet further. The net result of the prices, the crush and the character of the MCC is the *Lord's Effect*: a general perception that international cricket in England and especially London is a members-only affair for wealthy upper-middle class white males. Furthermore, it communicates that cricket is a minority activity pursued by public schoolboys and other flannelled fools rather than what it actually is: a mass-participation and mass-audience national sport.

My companion is now an Arsenal fan and is unlikely ever to go to an England cricket match again. Me, I go to Trent Bridge.

## Olympics

When the UK team bidding for the 2012 Olympics went over to Singapore for the last round in early July 2005, in the team were Sebastian Coe, Tony Blair and Ken Livingstone, three people who know how to win races. By contrast, the French side came across as arrogant and blasé. Their body language communicated their conviction that Paris, with its 186 mph infrastructure already in place, would trounce London and its paper stadium.

The marketing aspects of our bid were a triumph. The promotional video was a masterpiece, featuring London's multi-ethnic population and emphasising the role of sport in inspiring children. In Singapore, our bid team wore the same nifty linen suits and ties or scarves. They had organised themselves to win and, evidently, had developed the will to win of the Australian cricket team.

Ten weeks later, a last-day crowd of ordinary fans with £10 tickets witnessed England draw at the Oval and win the series against the

Australians 2–1. Millions more watched on the TV. The day after, Trafalgar Square was filled with euphoric fans as tens of thousands lined the route of the buses carrying the England men's and women's teams. There was ticker-tape, singing and drunkenness in the bright sunlight.

I watched these celebrations with a strong feeling of déjà vu. The next day, a newspaper columnist opined that 100,000 cricket fans on the streets of London, the earlier Olympics win, as well as the 2003 Rugby World Cup triumph, meant that sport in Britain was alive and kicking. Certainly, the habitual English sporting cringe towards Australia was in abeyance.

Above the article was a picture of the crowds from the day before. This picture and the words *Olympics, cricket* and *100,000* in close proximity reminded me of the Barmy Army at the MCG, whose capacity is 100,000 and which was used for the 1956 Olympic Games. When I looked them up, the 2012 bid documents revealed that the legacy use for our Olympic Stadium was far from finally decided, although it would certainly include athletics. The design showed that the jump events would be placed outside the track, making the arena[1] an oval rather than racecourse-shaped. The plan was to remove the upper stands and reduce the capacity to 25,000 seats, but this was a paper stadium and plans could easily be altered. The UK athletics schedule was so thin that plenty of time could be left for cricket.

Athletics and cricket could share the 80,000-seat 2012 London Olympic Stadium. A few England days there would dramatically improve crowd capacity in the whole country and mean that the Barmy Army and ordinary fans could turn up *en masse*.

I co-opted my friend Robert Franklin to help. He suggested launching the ground during the 2013 Ashes when there would be no problem filling it. For games against Bangladesh, a drop in prices and a marketing campaign would bring in local Anglo-Asians and two other neglected groups – women and children. Franklin also realised that the bigger stadium would be ideal for any Cricket World Cup that was staged in England.

We had no desire to become commercially involved ourselves, so we decided that our goal was to get the ECB and the UK government to open negotiations. We had no public forum of our own, so we went for two experienced sponsors. The first was Mike Atherton, who had a newspaper column and was unafraid to speak out. The second was Tony Banks[2], formerly the MP for Stratford (where the stadium would be built). As Sports Minister in 1997, Banks had forced the MCC to admit women to its membership.

But first came the research phase. This showed that there is easily enough demand for a giant cricket stadium in London. It also revealed the political muddle that afflicts English national sports stadiums in general and English cricket grounds in particular.

## Stadium shape

There are two fundamental stadium shapes: the rectangular and the oval. Rectangular stadiums are designed for most of the various codes of football—Association, Rugby, American and Gaelic—and their arena is a rectangle 110 metres by 75. Oval stadiums are designed for cricket, athletics and Australian-Rules football and their arena is an oval 180 metres by 135. Under the MCG model, the athletics track is buried underneath the outfield and is dug up for a major athletics event and then covered with turf again for cricket and Aussie Rules. The cricket square is protected by a layer of turf or by matting, or drop-in pitches are used.

The MCG—officially branded 'The People's Ground'—is used for Aussie Rules, cricket and athletics and is by a distance the world's premier multi-use stadium. It was used for the Commonwealth Games in March 2006, and I found a photograph, dated November 2005, of a new athletics track being installed at the ground less than four weeks before the Boxing Day Test against South Africa.

There were a few complexities[3], but the decision to keep the 2012 stadium for athletics after the London Olympics meant that only an oval sport could share it. Football and rugby were therefore ruled out from the beginning, leaving only cricket. We therefore reckoned that cricket's bargaining power was strong and would get stronger the more the UK government failed to ensure a proper legacy. We felt that the government might make it financially easy for cricket so long as the stadium remained athletics-compatible like the MCG. This meant, in turn, that convincing the ECB should be a doddle.

## Stadium economics

To convince the various parties that our idea was financially viable, we had to get into stadium economics. This apparently tricky subject can be summed up by two laws. The first is obvious: anyone who owns a stadium should use it as often as possible. The second is less obvious: assuming that there are enough punters, the more the stadium is going to be used, the bigger it should be built.

Take Arsenal's[4] new 60,355-seat ground, which was under construction during 2005. The cost of providing each seat at this stadium breaks down into two parts. The first is a fixed, annual cost mostly made up of construction and maintenance expenses. It is the same whether the stadium is used 50 times a year or just once. The second is a per-event cost consisting of stewarding, policing, cleaning and the other costs of putting on the actual show.

At Arsenal, the annual fixed cost per seat is about £550 and the cost per event about £7. Table 1 shows the cost of providing each seat at each event as the number of events per year varies. Column 1 is an example of a sports team that plays the number of events shown in column 2.

### TABLE 1: COST PER SEAT AT ARSENAL

| Example sports team | Events | Cost per seat per game |
|---|:---:|:---:|
| Two Premier League teams | 50 | £22 |
| One Premier League team | 25 | £35 |
| England at Lord's | 12 | £65 |
| England at the Oval | 6 | £120 |

The table shows that adding more events reduces the average cost of providing each seat at each event.

For example, if Arsenal had planned to use this stadium as little as England uses the Oval (6 days), each seat would cost £120 to provide. The club could have sold maybe 10,000 seats a game and a stadium of that size would have been appropriate. Upping the use to 12 days (England at Lord's) brings the cost down to about £65, and 30,000 seats would have been about right for Arsenal. At the other end of the spectrum, had the club got together with neighbouring Spurs and put on 50 games, each seat would have cost £22. They could have built 100,000 seats, charged an average of £35 and made £65 million a year between them.

Arsenal counts on 25 home games and each seat therefore costs it about £35. In 2006/07, the first season, the club sold nearly all its seats and made an economic profit of over £25 million from the ground. The Chairman, Peter Hill-Wood, said in the annual report that the move 'now provides Arsenal with the increased income, profitability, cash generation and firm financial foundations from which we will continue to build trophy-winning Arsenal teams for many years to come.' Arsenal dubbed this, an example of the virtuous circle between access, success and finance, the *Emirates Effect*. Other clubs which haven't already expanded their grounds, such as Spurs, are now planning to follow suite.

This particular example of the virtuous circle works because of the second law of stadiums, which runs:

*More events means cheaper seats means more punters means build a bigger stadium.*

If, by some mischance, a sports team runs a stadium but only stages few events, then the second law kicks in viciously:

*Fewer events means more expensive seats means fewer punters means build a smaller stadium.*

The second law has an important consequence. Sports teams should concentrate their games in as few stadiums as possible and build those stadiums up. Ten games in one big stadium provides much more capacity than five games each in two small ones, and makes much more money too.

In the tricky world of stadiums, less is more.

## Cricket

Australian cricket benefits from the second law because the sport shares its grounds with Aussie Rules. This adds events, lowers the cost per seat and allows the stadiums to be expanded, to the great benefit of the Australian cricket public. With five big grounds and one main outlier (Tasmania), Australia's total capacity for a typical home season is just under two million seats, making 93 seats per thousand population. Thousands of fans can sit *en bloc* in Australian grounds for a few dollars each. This is one reason why the Barmy Army exists.

England systematically defies the second law. It has too many grounds, each one gets few England games and as a direct result the grounds are smaller and fans as a whole lose out heavily. England's 47 home days (seven Tests, 10 One-Day Internationals and a pair of Twenty20 games) have in recent years been allocated to the six historic grounds (Lord's, the Oval, Edgbaston, Trent Bridge, Old Trafford and Headingley), two new grounds (Riverside and The Rose Bowl) and two small county grounds (Bristol and Cardiff). Total seating capacity[5] is just under one million, equal to 21 seats per thousand population, under a quarter of Australia's 93. This is why our grounds, especially in London, are almost always jammed. This is another reason why the Barmy Army exists.

The one good outcome is a wide geographical spread that allows a few thousand fans in the far northeast (Durham) and the middle west (Bristol) nearby access. The Oval, though, has sold all its advance tickets every year since 1987. At Lord's, the MCC has a membership of 18,000, a waiting list of 9,000 and an average wait for membership of about 20 years. To get a seat at a big game, members have to queue at The Grace Gates early in the morning, a farce known in the trade as *The Pensioners' Derby*. Even if he has waited for hours, a member is still not safe because the rules state that another member can snaffle an unoccupied seat. The cadaverousness of MCC members when the Mexican wave goes around may be because they are all dying for the lavatory.

The worst-served region in Australia, New South Wales, with 57 seats per thousand, is much better served than the best England & Wales region, the East Midlands, with 37 per thousand. Trent Bridge is the best ground in the country for the ordinary fan because it has the most capacity in relation to its hinterland and is therefore less jammed than the others. For the time being, one can get a seat there nearly as good as at the MCG, albeit at great cost.

England fans lose out for another reason. Below an elevation of seven metres the only places from which the spectator can see the red ball properly are the 25% of seats at one of the ends. From the side, the ball is lost against the stands and spectators on the other side. Above seven metres, though, the spectator can see the ball against a grass background from more than 90% of the seats. Big grounds by definition have most seats above this height, meaning that a greater proportion of seats offers a good view. Perhaps 80% of the MCG's seats afford such a view and about 50% at Sydney. Maybe 40% at Lord's are good, and 25% elsewhere in England. Most of these are taken by members, leaving the low, side-on dross for the public. In England, it really is better on the TV.

Furthermore, England's six historic grounds are in closely-spaced pairs: Lord's and the Oval in London are four miles apart, Edgbaston in Birmingham and Trent Bridge in Nottingham are 47 miles apart, and Headingley in Leeds and Old Trafford in Manchester are 33 miles apart. Were England to merge these six grounds down to three, then it could concentrate its games and build these three venues up, dramatically increase national seat capacity and cut the proportion of seats with a poor view.

Had Arsenal kept its Highbury ground as well as building the new Emirates stadium, and shared its games equally between the two venues, then its fans and the press would have clamoured for the incarceration of the club's management in Pentonville. Instead, of course, the club successfully seeded the virtuous circle of access, success and finance and is, in passing, making a lot of money redeveloping its old ground.

England cricket has operated three sets of geographically-paired stadiums for more than a century.

## 2012 plan

This poor state of affairs was the background to our proposal for the legacy use of the 2012 Olympic Stadium. The essence of the plan was to expand England's limited capacity by using the Olympic Stadium at its original Games size and filling it every time. We produced two options for the ECB. The modest one was to put on six England One-Day Internationals. This left the existing distribution of Tests unaffected but removed One-Day Internationals from the venues outside the historic six. It increased the number of seats in England & Wales by 30%, and in London almost doubled them.

The ambitious option was to use the ground as the National Cricket Stadium, with 17 days including two Tests. This meant abandoning Headingley altogether, stripping Lord's of one of its two Tests and leaving Trent Bridge and the Oval to share one per year, with the Oval getting the Ashes game for tradition's sake. This option more than doubled the capacity in England & Wales to over two million seats, meaning that a more diverse audience by age, ethnicity and gender could be admitted to the live game while preserving the privileges of most of the existing audience.

We calculated that, if 75% of the seats were sold and 10% of the days were lost to rain and early finishes, the modest option would break even and the stadium would produce a profit of £1.2 million[6] for each additional day.

We worked out how many cricket fans reside in range of London and its grounds, arriving at a figure of 750,000[7] serious fans, who would go to a game on their own initiative, and 1.5 million casual fans, who would go to a game if invited. Most of these fans do not currently go to Lord's and the Oval because of price, lack of seats and the *Lord's Effect*. Variable pricing (seats between £10 and £60) and direct marketing to women, children, less well-off white males and Anglo-Asians and Anglo-Caribbeans would get over all that.

The finances were excellent because the UK government had to build this stadium anyway. All the ECB had to do was put back the upper stands, or get the government not to remove them after 2012. Each year, it could simply turf over the track in June for a seven-week season beginning in July and then give the stadium back to athletics for a couple of events in late summer.

## Sales pitch

A trial marketing campaign using the photo of the MCG with an athletics track under the outfield convinced anybody who doubted the technical feasibility of this idea. A reminder of the scenes at Trafalgar Square and a dose of audience statistics convinced anybody still labouring under the *Lord's Effect* that this place could be filled.

Two killer lines drove the points home. How often does the UK government build an 80,000-seat cricket stadium in the country's main city and then cast around for someone to use it? Not that often. How many London football clubs provided their fans more seats than England cricket did in London? Eight. All six Premiership teams at that time provided more seats, as did both QPR and Millwall. We worked our way down the divisions and found that a west London club in what used to be known as Division Three, Brentford, was the first club that provided fewer seats in London than England cricket.

Finally, we appealed directly to Livingstone, the UK government and the London Olympics organisers. The last two paragraphs of the pitch read:

> *London is then home to giant stadiums for each of the big three British team sports at Stratford, Twickenham and Wembley respectively. Athletics, too, gains a commercially viable national stadium of the right size for major international events. The London Olympics gets a secure legacy for the stadium as originally constructed. Last but not least, the owner of the stadium generates many millions more than under present plans, depending on the arrangement made with cricket.*

> *With 320,000 low-priced seats each year at the London Olympic Stadium, schoolchildren would return in droves to live cricket. In this way, the spirit of the 2012 London Olympics can be sustained for many years to come.*

With these arguments in our kitbag in November 2005, we set out on a crusade to convince Atherton, Banks, national newspapers, the ECB, the 2012 Olympics people, Government ministers and the Mayor of London of the sense in copying what Melbourne has had since 1956.

## Lobbying

Within a month, Atherton responded positively, a national newspaper agreed to run a feature and a mid-level official at the ECB agreed to a meeting. Banks was more difficult to reach, though, and the 2012 Olympics bid team had broken up but not yet been replaced. Furthermore, the Sports Minister (Richard Caborn), his boss the Secretary of State for Culture, Media and Sport (Tessa Jowell), Livingstone and Coe were inaccessible to members of the public. Whenever we got in the queue to see one of them, thick-shouldered representatives of vast construction firms seemed to be ahead of us.

At the ECB meeting, the photos did the trick. The official promised a follow-up meeting with the Commercial Director, John Perera, and the Chief Executive, David Collier. Then, getting more excited than he perhaps should have done, the official proposed that we launch a press campaign. When told that this was well underway, his face fell. 'That's bad,' he said. 'That will not go down well.' Naïvely, we told him the name of the national newspaper and left. A day later, the newspaper pulled the story. The writer lost interest in it, apparently.

Atherton was away for a month and out of contact, and the follow-up meeting with Collier and Perera did not materialise within a fortnight. I called the ECB official only to find that he was not prepared to discuss the subject further. Just before Christmas, Kevin Mitchell of *The Observer* gave the plan a positive write-up. Mitchell, an Australian, concluded his piece with the sentence:

> *It would be a shame if, when the Australians tour in 2013 and the entire nation is clamouring for tickets, they are still going to be crammed into tiny grounds designed for Victorian gentlemen of leisure.*

I was then interviewed on *BBC Radio Five Live*. While sitting in the studio I could see the 2005 Boxing Day Test at the MCG on a monitor. A thin line of light-green grass described a circle about 30 metres from the centre of the square. Outside the line, turf had been laid above the newly-installed athletics track, and it hadn't yet merged with the untouched turf in the centre. The proof of the technical viability of the proposal was there on screen.

I was about to point this out on air when the presenter went to the news. However, the former England cricketer Angus Fraser, speaking from a ski slope, was asked for his opinion. He too was positive, saying that the venue would be ideal for one-day cricket.

## Failure

A week into 2006, Tony Banks died of a cerebral haemorrhage and the number of decent politicians in this country dropped by an appreciable percentage. We left a series of messages with ECB officials, none of which was returned. In March, a message came back from the Department for Culture, Media and Sport via an intermediary. Although the proposal was interesting, they wouldn't talk to us. The message was loud and clear: bring us the ECB.

We had reached the end of the road. In May, the ECB announced that a Test match in the 2009 Ashes series would be played at a new 15,000-seat ground in Cardiff. By substituting Cardiff for Old Trafford, the ECB was actually cutting the already inadequate capacity provided in 2005. More strategically, it was defying the second law of stadiums by spreading days more thinly across yet more small stadiums rather than concentrating them in fewer, bigger stadiums such as the one in East London.

The decision reduced Franklin and me to a state of bewilderment and speechlessness, and we decided to give up.

## Spreading exclusion

I had no idea what was going on at the ECB and why the officials hadn't even asked us to give them a presentation about an idea which could make them money and serve their customers. But I gained another insight into English cricket when I went to see the second day of the First Test versus Sri Lanka at Lord's in May 2006, courtesy of an MCC member, after my public ballot application had been unsuccessful for the second year in a row.

England ended the first day at 318–3 with Kevin Pietersen 53 not out. Like many fans, I was more than keen to see Pietersen in the flesh. Few players are caught on the boundary in each of their first three Test innings, and his 2005 innings at the Oval contained several shots of almost superhuman hand-eye co-ordination. Two weeks before, Pietersen had told a journalist: 'I'm not interested in being a short-term success, I want long-term success. I want to be the best batsman in the world and that requires complete determination, hard work and making sure I keep doing the right things.' I saw a strong similarity to Viv Richards in his leg-side bias, his inventiveness and his professionalism, and his determination to be number one was refreshingly not Pommy.

Nothing had changed at Lord's since 2004. In our stand, huge quantities of drink were chugged from 10.30 onwards, and we had some ourselves. When at Lord's, do as lords do. Out in the middle, Pietersen was back in the groove within a few minutes. Trademark on-drives and shots from three yards down the wicket thudded into the boundary. With a slog-sweep against a quick bowler, he began to resemble a battleship sailing through a regatta of small yachts. Even Muttiah Muralitharan was made to look like a one-gun cutter.

At lunch England were 432–4 with Pietersen 120 not out. At 1.35 I went back to my seat to see what he would do next. For the next hour, 15,000 people enjoyed the display of big batting. Another 14,000 people preferred to carry on scoffing and quaffing round the back and in nearby pubs and restaurants. Also not watching were thousands of people on the waiting list for MCC membership and thousands of ordinary fans who, like myself, had been unable to obtain a ticket through the application process. Then there were thousands of others who couldn't afford the £50-plus price caused by the lack of capacity at this ground. Plus untold more put off by the *Lord's Effect*.

This match was the first to be broadcast on Sky Television as part of the four-year deal between the ECB and BSkyB. Viewing figures for the First Test in 2006 are confidential, but press reports suggest a continuous average[8] of about 250,000 for the whole summer. Since the average audience for Channel 4 was 1.3 million, at least another million people were not watching this epic battle between Pietersen and Muralitharan.

When Pietersen holed out for another 158, I went for a walk around the ground. I called my uncle, Don Tandy, to see if he had enjoyed the duel. He had, courtesy of Ceefax and the 'wireless'. Then, walking past the MCC shop, I realised that I had seen no Blacks and Asians at all in thirty degrees of circumference.

In the food court, I spotted a tall, athletic man standing at the betting shop almost directly underneath the Media Centre. He had his back to me but the dark black hair was a giveaway. By now insatiably curious about why there were so few non-whites, I moved in surreptitiously, feigning an interest in the odds on offer at the betting shop. Out of the corner of my eye, I could see that the man was looking down at his betting slip. He was middle-aged, serene and academic, like a professor at UCL, and he was most definitely West Indian. The man looked up and for a brief moment I caught the eye of Michael Holding.

I continued around the ground in an anti-clockwise direction. In the lower Grand Stand I clocked a knot of teenagers wearing the Sri Lankan one-day kit. They looked well-to-do. By the time I arrived back at my seat, I had totted up one West Indian former fast bowler and six Sri Lankan teenagers. This number is so low that non-whites in the London area must be excluding themselves[9] from England games. As with censorship, there is no exclusionary force as powerful as self-exclusion. But why?

I already knew about the exclusive nature of the MCC and Lord's from previous trips to this ground and my work on the stadium proposition. In May 2006, this exclusiveness seemed to have spread from Lord's out into the country, infected the whole of England cricket and taken the *Inspiration Effect* with it.

After 68 years (1938–2005), free television access to the national cricket team for all was gone. Most of the people who watched Pietersen at the Oval in 2005 will never see him bat live again. Unless the England team is restored to free-to-air television, more Australian fans than England fans will see him in Ashes Tests.

## Strange

Almost every week during summer 2006 press reports suggested that the 2012 stadium legacy was in a frightful muddle. The government was out chasing football teams such as Spurs and West Ham when right in front of its nose was cricket. We felt football had effectively been ruled out a year before but, to our great frustration having put our pitch out far and wide, there was no mention of cricket. I detected the *Lord's Effect* at work.

A letter to David Higgins, a Sydney Olympics official who had just become the Chief Executive of the UK's new Olympics Delivery Authority (ODA), produced a press report with the quote: 'I mean look at the MCG. It must be one of the best venues in the world. It is owned by a trust. You have Australian rules football, rugby, both league and union, cricket, of course, and if Madonna comes along she can perform. For the Commonwealth Games they tore the pitch up and put it down again for the Boxing Day Test.'

A meeting with one of Higgins' people served only to reinforce the message 'Bring us the ECB'. Then, a letter to Giles Clarke, the ECB person responsible for grounds, finally brought a response from ECB Commercial Director John Perera in September 2006. It was negative. The government was out on the dance floor but the ECB was hugging the wall and refusing to make eye-contact.

As I looked at this letter (for an analysis, see the notes to Chapter 6), I recalled a well-known maxim uttered by an Ian Fleming character, Auric Goldfinger, that provides a rough but useful way of sorting out cause and effect from a noisy blizzard of information. The saying runs:

> *Once is happenstance, twice is coincidence, three times is enemy action.*

This is also a useful way of looking at reasons. The more reasons that are given for something, the fishier it gets. For instance, if one's partner arrives home at 11.45pm and says he worked late, that's fine. If he says he worked late and got lost on the way home, some scepticism is in order. If he says he worked late, had a drink with Leonard from Accounts, and got lost on the way home, then it's time to check into a hotel.

The rule of three works. But if Leonard also broke his ankle and had to be carried to hospital, call the police. If the weight of Leonard on one's partner's back caused him to … call the doctor.

The curious thing was, Perera gave five reasons for official ECB inaction.

## 2006/07 Ashes

Later in 2006, the England team was treated to a proper drubbing over in Australia. The 4–1 of 2002/03 was turned into 5–0 as a wounded Australia went for the kill and did not let up in the last game.

From the moment Justin Langer walked on to the field in Brisbane, grinning like a hyena about to tear out the first chunk of English flesh, to the moment where the same Langer walked off the field in Sydney in floods of tears, it was an Aussie *tour de force*, a textbook demonstration of sustained brutality as comprehensive as anything achieved in sport. Our 2–1 victory in 2005 was repaid with interest and a kick in the arse, and only Kevin Pietersen and Monty Panesar were left standing. Only Pietersen, like Michael Vaughan four years before, would have made a combined team.

At the end of the series, Steve Harmison announced his retirement from the one-day game and said he would go home from the Ashes tour and would not be going to the World Cup. He then gave an interview to Mike Atherton in which he was nervous, off-hand and not-bothered, all at the same time. In years gone by, Ashes tours and World Cups represented the pinnacle of a player's career. But Harmison was the third England player to bail out of an Ashes tour in four years after Graham Thorpe and Marcus Trescothick. To my mind, this activated the rule of three.

During the tour, my co-conspirator Robert Franklin went to the Gabba and watched England being put to the sword in the First Test. His Australian colleagues liked our idea but said it was obvious. Absolutely it is, but only to them. Someone reminded Franklin that Sydney had also staged an Olympic Games. What had happened to that stadium?

That ground is now called the Telstra Stadium and is used by a variety of sports teams, including the New South Wales side for one-day matches. The long-term future of the Sydney Cricket Ground seems rather precarious, and *Your Gracious Queen* may well be sung at some point in a second gigantic cricket ground Down Under.

Table 2 opposite lists the five large cricket grounds in England and Australia.

That's another 5–0 to them. And, I understand, the South Australia Cricket Association is increasing the capacity of the Adelaide Oval to 37,000.

## Investigation

In February 2007, the ODA board reaffirmed its commitment to an oval stadium legacy and confirmed that a Premiership football club

TABLE 2: GROUNDS IN ENGLAND AND AUSTRALIA WITH MORE
THAN 30,000 SEATS

| Ground | Capacity |
|---|---|
| Melbourne Cricket Ground | 100,000 |
| Telstra Stadium, Sydney | 78,000 |
| Sydney Cricket Ground | 43,000 |
| The Gabba, Brisbane | 40,000 |
| Adelaide Oval | 32,000 |

would not play there. The most likely outcome now is that a small football club like Leyton Orient will agree to play inside the track of the reduced 25,000-seat stadium. Its fans, once they realise how far they will be from the action, will probably revolt. A football club is still unlikely, therefore, and it seems that there will be no legacy user other than athletics.

If the ODA builds the stadium so that the upper tiers can be re-erected at a reasonable cost, then the opportunity to use it for cricket will continue to exist indefinitely. Then, should there be a change of management at the ECB, or a change in the ownership of the professional game, this golden opportunity can be revisited. Someone, somewhere, can make a lot of money and a lot of people can watch Kevin Pietersen and his successors bat.

That lies in the future – maybe. For me, the questions about the management of the game in this country were multiplying. Between the two Ashes series in 2002/03 and 2006/07, England cricket achieved a single great feat. But we lost the next series against Australia 0–5 when we had a great squad. Why? We are behind 0–5 in stadiums and remain 0–3 down in wrist spinners. Why? Two more players walked off an Ashes tour. Why? England cricket disappeared off free-to-air television screens on the very same day that it achieved the Ashes victory, while cricket in Australia remains solidly on free-to-air Channel Nine. Why?

The gap between England and Australia in success and access, already vast in 2002/03, had only increased in the following years. But England, with its larger population, should surely have a bigger talent pool and its larger audience should surely generate greater financial resources to invest in the professional game.

What's more, I had in my hand a five-excuse letter from the governing body of the sport in this country explaining why it wouldn't take up a proposal that would help close that gap. Why was a senior executive at the ECB giving me and Franklin five reasons for doing nothing when a single one would do?

I was left with an overwhelming sense of curiosity about the management of England professional cricket. It seemed likely that the cold reception given our proposal was somehow related to the BSkyB deal. How these access problems related to England's deficiencies in the playing arena was also not clear. I felt I had only scratched the surface of something deep and not necessarily pleasant.

So I decided to look a little further into the business of cricket and try to discover why Australia has achieved the virtuous circle of success, access and finance and why England cricket has not. My investigation covered all the factors that affect the success of the England side and access to it for England fans. In particular, it obeyed the golden rule of all investigations: follow the money.

Finally, I looked at how we in England can create a virtuous circle of our own.

## Ashes history 1877–2007

Three sets of statistics illustrate three differences between the two countries. The results history shows that Australia has consistently had the upper hand over England since 1877, despite using far fewer players. Since the early nineties, England has produced many high-scoring batsmen. But it has failed to produce any bowlers who have matched the achievement of Derek Underwood, Bob Willis and Ian Botham in taking 250 Test wickets.

Figure 1 shows the performance of England and Australia in Tests between the two countries between the first game at the MCG in 1877 and the 316th at the SCG in 2007.

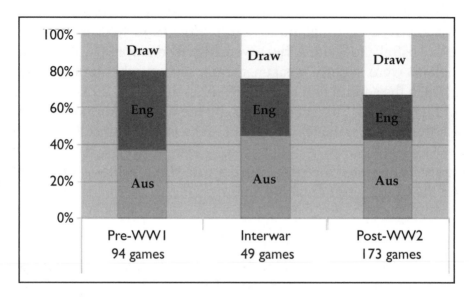

FIGURE 1: AUSTRALIA AND ENGLAND WIN, LOSS AND DRAW
1877–2007

Australia leads by 131 to 97, with 88 draws and no ties so far. Over the years, it has consistently won about 40% of the encounters, whereas the proportion of England victories has steady declined.

In the games before the First World War, England squeaked ahead by 40 to 35 (England won 43% of the games). In the interwar period, Australia reversed that result, winning 22 to 15 (England 31%). Since the Second World War, Australia has marched ahead and with the 5–0 result in the latest series in 2006/07 has established a commanding 74 to 42 lead (England 24%). Since the Second World

War, Australia has won four games in a series on nine occasions compared with just one by England. On that occasion, 1978/79, Australia put out its third team after its first two teams defected to Kerry Packer's World Series Cricket.

The post-war period includes a decade from 1977 to 1988 where Australia (three times) and England (once) were heavily weakened by defections either to Packer or to rebel tours to South Africa. In that period, only the 1979/80 and 1981 series involved teams that were both selected from all fit players. The remaining series, 1978/79 (Packer), 1982/83 (England to South Africa) and 1985 and 1986/87 (both Australia to South Africa), were heavily disrupted by defections. England were slightly weakened by a second rebel tour to South Africa in the second half of the 1989 series and in the 1990/91 series, but I ignore that. This set of results, by the way, means that England beat the full Australia team only once between 1977 and 2005.

Figure 2 separates the post-war era into the rebellious 1978–1988 and the two periods on either side.

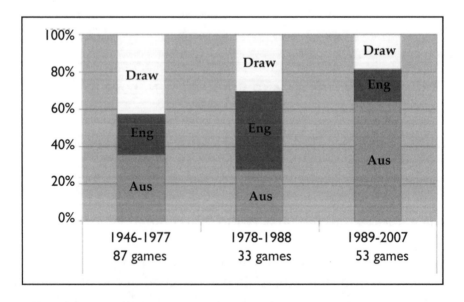

FIGURE 2: AUSTRALIA AND ENGLAND WIN, LOSS AND DRAW
SINCE THE SECOND WORLD WAR

In the 30 years before the rebel interruptions, Australia led England by 31 to 19. The rebel decade was then won by England by 14 to 9. Since 1988, Australia has won 34 to 9, with only 10 drawn. In that period, Australia won by 17 games to four in the five series between 1989 and 1997 and again by 17 to five in the five series to 2007. There has been minimal progress by England during the last 20 years, and the lone England victory in 2005 was quickly negated by the beating meted out in 2006/07.

In the 130 years of this great sporting rivalry, then, Australia has the upper hand over England and has frequently inflicted on our team a comprehensive thrashing. If the Ashes is an everlasting two-horse race, then Australia is so far ahead that it could lose all six series between 2009 and 2018/19 by four games to nil and still lead 131–121 overall. It would, also, still be ahead since the Second World War (74–66) and since the end of the rebel period in 1988 (34–33).

## Coming second to them

During the 2003/04 season, the England rugby union team won the Rugby World Cup final in Sydney against Australia. The outstanding England team was well-supported by a second XV that in the months before the tournament beat New Zealand Māori away and nearly beat France's full-strength side in a warm-up game in Marseille.

The coach, Clive Woodward, did another year before quitting when the RFU would not accept his management plan to defend the trophy in 2007. In a 2005 lecture at the Foreign Office in London, Woodward talked about the fatal effect of compromise in international sport:

> If you do compromise, you can be sure that somewhere else in the world, there is someone who is not compromising. That means you are going to come second to them.

After Woodward quit and his deputy Andy Robinson took over, the club-country conflict that had bedevilled rugby since the onset of professionalism in the nineties continued and team performance collapsed. In December 2006, Woodward again ventured his opinion on what had happened:

> When England won the World Cup in 2003, it probably seemed to the outside world that we were travelling on a gleaming, modern cruise liner. We were not – we were on the Titanic ... The truth is that we won the World Cup in spite of the system ... We won it because we had an awesome group of players ... and a fantastic management team, many of whom led the world in their areas. We got the job done against all logic and common sense. The roles the clubs and the RFU play are clearly important, but it is not a system that puts international rugby first.

As well as despising compromise, Woodward had no time for any notion that success comes and goes of its own accord.

> I am driven mad when I hear that success is cyclical. It is complete nonsense. Cyclical fortune was a phenomenon of the amateur days. Rugby is now a business, and you can go out of business.

He also despaired of the treatment of England's top players:

> Then I hear that we have had bad luck with injuries. Again, nonsense. There will always be injuries, but why can New Zealand and Ireland field their full first XVs at present? Why are so many England players unavailable? Are the other nations playing to different safety laws? Our players are playing far too much rugby, they are playing and training when exhausted and when injured. That is not bad luck, that is lack of elite planning and care for the athletes – and on the verge of exploitation.

Many of Woodward's concepts seemed also to apply to England cricket. In particular, the modern gleaming cruise liner that was the 2005 team broke up immediately afterwards and team performance deteriorated.

A good second team, a domestic second tier that supports the national side, good injuries management and a refusal to compromise on the primacy of the national team all lead, as Woodward suggests, to sustained success. A poor second team, an introverted second tier, poor injuries management and compromise together make performance dependent on external factors.

Sometimes these external factors are favourable and a windfall player like Kevin Pietersen suddenly turns up. Sometimes they are unfavourable, two bowlers fall injured and Wasim and Waqar are both fit. The result of letting Lady Luck have her way is a haphazard, cyclical performance.

Has England cricket relied inordinately on Lady Luck?

## Against everybody since World Series Cricket

Figure 3 overleaf is a graph of the performance of both England and Australia in Tests against all opponents since the end of the Packer revolution in early 1979. The upper line represents Australia, and the lower line England. The lines, to be clear, represent each country against all opponents, including each other. They do not represent just the Ashes.

Each point on a form line[10] represents the average result of that country in every five Tests over the previous two years. For example, England's form line starts at 3–1. This means that from September 1977 to September 1979 the team averaged 3–1 in every five Tests, with one draw. England's low point came in the two years from March 1992 to March 1994 when it averaged between 0–2 and 0–3 every five games. Its high point came between December 2002 and December 2004, when it averaged better than 3–0. Please see the notes for details of how the lines were calculated.

After World Series Cricket finished in early 1979, England and Australia followed a similar downward trajectory, with England's being more cyclical. In 1987, Australia broke upwards to between

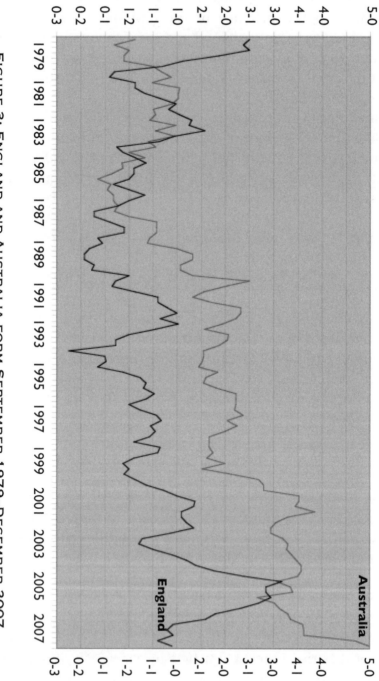

FIGURE 3: ENGLAND AND AUSTRALIA FORM SEPTEMBER 1979–DECEMBER 2007

2–1 and 3–1 and remained there until 1999. It then broke upwards again to between 3–0 and 4–0, remaining in that range except for a brief dip in 2005 caused by you-know-what.

England, by contrast, followed a cyclical path around the 0–0 line between 1987 and 2003, sometimes sliding down to 0–1 or 0–2 and sometimes drifting up to 1–1 or 1–0. In 2003, England suddenly broke upwards and actually crossed the Australian line in December 2004, a few months before the 2005 Ashes. But the England team could not sustain this performance for longer than nine months, and in late 2005 began to slide back down whence it came.

Since its 2005 Ashes defeat Australia has won 19 of its 20 Tests, with one draw, and was at 5-0 on the form chart at the end of 2007. England has won eight and lost 11 of its 28 games and was between 1-0 and 1-1. In the 28 years covered by this chart, the gap between the two sides was at its greatest in the second half of 2007.

These two lines represent the hard reality of England's relative decline as a Test nation after the end of the Packer revolution and Australia's ascent to world domination of the sport. Since 1987, Australia has built towards and then sustained excellence. England has cycled through a succession of phases but has always reverted, in time, to mediocrity.

What has been going on?

## Less is more – again

Since 1877, Australia has fielded 398 players in Test cricket compared with England's 638. Both suffered comparable war interruptions and have faced the same set of oppositions, except each other, but England's total is 60% greater. Since World Series Cricket ended in 1979, Australia has fielded 93 new players to 158 by England. The difference here is even greater: 70%.

Figure 4 shows the number of Test debutants for each country since

1980, the first year after World Series Cricket. Points on this graph are yearly. The figure for each year[11] is the number of new caps awarded in the five years up to and including that year. In the five years from 1999 to 2003 inclusive, for example, Australia awarded seven new caps compared with 27 by England.

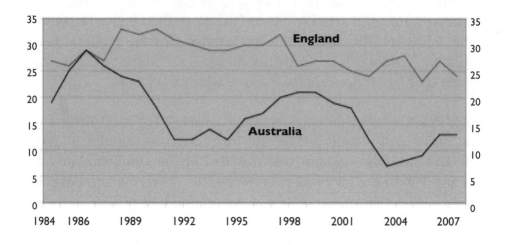

**FIGURE 4: ENGLAND AND AUSTRALIA TEST DEBUTANTS
1980–2007**

A perfectly-selected national squad of 24 with an average tenure of eight years would require three new players a year on average, or 15 every five years. England has awarded between 25 and 35 new caps every five years throughout, but Australia oscillates around 15 from 1990 onwards. In fact, the average number of Australian debutants from 1987 to 2006 was, to two decimal points, 3.00. Interestingly, the year in which the two countries diverged here, 1987, is also the point at which their performances diverged.

International cricketers are produced by each country's elite youth development system and by its domestic second tier below the national side. Over the years, 398 Australians have consistently out-performed 638 Englishmen, suggesting that, so far as the production of elite players is concerned, less is more.

Why do we employ so many more international cricketers than Australia? Is this one of the reasons that we keep coming second to them?

## Bowlers

More straightforwardly, the ancient lore of the game says that bowlers win matches and batsmen draw them. After all, 20 Test wickets have to be captured unless the opposing captain makes a declaration. The four best teams in recent years—West Indies in the eighties, Australia from 1999 onwards, Pakistan in the late nineties, and England between 2003 and 2005—all featured extra-strong bowling attacks.

The top two England bowlers in the history of Test cricket are Ian Botham (373 wickets) and Bob Willis (325). They retired in 1993 and 1984, respectively, but since Botham no England bowler has attained 250 Test wickets. Matthew Hoggard is currently the top-placed, with 247.

Since 1993, though, 16 other bowlers have got to 250 wickets. Five are Australian, three South African, two Indian, two West Indian, two Pakistani and two Sri Lankan. The only other nations that have not produced a 250-wicket bowler in this period are New Zealand, Zimbabwe and Bangladesh.

Shane Warne and Glenn McGrath have won many games for Australia since the early nineties, prompting many in England to cite this pair as the main cause of Australian success. These two players have indeed been exceptional, but not that different from Anil Kumble and Muttiah Muralitharan and from Courtney Walsh & Curtly Ambrose, Wasim Akram & Waqar Younis and Allan Donald & Shaun Pollock. All of these men have taken over 300 Test wickets and in several cases a great deal more.

Looking at the list of top bowlers, the absence of any England 250-wicket bowlers since Botham is much more notable than the presence of two Australian 500-wicket bowlers. It is likely that this absence has contributed to England's generally mediocre performance.

Where have our bowlers been?

## Where to start?

Australia was where my view of the game irrevocably changed and seemed like a good place to start. They obviously know a few things that we don't, about us as well as about this game.

There was an Australian, once, who had something to do with cricket and money. He was pretty successful, too. People still watch cricket on his television station, although it was recently sold. He's dead now, this man, and he hardly ever spoke about what he did. But others have, and in their stories there lie some truths that are worth extracting.

# SECTION 2

# Causes
## 1972–2002

# CHAPTER 3

# REVOLUTION

*Packer was not interested in cricket. He was only interested in TV rights, but he was the best thing that ever happened to cricket.*

Don Bradman, date unknown

The 1976 Oval Test between England and West Indies is covered in the 1977 edition of the *Wisden Cricketers' Almanack*. Many years later, Don Tandy found a copy of this edition in a second-hand book shop and bought it for me as a memento of our trip.

Inside its yellow dust-jacket is revealed a cricket world little changed since the end of the Second World War. Cambridge and Oxford still provided a training ground for future first-class players. Seven of these represented the Varsities in 1976, of whom Vic Marks and Chris Tavaré went on to play for England. The national team still toured abroad as the MCC and the 17-county Championship[1] was much the same as it had been in 1899.

There were six Test-playing nations. England and Australia had invented and still dominated the international game, India and the West Indies were on the up, but Pakistan seldom played and New Zealand had won only nine of its 119 Tests. Sri Lanka had only recently changed its name from *Ceylon*, Zimbabwe still had three years to go as *Rhodesia* and Bangladesh had only emerged from East Pakistan five years before. Pakistan itself had only been playing Test cricket for 23 years, and South Africa, to the chagrin of many within the English cricket Establishment, was seven years in to what would turn out to be a 22-year suspension from international cricket. The global game was administered by the International Cricket Conference (ICC). This body, which had changed its name from

*Imperial Cricket Conference* 11 years earlier, was based at Lord's and run on a part-time basis by the Secretary of the MCC.

At home, the game was governed by the Cricket Council. Started in 1968 when the Labour government insisted that the sport could not be run by a private members' club (the MCC) if it were to receive public money, the Council had five representatives from the MCC, five from the professional game (the Test and County Cricket Board – TCCB) and another five from the recreational game (the National Cricket Association).

This English compromise had left neither the MCC nor the TCCB in charge.

## Still amateur

The business model of England professional cricket was simple. Like any professional sports team, cricket made money in 1976 in three ways: ticket receipts, broadcasting rights and sponsorship & advertising. It also spent money in three ways: on players, grounds, and administration & marketing.

Test match tickets cost about a pound. But, unlike rugby and football, there was no National Stadium. Instead, the England team played at grounds owned by either the MCC (Lord's) or a county club (Edgbaston, Old Trafford, Headingley, Trent Bridge and the Oval). There was some sponsorship of county tournaments but none of England, and the one TV operation prepared to cover the national team (the BBC) paid almost nothing. Counties employed all 300 or so cricketers and made what they could from their games. The TCCB, owned and controlled by the MCC & Counties, put on England games and paid the counties a dividend from the profits.

The game was run on a shoe-string, generating a little under £2 million[2] in 1976, mostly from ticket receipts and memberships. England captain Tony Greig made £210 per Test and neither he nor any of the other England players enjoyed any financial security beyond the length of their county contract. The whole game spent whatever it earned and kept little or nothing in reserve. Importantly, though, the counties made 50% more revenue from their games than England did.

Long-term decline in attendances at three-day County Championship matches from 2.2 million in 1947 to half a million in the mid-sixties had required changes in the county product to increase audience appeal. The first Gillette-sponsored one-day tournament took place in 1963, the year the amateur / professional distinction was abolished. In 1967, the counties agreed to permit overseas players. The first John Player League Sunday tournament was in 1969 and the first Benson & Hedges Cup in 1972. The John Player League was particularly successful, with the 280,000 spectators in its first year almost matching the 327,000 who went to first-class matches.

The England team in 1976 was a pure representative side rather than a coherent team in the modern sense. A group of selectors picked from the counties and the selected players turned up at the ground the day before. There was no coach and little administrative and managerial backup, and players were responsible for their own fitness and development. Television coverage was threadbare, with both the BBC and the Australian Broadcasting Commission (ABC) in Australia using one camera at one end and another somewhere to the side. The television viewer therefore had to watch half the game from the batsman's end.

In Australia, five states played a first-class four-day tournament called the Sheffield Shield, and the Australian Cricket Board (ACB) ran the national team. The ABC paid a little over $30,000 a year, there were few sponsors, and total revenues amounted to less than $1 million. Players had no contracts with their states, unlike in England, and were instead paid piece rates of a few tens of dollars for each game. Test match player fees were so low—$200 per game until 1975—that national captain Ian Chappell regarded them as 'fish and chip money'.

Australia had no full-time professional cricketers. Fast bowler Dennis Lillee ran an office-cleaning business, batsman Rick McCosker worked in a bank and bowler Max Walker was an architect. This left top Australian players in a *Catch-22*, unable to commit either to cricket or to a regulation job. To get out of it, Chappell's predecessor Bill Lawry had suggested in 1968 that leading Australian players be contracted. That proposal went nowhere.

Things were the same in the West Indies. Colin Croft earned only US$600 for the five-Test series against Pakistan in early 1977, while Michael Holding, even after his historic effort at the Oval in 1976, was uncertain about a career in cricket. The best Caribbean players depended on English county cricket for their living, but Holding 'was not interested in county cricket, that grind. I played because I loved it. Andy [Roberts] had been used at Hampshire, bowled into the ground, because he was such a great wicket-taker.' Holding had done the first year in a computing course at the University of the West Indies and was considering a career in the field.

To all intents and purposes, cricket was still an amateur sport.

## Backwards

In *Wisden* 1977 there is little mention of the bubbling question of money. Instead, a series of articles looks back into the distant past. One marks former England captain Gubby Allen's retirement as MCC Treasurer after 12 years. Two others mark the passing of Arthur Gilligan and W.A. Oldfield, both of whom were born in 1894 and who played their cricket in the years after the end of the First World War. There is an article entitled *Tales of W.G. Grace*, and another looks back at 100 years of the Scarborough festival.

In two concessions to modernity, Gordon Ross reviews the history of the Gillette Cup since 1963 and a Richie Benaud article about *The Really Great Fast Bowlers* covers Frederick Spofforth, Frank Tyson, Dennis Lillee et al but somehow contrives not to mention the man who took 14 wickets at the Oval the year before.

The biggest article is about *The Cricket Rhymemaster*, a man named A.C. Craig who was known as the *Surrey Poet*. *Wisden* reproduces dozens of lines of verse like this:

> *I remember one County fixture, a regular grand affair,*
> *Holiday folk in their thousands with the rank and file were there,*
> *Our five best batsmen had fallen most lucklessly in the fray,*
> *And our score was a modest thirty, not a man had made a stay.*
>
> *I was seventh to take up the willow, but wasn't a bit depressed,*
> *A score of admirers whispered – 'take courage and do thy best',*
> *I felt nerved when the great assembly were cheering me all the*
> *while*
> *Still I ran up my century in fine and brilliant style.*

## Great men speak alike

When Ian Chappell first went to meet Kerry Packer in late 1976, Packer had his feet on the desk and wasted no time getting to the point.

'What are you, a fucking cowboy? Well, who do you want in this fucking team of yours?'

Chappell had been called to Packer's office at short notice with no time to change out of his casual clothes. When he protested that he had stepped down as Australia captain earlier in the year and that his brother Greg was now the national captain, Packer would have none of it.

'What do you think this is, son, a fucking democracy? You're the fucking captain.'

Chappell himself was no slouch in the profanity department. According to Kerry O'Keeffe, Chappell's strategy[3] each England bowler in a recent Ashes series was to 'slog the cunt'. For each batsman, the plan was to 'bounce the cunt'.

Chappell, 32 at the time of this meeting, first captained Australia in the Seventh Test versus England in February 1971, just after the first One-Day International at the MCG, and went on to captain Australia in 30 Tests between 1971 and 1975, winning 15 and losing 5. He did not lose a series.

Packer, 39, was the son of Frank Packer, a media tycoon who had owned *The Daily Telegraph* (a major Sydney paper) and had been heavily involved in the early days of television in Australia. In 1974, Frank died and Kerry inherited control of the family company, Consolidated Press Holdings, which owned a portion of Publishing and Broadcasting Ltd (PBL). This firm in turn owned Channel Nine and a stable of magazines.

The two men agreed to work together. Their business relationship continued through to Packer's death in 2005, interrupted only by a dressing-down that Packer gave Chappell when he swore on air by mistake.

## Their problems

Packer and Chappell both had grievances with the Australian Cricket Board. Chappell, like most Australian players, was disenchanted with the poor pay and conditions, whereas Packer wanted to secure the television rights for his Channel Nine. Both problems were fundamentally commercial, but the game was run on a gentlemanly and non-commercial basis.

In the 1972/73 season, Chappell suggested to the ACB that it create a system of player contracts and a provident fund for retired players. As with Bill Lawry's proposal in 1968, this made little progress. Things festered and then came to a head in the 1974/75 Ashes. With Lillee and Jeff Thomson bowling in tandem, Australia won two of the first three games. But on the morning of the first day of the Fourth Test at Sydney in January 1975, ACB Secretary Alan Barnes was quoted in *The Australian*:

*These are not professionals. They were all invited to play, and if they don't like the conditions there are 500,000 other cricketers in Australia who would love to take their places.*

Chappell told the ABC in 2002 that this statement did for him and his players.

*I went out to the nets and I'm fuming. I'm batting in the nets and every ball that's coming down I'm whacking them as if they're Alan Barnes' head. And I walked back through the dressing room and I walk through the door and there was Ian Redpath, one of the milder blokes you would think in the Australian team. He has got Alan Barnes up against the wall by the bloody throat saying to him, 'You bloody idiot. Of course there are 500,000 out there who would play for nothing. But how bloody good would the Australian team be?'*

Australia won that Sydney Test to go 3–0 up and reclaim the Ashes. The ACB provided a healthy bonus, but the cricketers noted during the Sixth Test at the MCG that their collective remuneration for the match was around 1% of the ticket revenue generated by the total crowd of 250,000. Lillee told journalists that the top players should be on contracts worth at least $25,000 a year.

In October 1975, Bob Hawke, the President of the Australian Council of Trade Unions and future Australian Prime Minister, told the players that they had been exploited for years. Later in the 1975/76 season, Australia beat the West Indies for the last time in 19 years, taking the series 5–1 with Lillee and Thomson again rampant. Even though the ACB doubled player fees to $400 a game, Ian Chappell retired at the end of the series saying that he could make more money coaching. His total cricket earnings were about the same as the average Australian male made in private sector employment. Batsman Ian Redpath, Man of the Match at the Sixth Test with a century and a fifty, also retired pleading poverty.

In his book *Chappelli*, Ian Chappell delivered a parting shot:

*I think it's time that the Board carefully considered the principle of binding the leading Australian players to full-time contracts in much the same way as other sportsmen, businessmen and celebrities are contracted.*

At almost the same time, in February 1976, Kerry Packer asked to meet the ACB to discuss the upcoming three-year contract to televise Australia's home games. This contract traditionally went to the ABC on the nod, and the Board refused to meet Packer. When the two sides did meet, in June, there were two offers on the table. One, from the ABC, was for $69,000 per year non-exclusive. Packer's offer was for $500,000 a year, exclusive.

This meeting has entered Australian sporting legend. Packer is reported to have said to the assembled dignitaries, 'Come on now, we're all harlots. I know you haven't signed the contracts. What's your price?' When told to come back in three years for the next contract, Packer is reported to have said: 'Well damn, I don't know why we don't put on our own cricket Tests.'

## Start

The chain of events that turned cricket from a largely amateur sport into a global business can be traced back to a social encounter between Dennis Lillee, his joint agents John Cornell and Austin Robertson, and TV and film star Paul Hogan. Cornell was also Hogan's manager and occasionally appeared beside him on the *Paul Hogan Show* on Channel Nine. He was later the producer of *Crocodile Dundee*.

Lillee told Cornell and Robertson that Australian players should play extra fixtures to help them escape the *Catch-22*, adding that the new games could be scheduled not to compete with official cricket. Cornell then told Packer that the players were poorly paid and passed on Lillee's suggestion. Packer replied, 'Why not do the thing properly? Let's get the world's best to play Australia's best.' But when Cornell and Robertson went to see Ian Chappell, he told them that the authorities had a lock on the game through their control of all the major grounds. According to Chappell, the response was:

*Fuck that! We'll get the grounds. We are not going to the Board.*

Then came the meeting between Packer and Chappell. At Packer's invitation, Chappell made a list of 28 Australian players, all of whom were successfully recruited. Dennis Lillee was among the first, signing in January 1977 for three years at $35,000 a year. Captains were to be offered $30,000 and players $25,000.

Packer also achieved another coup against the Australian cricket authorities by securing the television rights for the 1977 Ashes series, despite an attempt by the Board to assert control over the rights for overseas matches. When Packer doubled his initial offer, the TCCB agreed that the 1977 Ashes would be shown on Channel Nine and not the ABC. It was the first cricket to go on that channel.

Packer was not impressed by the ACB's refusal to meet him in the first half of 1976, its rejection of his offer of $500,000 a year, and its clumsy attempt to keep all cricket out of his reach. He later said:

*Three times the stiletto went in, and at the end of the third time, I said that's it.*

## England

The Centenary Test at Melbourne took place from 12–17 March 1977, attended by 200 former players. At the game, according to Bob Willis, Australian players moaned that they were being paid less than the cleaners. Afterwards, Tony Greig went to meet Packer and was offered $30,000 a year for three years to captain a World XI. In early April, Greig went to the West Indies / Pakistan series in the Caribbean with Austin Robertson to scoop up more players. For Greig's nemesis from the year before, Michael Holding, the sum of $25,000 was completely outside his imagination. He signed on.

On 6 April 1977, Kerry Packer called Richie Benaud. The Aussie-captain-turned-commentator initially advised a co-operative approach and, like Lillee, suggested that Packer organise games on different dates from official ACB cricket. Then, after thinking about it overnight, Benaud agreed to help.

For Packer, this was another coup. Benaud was an Establishment figure who could confer credibility on the project, and he was more than useful on the cricketing front too. Benaud wrote later: 'Everything that happened I had something to do with, that was part of my job. Everything would be run by me.'

Having recruited a battery of West Indian players, including Clive Lloyd, to staff one of Packer's three sides, Greig returned home in April 1977 to begin the recruitment of his colleagues. A little later, the Australian tour party flew to England for the 1977 Ashes series with few players that had not signed for Packer.

On the flight over, Doug Walters set a new benchmark for the number of cans of beer[4] drunk on a Sydney-London flight, with 44. Wicketkeeper Rod Marsh's claim also to have sunk 44 was not supported by his team-mates.

## Into a meat mangler

On 24 April 1977 the *South Africa Sunday Times* reported under the headline 'Howzat' that over 30 top players, four of them English, had signed playing contracts with an external organisation. News did not travel fast in those days, and it was not until 9 May that the *Daily Mail* broke the story in the UK. Under the headline *World's Top Cricketers Turn Pirate*, Ian Wooldridge revealed some names and details provided to him by Benaud on Packer's authority. Wooldridge reported a guarantee that 'not a ball will be missed' by television and concluded that 'Cricket leaders throughout the world, therefore, are this morning confronted with a brilliant and ruthless coup.'

On the same day, Packer told a press conference:

*We'll do all we can to co-operate with the cricket board. And, if they co-operate with us, there is no reason why Test cricket as it is now will be affected. But, if they don't co-operate, they'll walk straight into a meat mangler.*

In all, 35 players had been recruited, including the captains of the big three teams. Reaction in England was strongly antipathetic. There was a feeling that Tony Greig, already held to be an outsider fortunate to be allowed to play for England, had polluted the Centenary Test with money-grubbing scheming and treachery. Christopher Martin-Jenkins wrote:

*For those of us who admittedly take the game (which is or was, just a game) too seriously, it was like learning that a wife whom one loved and trusted had been secretly, and for some time, making love to another man.*

Expectations for Packer were low. John Arlott wrote in *The Guardian*:

*It is virtually certain that if a circus scheme were launched in competition to Test cricket, it would fail … The English cricketing Establishment could almost certainly destroy any such threat to the international game.*

In late May, Greig was sacked as England captain and replaced by Mike Brearley. Greig did his best to present Packer's plans as positive for the game, but later wrote: 'For the first time in my life, I experienced the odd sensation that many of my listeners did not believe a word I was saying … When I insisted that cricket would benefit in the long-term, they stared and muttered as if I was a creature from another planet.'

Packer himself flew to the UK to meet the ICC, saying that cricket 'is the easiest sport in the world to take over. Nobody bothered to pay the players what they were worth.' At the ICC meeting, he reassured delegates that he only wanted the television rights. When told to bid for them like everybody else, he left the meeting saying, 'I will now take no steps to help anyone, every man for himself and the devil take the hindmost.'

Six England players committed to Packer: Greig himself, Bob Woolmer, Derek Underwood, Alan Knott, Dennis Amiss and John Snow. Bob Willis was offered a five-year deal but ultimately rejected the offer when his county, Warwickshire, co-ordinated a counteroffer that provided him with the security he wanted. In July, the ICC banned those who played for Packer from official international cricket, and in August the TCCB did the same with county cricket, despite receiving legal advice that enforcement would be difficult. Crucially, both organisations executed the bans via a change in their rules.

A month later, Greig, Snow and Mike Procter took the authorities to court in London. Backed by Packer, the three argued that the rule changes by the ICC and the TCCB were invalid. Mr Justice Slade ruled that none of the players had any contract that prevented them from playing for Packer. He then declared the rule changes by the ICC and the TCCB to be void and awarded costs against the defendants. The winning barrister was Bob Alexander, who was to become President of the MCC in 2000.

Meanwhile, the first effect of Packer's action had already been felt in England. Cornhill Insurance agreed a sponsorship deal of about £1 million over five years with the TCCB, and player fees rose nearly five-fold to £1,000 per game.

## Setup

While he was fighting court battles and recruiting personnel, Packer's team organised the 1977/78 season. The overall objective was to use his superior financial resources to spend the ACB into the ground and force them to cede. His strategy was to swamp the public with high-quality cricket, bring in the punters *en masse* and develop new sources of revenue with which to pay the players their increased fees.

World Series Cricket (WSC) started life with just two assets: the players and Channel Nine. Although it had no grounds, no audience and no reputation, the team was reassured by a statement from Packer that 'It's not lack of money that will determine the future of World Series Cricket. It's the standard of play.'

To this end, Australia, West Indies and a World XI would play six Supertests and fifteen one-day games in the main urban centres. For one-day games, a white ball would be used so that fans whose eyes were not cricket-trained (especially women and children) could more easily see what was going on. Because most fans were normal people with jobs, WSC decided to schedule matches during the evening. For the same reason, it decided to play five-day games straight through the weekend with no interruption on a Sunday.

Richie Benaud decided to write new laws instead of using The Laws of Cricket which were, and still are, owned by the MCC. Against Benaud's advice, though, Packer decided to schedule the Supertests against the official ACB cricket programme. However, none of the main venues was available, proving Ian Chappell's point. Instead, WSC rented four other grounds, including Aussie Rules[5] grounds in Melbourne (VFL Park) and Adelaide (Football Park), a harness racing ground in Perth and a showground in Sydney.

With no cricket grounds available, pitches were a big problem. An assistant groundsman at the Gabba named John Maley invented the solution. His idea was to grow turf in a concrete tray inside a greenhouse, place the 25-ton tray on to a low loader and then drop the tray into a hole in the middle of the playing arena using a crane. Hence the drop-in pitch.

Channel Nine would earn most of the revenue in the form of sponsorship and advertising, and so the design of the television operation was critical. Packer himself had trenchant views on how the game should be televised, having long derided the established practice of one-ended coverage as filling the screen with 'the batsman's arse'. He also disparaged dull commentary and the minimal number of cameras.

The television team decided to use a camera at both ends and two more at the side for run outs and stumpings. A roving camera was to follow a dismissed batsman back to the pavilion, and another would provide a bird's eye view. A total of eight cameras would provide far richer coverage of the game and, together with pitch microphones and player interviews, establish a stronger connection between the players and the viewers.

For the first season, WSC adopted the slogan 'See the white ball fly'. Sponsorship deals were secured with Qantas and McDonald's, and Channel Nine introduced advertisements between overs.

## First season

Packer's first season involved 51 cricketers and lost PBL over $3 million. WSC also lost the live audience battle, generating an average Supertest gate of 5,300 compared with 11,500 at official games. On the other hand, Test takings were down by two-thirds from the year before and the ACB also had to support domestic cricket, pay its share of the legal bill incurred in London and swallow the costs of an unsuccessful court action to stop Packer calling his games 'Supertests'. Furthermore, Sheffield Shield attendances fell fast, despite the admission of Tasmania, and the states incurred big financial losses as a result. Official cricket was starting to buckle under the weight of Packer's financial assault.

The campaign started with an advertisement in the Packer-owned *Australian Women's Weekly* on 28 September 1977. In this ad, WSC extended an open invitation to the female half of Australia's population to join in the party that is a big cricket match.

The first two games were played on 24 November 1977. In the official first game, WSC Australia faced the World XI at VFL Park on a drop-in pitch. The toss was run by Garry Sobers, hired to play the role of WSC elder, and Bill Lawry and Richie Benaud were the first two commentators.

Three weeks later, on 14 December, the first game under lights was played between Australia and the World XI, an extraordinary team featuring the six England players and the five Pakistanis. A crowd of 6,400 watched the white ball fly. Packer was pleased, telling reporters, 'For the first time in a lifetime of watching cricket, I could see the ball from the moment it left the bat. It must be a great innovation for cricket and I can't see why it can't be used all the time.' That ball is now in the museum at the Sydney Cricket Ground.

In order to enhance the spectator experience, WSC instructed umpires to tolerate the bouncer. But, during the second Supertest at Sydney in December, David Hookes was hit by an Andy Roberts bouncer and suffered a broken jaw and cheekbone. To protect his players, Packer ordered a batch of helmets of the type used by Dennis Amiss, who had also been hit by Roberts at the Old Trafford Test in 1976.

## Divide and rule

Official England went to Pakistan in December, and Packer decided to let his Pakistani players take part in the Third Test at Karachi in January. This inspired move signalled to the governing boards outside Australia and England that he had no beef with them. The England team protested and in the ensuing row Greig blamed Geoff Boycott and accused him of running away from the world's fastest bowlers. Sussex promptly sacked Greig as captain and his career as an un-person in England began.

Official Australia was due in the West Indies in February under Bob Simpson, brought back from retirement at 41 by Don Bradman. As the WSC season was over, Packer made his West Indians available for selection for the official West Indies side but held his Australians back. This reinforced Packer's image as a co-operative man compared with the would-be monopolists of the ACB.

The West Indies won the first two Tests, but the West Indies Cricket Board of Control (WICBC) then wanted to know whether the Packer players would be available for a tour to India later in the year. The players and the Board fell out, the players withdrew from the next game, and a spectator boycott began. Tony Cozier commented that 'the public was overwhelmingly in favour of Packer'. WSC then signed a deal with the West Indies Board to co-operate on a series in the Caribbean the following year. The WICBC, which had promised the ICC not to deal unilaterally with Packer, had effectively switched sides.

Despite the $3 million loss, Packer ended his first season well ahead. Day / night cricket, the white ball and the drop-in pitches all worked. The opposition was growing poorer by the day and its overseas support was fragmenting. WSC players stayed in the best hotels, their partners and guests were welcomed and they could write freely for the press. Packer let the players use his house and pool and on occasions was seen mowing outfields himself. This open, egalitarian approach compared favourably with the aloof superiority of ACB officialdom, and player relations were consequently good. The cricketers as a group showed their appreciation with a signed bat and the West Indians gave him a voodoo doll.

Altogether, it was an *Annus Mirabilis*. Packer concluded that 'We are still amateurs, but we are more professional than we were, and will become even more professional.'

## Second season

England was due in Australia for the 1978/79 Ashes, setting up a showdown between official and WSC cricket. In the off-season, WSC pulled off another coup with deals that secured both the Sydney Cricket Ground and Brisbane's Gabba. For the season, both the ACB and WSC scheduled more than 80 days, half of which were to be televised. The battleground would be the audience, and marketing was the key.

The ACB launched its campaign under the slogan 'Battle for the Ashes' and portrayed the bearded Mike Brearley as a knight. For its part, WSC spent $2.5 million on promotions, more than twice the revenue of official Australian cricket. It introduced a national cricket song entitled *Cmon Aussie Cmon* and produced T-shirts with slogans aimed at women such as 'Big boys play at night' and 'Your pad or mine'. It set up a children's cricket club, was the first advertiser to use hoardings on the backs of cabs in Sydney and launched a logo-decorated balloon above that city.

WSC scheduled a huge volume of cricket between 23 November and 3 February, with an average of more than one game per day completely swamping the audience. This volume of cricket demanded new fitness standards of the players and Packer decided to set targets for weight, stamina and speed, with fines for the recalcitrant. Dennis Lillee decided to get fit and took running lessons.

The finest moment for World Series Cricket came on 28 November 1978, when the first televised day-night game took place under floodlights at the Sydney Cricket Ground. Lillee later wrote:

> *We played the first game of the season at the SCG. During a break in play, Cornell said Packer wanted to see me. There were about 7,000 or 8,000 people in the ground, far from full, and I wondered if this was the end of the road for a brave and bold idea.*
>
> *When I arrived in his room upstairs … he called me over and took me to a window that looked out over the parkland at the back of the SCG. There were about 20,000 people trying to get in, with huge queues waiting at the gates. He put his arm around my shoulder and said, 'We've made it.'*

Tony Greig choked back tears. Michael Holding, who was injured but at the game, later wrote: 'The thrill of that night will always remain with me.' Packer ordered the gates opened and over 44,000 watched Australia beat the West Indies, with women allowed into the members' area at the SCG for the first time.

Three days later, the official Australian team was bowled out by Bob Willis and Ian Botham for 116 on the first day of the First Test in Brisbane. The new captain, Graham Yallop, had played only eight Tests, and the whole Australian side only 55 between them. Fewer people went to see official Australia's third XI during the whole First Test than to WSC's one-day game at the SCG.

Official Australia went two down in the first two Tests, but on 29 December pulled off a remarkable victory at the MCG. The ACB struck a blow back by attracting over 100,000 people to that game against the 50,000 achieved by WSC in the five one-day games scheduled at the same time. But, when England won the Fourth Test on 11 January to go 3–1 up and retain the Ashes, the two remaining Tests became dead games, giving the advantage back to WSC. On 17 January, 45,000 spectators saw the first coloured-clothing game at the SCG. Three weeks later, Tony Greig signed off from the international game at the Supertest final between Australia and his World XI, 'caught Marsh, bowled Lillee' for nought.

For the ACB, the 1978/79 season was a disaster. Although WSC only beat the Board narrowly in the live attendance stakes, by 585,000 to 551,000, Sheffield Shield numbers collapsed from 350,000 to 135,000. Profits fell by 75% compared with the previous Ashes tour, and finances became so tight that the New South Wales Cricket Association considered the sale of its headquarters building, Queensland was on the verge of insolvency and Victoria was also in trouble. The ACB itself went into negative equity.

The World Series bandwagon then went off to the West Indies for the series arranged the year before. Packer compensated the WICBC for the loss of West Indian players from its domestic tournament and paid over the odds for the use of its grounds, thereby keeping this Board happy. In England, a new cricket magazine, *Wisden Cricket Monthly*, started in June 1979. Fresher and less inhibited than the Almanack of the same name, it sent a female reporter, Wendy Lloyd, to cover the WSC Caribbean tour for its first issue. Lloyd reported back:

*The WSC organisation is a professional business geared to good financial remuneration. There is, however, an obligation to give value for money. Cricket is seen as an entertainment in a commercial world ...The most striking thing to me as the players took the field for the first of the one-day games was their fitness. The Australians were smart and svelte ... the West Indians were like panthers ...My experience of WSC has shown it to be very much alive, with much to offer the cricket world as a whole.*

## Rapprochement

The dire financial situation of the ACB, along with the ICC's wish for a successful 1979 World Cup in England, forced the authorities to reconsider their stance. In the background, too, there lurked a dreadful threat. Packer had told ICC officials that he might take WSC to England if officialdom there caused any trouble. Had he done so, two worlds would have thudded together in an epic collision. There could only have been one winner.

The expiration of the television deal that had caused all the fuss in the first place provided the opportunity. In February 1979, after refusing to deal with the MCC-run ICC, Packer met the ACB Chairman, Bob Parish, and on 24 April Parish announced a deal. For the next 10 years, the ACB would select the national team and PBL would take charge of the commercial side. The format of two visiting teams was to be retained, with a programme of Tests and a triangular one-day series with finals. The Board also agreed to consider fielding circles (invented by Tony Greig), day-night games and coloured clothing. Channel Nine was granted an exclusive right to televise home cricket for three years and, most importantly, the Board was to set up a system of Key Player contracts with the top cricketers. The same players would then sign a contract with PBL to cover off-field duties.

This deal was hugely advantageous to Packer. It provided the ACB $1.15 million a year, non-indexed, for 10 years, of which the television component was $420,000 – less than Packer had offered in 1976. Under PBL management, cricket revenues grew so fast in the eighties that the ACB forced a renegotiation in 1986. It is likely that Packer made his WSC losses back many times over.

Packer concluded his involvement in the direct management of Australian cricket by paying his players the third year of their WSC contracts. In return, he received a bat signed by all the WSC players which he named the 'Six million dollar bat'.

Looking to the future, Packer's managing director, Lynton Taylor, told a reporter that 'The big input is in the younger generation and females. It's our job to see that we introduce all those people to the traditional game now, and induce a new lot of people to come to cricket.'

## Retrospective

In the years since, many of those involved in World Series Cricket have written about their experiences. Tony Greig was not alone in feeling the hostility of the English press and cricketing Establishment. Bob Woolmer, interviewed in the second issue of *Wisden Cricket Monthly*, said that the English press was the most disappointing aspect of WSC, adding, 'Most of the writers were dead against it as though they'd made their minds up in advance.' Clive Lloyd agreed, saying, 'The campaign against Mr Packer was quite outrageous. It just made many of us more determined. Instead of making World Series Cricket weaker, it made us stronger.'

Others have stressed the competitiveness of the cricket. Richie Benaud wrote: 'Some of the best and most competitive cricket I have ever seen was in the time of World Series Cricket which followed Richards' wonderful tour of England in 1976'. Bob Woolmer, who mostly played for the country touring side, the Cavaliers, said, 'It may have been in the bush but the West Indies would still have an attack of Holding, Roberts, Croft and Garner. It was the toughest cricket I've ever played.'

The commercial people have been scathing about the role of the England Establishment. Andrew Caro, PBL Managing Director for most of WSC's short life, commented, 'Parish and the board were the losers that summer. I mean, we out-marketed the bastards. But the Poms were absolutely pusillanimous and they delivered Bob Parish's head on an absolute platter, like John the Baptist.'

Lynton Taylor said, 'It's not just the English Press. It's the English administrators as well. Having tried unsuccessfully for some rapprochement between WSC and the Establishment, they took umbrage when the ACB took the initiative and brought about that rapprochement. I think they are now envious of the situation which exists for the ACB here. There is no doubt the centre of cricket has moved out of England and is now in Australia.'

Ian Chappell disagrees slightly with that last comment. His view is that England permanently lost its leadership of the game when it conceded a 2–2 draw against his team at home in 1972, five years before World Series Cricket.

## Afterwards

In the subsequent five years, England, Australia and West Indies followed three distinct trajectories. Figure 5, an expansion of the earlier part of the form chart in Chapter 2, shows England and Australia's form in official Tests between 1979 and 1986.

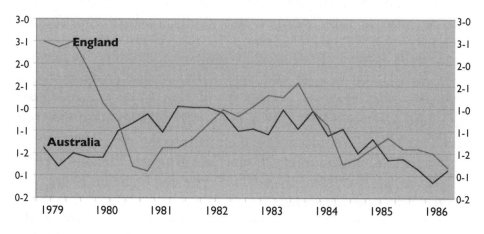

FIGURE 5: ENGLAND AND AUSTRALIA FORM SEPTEMBER
1979–JUNE 1986

The West Indies forged ahead with its battery of fast bowlers, England followed a cyclical path as if nothing had happened and Australia recovered but then collapsed. Players from all three countries went on rebel tours to South Africa, whose top players had experienced international cricket with WSC and wanted more, and whose government craved international sporting contact for political reasons of its own. By 1985, both England and Australia were in the doldrums.

The West Indies won the 1979 World Cup, beating England in the final at Lord's thanks to 138 from Viv Richards. Then, at PBL's insistence, the West Indies and England were both invited to tour Australia again in 1979/80 to restart official world cricket. The TCCB assented but insisted on white clothing and fewer one-day games. It also refused to stake the Ashes in a series with only three Tests.

This season was Year Zero for Australia, and the construction of new traditions out of old began. In the Tests, the Aussies beat England 3–0 in spite of a stupendous performance by Ian Botham, with 19 wickets at under 20 and 187 runs at 37, but lost 0–2 to the West Indies. A clear pecking order based on fast-bowling resources was thereby established: Andy Roberts, Michael Holding, Colin Croft and Joel Garner trumped Dennis Lillee, Jeff Thomson and Len Pascoe, who in turn trumped Bob Willis, Botham and Graham Dilley.

England played its first One-Day International under lights at Sydney exactly one year after the momentous game of 1978, narrowly beating the West Indies by two runs. Overall, PBL put another $2.5 million promotional effort into the programme of six Tests and 15 One-Day Internationals, securing an attendance of 1.3 million at the six Tests (over 40,000 per day) and an average of 20,000 at the one-day series.

Holding discontinued his studies at the University of the West Indies, and wrote in his autobiography: 'In fact, had it not been for

Kerry Packer, I would not have played the game for as long as I did. There was no money in it before he came along, and it offered me no great future as a career since I wasn't interested then in professional cricket in England or in becoming a full-time coach at home.' He went on: 'WSC was the making of the West Indies team of the nineteen eighties. Kerry Packer gave us pride.' The other reason for West Indies' success was improved coaching and fitness. 'We'd never had a single person dedicated to us before. And in those days we'd never heard of track suits. You played in whites. But Dennis [Waight, the West Indies trainer] told us that we weren't fit enough. He got us running and stretching and training, and learned what each of us needed.'

Croft told the BBC in 2002 that 'Kerry Packer's World Series Cricket was the genesis of Clive Lloyd's all-conquering team, using all of the elements of natural athleticism with the attitude of professionalism.' Viv Richards said, 'I think our experiences there, at the very highest level, helped us when we came back to Test cricket.'

The West Indies did not lose a series for 15 years from 1980. During this period, they played 115 Tests, won 59, lost 15 and established clear superiority over all other teams. In a run of seven series between 1983 and 1986, they played 35, won 23 and lost only one game, beating England, Australia and India both home and away and hammering England 5–0 on both occasions.

## Australia

After the 1979/80 season, the Australian side suffered from a combination of problems. World Series Cricket had forced the ACB to extract 20 players from domestic cricket and pitch them into the sink-or-swim environment of the Australian third XI, further starving domestic cricket of international players and disrupting the development system that had produced a strong national team for decades. Then, when WSC and official cricket merged, the hectic PBL-designed schedule kept the leading players out of domestic cricket. In 1975/76, for instance, the two Chappells, Lillee and Rod

Marsh each played all eight Sheffield Shield matches, despite a six-Test tour by the West Indies. In 1984/85, Allan Border played in only five out of 11 domestic games.

Almost all of the fill-in players were discarded in favour of returning Packer players, most of whom then retired within two years. Ian Chappell retired for the second time in early 1980, leaving his brother Greg, Lillee, Thomson and Marsh as the senior cricketers, with Border and Kim Hughes the most established of the non-WSC group. Captaincy problems stalked Australia too. Factions developed behind Greg Chappell, who was not consistently available for tours, and the alternate captain, Hughes.

Commercially, however, Australia went from strength to strength. Gate receipts rose from $3.5 million in 1981/82 to $5.3 million in 1982/83, partly driven by increasing numbers of One-Day Internationals. By 1982, the ACB and PBL had 20 players under contract.

Australia came repeatedly under the cosh on the field. After three successive visits in the seasons 1977/78 to 1979/80, the West Indies came three more times in the next five seasons and delivered further heavy beatings. Pakistan, too, drew level with Australia. In late 1982, a weak Australian side without Lillee and Greg Chappell was beaten 3–0 in Pakistan. The man who kept leg-spin going in the eighties, Abdul Qadir, took 22 wickets in that series.

## Back in Blighty

Business in England carried on as before. Committees met, reviews reviewed and the geological clock ticked on. As the 1978 season began, for example, a further move against the MCC got under way within the upper echelons of England cricket administration. A proposal was circulated to wind up the Cricket Council and re-constitute the game under a UK Board of Control composed of the first-class counties and the National Cricket Association. The proposal made little headway at the time, although it did eventually become reality in 1997.

Because only six players had been involved in the Packer circus, England was initially affected only in the personnel department. Ian Botham took the berth vacated by Tony Greig, perhaps two or three years early. Graham Gooch and David Gower took up the spots vacated by Dennis Amiss and Bob Woolmer, and Bob Taylor took Alan Knott's wicket-keeper slot.

Debate about the future was led by Bob Willis. In a remarkable book, *Cricket Revolution*, published in 1981, Willis worried about the balance of one-day versus Test cricket. He claimed that too many overseas players in county cricket were hogging the best spots and proposed the replacement of three-day cricket by four-day games played during the week, with limited-overs games on the weekends. He called for a salaried full-time team manager, an England Under-25 team, the end of the 'semi-feudal' benefit system and a transfer system. Separately, he called for an end to Test match rest days and criticised the TCCB for continuing with uncovered wickets because they did not prepare England players for Test cricket.

Willis was prescient in his diagnosis of the ills of England cricket and his forecasts for the future. Overseas players and the benefit system are still live issues in 2007, and most of his other suggestions have since been adopted. One prediction, that 'ITV-2 eventually makes the TCCB an offer it just cannot refuse', came true in 1998 when Channel 4, together with BSkyB, took cricket away from the BBC after 61 years.

WSC made itself felt in small ways. For 1980, the BBC decided to use five cameras, with one at each end for replays, although coverage was still one-ended. Middlesex and Arsenal played a game at Highbury Stadium under lights in front of 8,000 people, and another day/night game at Stamford Bridge between Surrey and the West Indies made a profit of £20,000. However, a TCCB floodlit tournament using football grounds at the end of the 1981 season flopped, bringing an end to this experiment.

In 1981, Kim Hughes brought Australia to England for an Ashes series. After winning the First Test, drawing the second and forcing England to follow on in the third, Australia were well set to go two-nil up in the six-match series. England won that third game and then the next two courtesy of the best three-match performance in cricket history by an individual player. Following his outstanding display against Australia in 1979/80 and another immediately afterwards against India, Ian Botham scored 336 runs at 67 in the three matches and took 18 wickets at 17.

Botham was not alone. In the Third Test, the fifth-day crowd hooted in amazement and disbelief as Bob Willis, in a bowler's trance, took eight for 43 in 15.1 overs of irresistible brilliance. Having taken the final wicket, Willis set off on a demented, elliptical run like a wild horse let out of its box after a long road journey. Had there been another four Australian batsmen, England would still have won.

Australia collapsed to a 1–3 loss in the series. Kim Hughes claimed afterwards that Botham was the difference between the sides, but that was incorrect. The difference between the two sides was England's last pair of world-class bowlers, Bob Willis and Ian Botham. England was not to beat the full-strength Australian side again for 24 years.

In February 1982 a rebel tour to South Africa was announced. The rebels increased from six in 1977 to 14, four of whom were repeat offenders. The squad—Dennis Amiss, Geoff Boycott, John Emburey, Graham Gooch, Mike Hendrick, Alan Knott, Wayne Larkins, John Lever, Chris Old, Bob Taylor, Geoff Humpage, Bob Woolmer, Derek Underwood and Peter Willey—was attracted by fees of up to £45,000. The TCCB banned them for three years, which meant that the 1982/83 Ashes team would be badly weakened.

Bob Willis again remained loyal, despite an offer of £60,000 to captain the rebel team. Under his captaincy, however, England lost the 1982/83 Ashes series by one game to two.

# England finances

Throughout the immediate post-WSC period, England cricket revenues were driven up by increasing sponsorship and ticket receipts. Cornhill's Test sponsorship and county sponsorships more than tripled between 1977 and 1985 and England ticket receipts quadrupled over the same period. In December 1983, the TCCB agreed a new deal with the BBC worth £1 million over three years, triple the amount collected in 1976. Overall cricket revenues rose from about £2 million in 1976 to about £8 million[6] in 1985, an average of 8% per year on top of inflation.

The England team and the 17 counties both generated £4 million, meaning that England had caught up for the first time. The game's business model remained in place, though. Money generated by the national side went straight out to the counties, which then spent it on their own circuit. The minimum salary for a capped county player rose in stages from £3,500 in 1977 to over £7,500 in 1985 and the total county salary bill went from £700,000 to £2 million. Little appears to have been put aside and the game continued to live from hand to mouth.

This business model, and the governance of the professional game in general, came under attack. In *Wisden,* a county Chief Executive named Philip Carling wrote that 'county cricket has lurched from one financial crisis to another'. The problem, he diagnosed, was that:

> *The game has survived for the most part in a form which would have been immediately recognisable to its practitioners in late Victorian England.*

Carling added that 'The somewhat unwieldy democracy of the TCCB committee system is hard-pressed to react quickly enough to the ever-changing demands of the eighties.' He suggested that 'The committee system ... could, I believe, be made more efficient at national level by an executive body which has foresight and teeth.'

But, without this, 'Cricket will continue to lurch from one financial crisis to another when there is no need. Until still more financial sophistication is applied, neither four-day Championship nor more limited-overs matches will provide long-term security.'

## First rows

In 1982, the silent war between the TCCB and the MCC broke out into the open. A two-year Working Party recommended that TCCB representation on the Cricket Council increase from five seats to eight and MCC decrease from five to three. An MCC bigwig, Gubby Allen, resigned in protest at the new TCCB majority, saying that the county clubs could now control the game and divert its resources to themselves.

The MCC launched a counter-attack by considering the dispatch of a team to South Africa. For the TCCB, host to upcoming tours by West Indies and Pakistan, a cancellation by either would be commercially disastrous. The MCC also put out the word that it was time the TCCB paid more for its offices at Lord's. However, in July 1983, the MCC voted not to tour South Africa.

After another review in 1983, the TCCB decided to ignore demands for four-day cricket by Bob Willis and others and opted instead to increase the number of three-day county games from 22 to 24. For most county club members, the crucial variable was the number of home games rather than the number of home days. They therefore preferred twelve games of three days to eight of four. Another Working Party considered a proposal by Ray Illingworth for a two-division championship, but at the end of the year the TCCB announced that no further changes would be made until 1986 at the earliest.

At the 1983 World Cup, England got through to the semi-final but were easily beaten by India. Bob Willis wrote afterwards: 'As I have been saying for several years, England's cup is fairly bare, and there is a huge gap between county expertise and consistent success at

Test level.' Australia had a poor World Cup, failing to get past the league stage, although Rod Marsh put away 45 beers on the flight from Sydney to London, one more than the 44 imbibed by Doug Walters six years before. In the first game, against Zimbabwe, Marsh took three catches and scored 50 not out.

Cricket writer Matthew Engel laid into the MCC in the October 1983 edition of *Wisden Cricket Monthly*, writing: 'Can you imagine how people in football would react if there was a Wembley Football Club whose members were entitled to automatic privileges at their Cup Final?' Noting that '50 per cent of the human race is excluded at birth,' Engel argued that 'If the members of the MCC want to divest themselves of all public responsibility they can do and restrict admission to Lords to red-headed left-handers if they wish. But in that event, the TCCB, with its wider responsibilities, should begin thinking of where else its major games might go.' Engel concluded:

> *The World Cup final might have attracted 50,000 or more had there been a stadium large enough; the NatWest final would regularly attract 40,000. Lord's holds 25,000. Melbourne and Calcutta can hold four times as many. How do you justify staging the World Cup final at Lord's?*

## Willis accelerates

Willis captained an England tour to New Zealand in 1983/84. With Graham Dilley and Neil Foster injured and Botham underperforming with the ball, England suffered its first series loss to New Zealand. In the Second Test at Christchurch, England ceded 307 on a poor pitch with bowling that Willis (who took 4–51) described as 'abysmal'. They were then dismissed by Richard Hadlee for 82 and 93 to lose by an innings. England went next to Pakistan and lost 0–1 there too. Two months later, Willis wrote: 'We have got to learn to win all over again, and change our domestic game to produce quality cricketers.'

Willis retired at the end of the 1984 home season, having

relinquished the captaincy to David Gower before the 0–5 beating by the West Indies. He took 325 wickets at 25 apiece in 90 Tests, and was responsible for the most inspiring bowling spell by an England player in living memory. As well as setting the agenda in his analysis of the game, he was one of the first players to emphasise England at the expense of his county, bowling only slightly more overs in non-England games than for England.

When no fast-bowling replacement presented himself, Willis got stuck in. In winter 1984, he complained that there was 'Not enough criticism of a system that throws up such mediocre resources.' He received backing from Pakistan and Sussex fast bowler Imran Khan who said, '... the structure of county cricket puts enormous demands on a young up-and-coming fast bowler. Seven-day-a-week cricket is just too much.' Imran pointed out that Alan Piggott and Neil Foster had had pins in their spines, that Graham Dilley was injured, Alan Ward and Chris Old had slowed down and that John Snow, like Willis, played hardly any county cricket.

Imran went on: 'Another side-effect of the over-abundance of cricket is the lack of competitiveness and aggression in English cricket. This is so obvious when viewed against the Australian and West Indian game. Consequently those countries—despite playing only a third of the amount of first-class cricket played in England—have consistently produced better pacemen. A competitive, aggressive atmosphere brings the best out of a fast bowler.'

In December 1984, the TCCB responded to the drubbing by the West Indies and the loss to New Zealand by setting up another Working Party to investigate the standards and quality of English cricket. This group, led by Cricket Council Chairman Charles Palmer, had nine members and included two England selectors. How exactly they were supposed to review themselves wasn't quite clear.

Despite the points made by Willis and Imran, *Wisden* editor John Woodcock, writing in the 1985 edition, blamed a surfeit of one-day cricket for England's decline. This sentiment, which ultimately sought to pin the blame for England's decline on World Series Cricket and its supposed obsession with money, had become the received wisdom in England cricket.

## Back to the present

In the winter of 2006, the BBC used Channel Nine as supplier for its Ashes highlights show. Bill Lawry, as is now traditional, led the coverage of the first game at Brisbane. Like 44,000 people in the Gabba and many back in England, Lawry waited for the inevitable crack in the England façade. He didn't have to wait long. Although there was a slight improvement over the 2002/03 series, when Nasser Hussain put the Australians in to bat, England wilted on the very first ball.

Another World Series Cricket commentator, Richie Benaud, did what are likely to be his last stints on British television. On the second day, Matthew Hoggard got Adam Gilchrist LBW for nought and on the BBC Daddles the Duck flopped across the screen to the sound of a croaking wheeze. The duck was first seen in 1977.

In 2007, two teams visited England, playing four and three Tests matches respectively and a programme of 10 One-Day Internationals. That format was first seen in 1977 too. A balloon floated above Regent's Park during both Lord's Tests. Throughout the summer, Sky showed advertisements between overs, used countless cameras and a stump microphone and tracked the dismissed batsman off the turf. There were no rest days during the Tests and a single rest break between innings in the one-day games. All the batsmen wore helmets. White balls, fielding circles and coloured clothing were used in the one-day games, some of which were day / night. All the players were supremely fit.

Two of Packer's top people have commented about the effect of WSC on Australia's performance. Richie Benaud has written: 'It's because of what happened then that cricket is so strong now.' Ian Chappell said recently, 'It's not the sole factor, but because WSC paved the way in opening up the game to a wider audience, I have no doubt that this contributed to Australia being well ahead of England all these years.'

The British Labour MP, Graham Allen, has said that Packer drove the transition of Australian cricket from feudalism to capitalism. Before World Series Cricket, the ACB primarily served its members – the five states. Packer cut out both the ACB and its members and served fans directly with a business model that linked access, success and finance. This model, designed for scale, exploited television sponsorship and advertising and generated greater ticket revenues at the existing set of large grounds. Then, through PBL's deal with the ACB, Packer controlled the commercial side of the Australian game into the nineties and prevented a counter-revolution by the forces of feudalism.

If cricket is a religious ritual, its grounds churches and its audience worshippers, then there is also a religious element to Packer's achievement. He overturned an ancient order, deposed the self-serving clergy and brought the common man, woman and child into the cathedral. And, although England fans have subsequently written better ones, Packer even provided the congregation with a song.

## C'mon Aussie C'mon

In May 2005, governing body Cricket Australia (which replaced the ACB in 2003) named Kerry Packer as one of the two most influential people in Australian cricket. The other one was Don Bradman.

Packer died on the first day of the 2005 Boxing Day Test at the MCG. The Australian team wore black armbands as they beat South Africa on the outfield that, like many of Packer's facilities, had just been re-laid.

On 17 February 2006, a state memorial service was held at the Sydney Opera House. The actor Russell Crowe read out:

*IF you can keep your head when all about you*
*Are losing theirs and blaming it on you,*
*If you can trust yourself when all men doubt you,*
*But make allowance for their doubting too;*
*If you can wait and not be tired by waiting,*
*Or being lied about, don't deal in lies,*
*Or being hated, don't give way to hating,*
*And yet don't look too good, nor talk too wise;*

*If you can dream – and not make dreams your master;*
*If you can think – and not make thoughts your aim;*
*If you can meet with Triumph and Disaster*
*And treat those two impostors just the same;*
*If you can bear to hear the truth you've spoken*
*Twisted by knaves to make a trap for fools,*
*Or watch the things you gave your life to, broken,*
*And stoop and build 'em up with worn-out tools;*

*If you can make one heap of all your winnings*
*And risk it on one turn of pitch-and-toss,*
*And lose, and start again at your beginnings*
*And never breathe a word about your loss;*
*If you can force your heart and nerve and sinew*
*To serve your turn long after they are gone,*
*And so hold on when there is nothing in you*
*Except the Will which says to them: 'Hold on!'*

*If you can talk with crowds and keep your virtue,*
*' Or walk with Kings – nor lose the common touch,*
*If neither foes nor loving friends can hurt you,*
*If all men count with you, but none too much;*
*If you can fill the unforgiving minute*
*With sixty seconds' worth of distance run,*
*Yours is the Earth and everything that's in it,*
*And — which is more — you'll be a Man, my son!*

Those words were written a few years before Australian

independence by an Englishman[7] born in another continent-sized colony that would in time also become a cricket superpower.

Then the assembled throng sang:

> *You've been training all the winter*
> *And there's not a team that's fitter*
> *And that's the way it got to be*
> *'Cause you're up against the best you know*
> *This is Supertest you know*
> *And you've go to beat the best the world has seen*
> *Lillee's pounding down like a machine*
> *Pascoe's making divots in the green*
> *Marshy's taking wickets*
> *Hooksey's clearing pickets*
> *And the Chappells' eyes have got that killer gleam*
> *Mr Walker's playing havoc with the bats*
> *Redpath, it's good to see you back*
> *Lairdie's making runs*
> *Dougie's chewing gum*
> *and Gilmour's wielding willow like an axe*
> *C'mon Aussie c'mon c'mon*
> *C'mon Aussie c'mon c'mon*
> *C'mon Aussie c'mon c'mon*
> *C'mon Aussie c'mon*

Hordes of school-children waved flags and Bob Hawke, John Howard, at least four Australian cricket captains, Crowe, Tom Cruise and dozens of other dignitaries got up from their pews and danced.

# CHAPTER 4

# DIVERGENCE

*No cricket country in the world has more working committees than England. No cricket country manages to pay less attention to the important things and more attention to the unimportant matters than England when addressing the question of cricket.*

Richie Benaud, 1995

## Changes in the game

The next 10 years in international cricket were afflicted by politics. When Sri Lanka became the eighth full member (temporarily the seventh, with South Africa suspended) of the ICC in 1981, Asia had three-sevenths of the members and power in world cricket began to shift east. A struggle for control of the game culminated in July 1993 with the separation of the ICC from the MCC and the appointment of the former West Indian cricketer Clyde Walcott as the first non-British Chairman.

South Africa continued to lobby for re-admission to world cricket and to organise rebel tours. An Australia team under Kim Hughes visited in 1985/86 and 1986/87 and a second England team under Mike Gatting went in 1989/90. The resulting bans devalued the Ashes series of 1985 and 1986/87 and also affected the 1990/91 series. After the release of Nelson Mandela in February 1990, the adoption of a new constitution and the abolition of apartheid, South Africa was permitted to play international cricket again. The rebel tours stopped and no Ashes series since then has been undermined in this way.

On the field, the West Indies remained strong. Pakistan produced two more great bowlers in Wasim Akram and Waqar Younis to follow Imran Khan and Abdul Qadir. India continued to enjoy the services of all-rounder Kapil Dev and, for New Zealand, Richard Hadlee won several series single-handed. The days when England and Australia could routinely beat these teams were gone, along with the control of the game that they had enjoyed before World Series Cricket.

The annual volume of One-Day Internationals doubled from 30 in the early eighties to 60 at the end of the decade. Australia, Pakistan, West Indies and India all increased their ratio of one-day games to Tests from one-to-one at the beginning to three-to-one at the end, but England stuck resolutely at a touch above one-to-one. There was little change in the number of days played by each country: five played around 60 days per year, New Zealand about 45 and Sri Lanka 35.

This volume of international cricket was not high enough, by itself, to burn out fast bowlers.

## England and Australia

Figure 6 shows the form of both countries between 1984 and 1993.

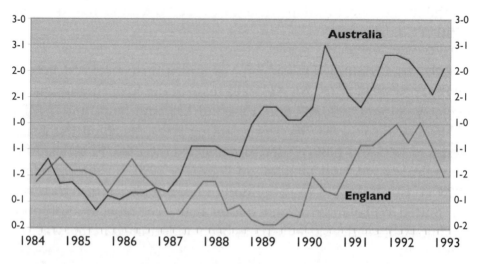

FIGURE 6: ENGLAND AND AUSTRALIA FORM DECEMBER
1984–JUNE 1993

England and Australia were at the same low point at the end of 1984, and both then wobbled around until 1987. At that point, the teams diverged sharply. England again followed a cyclical trajectory, plumbing new depths in 1988 and 1989, recovering in the following three years and falling away badly again from 1992 onwards. Australia, by contrast, ascended steadily in the four years to 1991. By the time Shane Warne (1992) and Glenn McGrath (1993) made their debuts it had achieved a consistently good level of performance. Against England, successive victories in the Ashes series of 1989, 1990/91 and 1993 ended Australia's two-part rebel nightmare once and for all.

The way in which Australia picked itself up off the floor, and England's continued cycling around mediocrity, has governed the performance of the two sides through to the present day. By 1993, the need for major structural reform in the England professional game was clear to several observers, three of whom pointed the way ahead. One was Graeme Wright, a New Zealander who edited *Wisden*, while the other two were fast becoming the usual suspects: Bob Willis and Ian Chappell.

## Australia falls apart

The 1983/84 season saw Australia host Pakistan to a return series after its 0–3 loss there a year before. State cricket produced a new fast bowler named Carl Rackemann to supplement Rodney Hogg, Geoff Lawson and Dennis Lillee, and these four helped Australia win the series 2–0. Australia won the last game at Sydney with a Greg Chappell century, six catches behind the stumps from Rod Marsh and eight wickets from Lillee. All three players then retired.

The next generation had been brought on too quickly to fill the empty ranks of the national team during World Series Cricket, leaving a huge hole five years later. Over the next four years Australia won only four games out of 33, with no series wins at all. Home and away defeats to both England and West Indies, already bad enough, were made intolerable by home and away defeats in the same season, 1985/86, to local punch-bag New Zealand.

Two series versus the West Indies started the slide. In spring 1984, Kim Hughes took a weak side to the Caribbean to face Michael Holding, Malcolm Marshall, Joel Garner and Wayne Daniel. They started well, drawing the First Test. Allan Border saved them in the Second Test with 98 in the first innings and a last-ditch century to stave off an innings defeat. But Australia was bowled out for 97 in the third game at Port-of-Spain to lose by 10 wickets, and the team collapsed in the Fourth and Fifth Tests. The side for the Fourth Test was one of the weakest ever to represent the country. To bat: Allan Border, Kim Hughes, David Hookes, Dean Jones. To bowl: Lawson. No other player in the side made any impression on cricket history. Aussie bowling throughout was so poor that the West Indies did not lose a single second-innings wicket in the series.

Between the two series Australian players agreed to sign one-year contracts binding them to the ACB and PBL until late 1985. And, under pressure from the government of Victoria, the Melbourne Cricket Club (the other MCC) decided to accept women members.

For the return visit in 1984/85, the West Indies brought an equally lethal combination composed of Holding, Marshall, Garner and Courtney Walsh. This quartet dismissed Australia twice in just over 100 overs in the first game at Perth to win by an innings and in 150 overs in the second to win by eight wickets. Criticism of Hughes' captaincy by ex-players in the media reached such a crescendo that in late November 1984 he announced his resignation of the Australian captaincy. At the press conference, Hughes burst into tears, passed his prepared statement to team manager Bob Merriman and left the room. For a brief moment, the captain and the rest of the Australian national cricket team were all at sea, like Pommies.

The Australian selectors passed the poisoned chalice to their best player. Aged 29 and with Australia 0–2 in the series, Allan Border inherited the captaincy by default. He lost the Third Test and the series with it but pulled back a game to register 1–3. Shortly afterwards, cricket fans were shocked to learn that a rebel tour of South Africa by an Aussie team had been scheduled for the 1985/86 season. The tax-free fee for two tours of $200,000 was so high—it was equivalent to over 10 years in the national team—that 16 players signed up.

Nine of these were in the party to tour England. Three promptly defected back when the ACB insisted on a loyalty declaration. Then, because Channel Nine had purchased the television rights and PBL was busy earning back what it had spent on World Series Cricket, Kerry Packer told the rebel organiser, 'I understand you are going up to Brisbane to sign up a few of my players for South Africa … don't waste your time.'

Packer coaxed three more rebels back into the fold and offered five of the most promising young players $45,000 to bind themselves to official cricket. One of these was a novice named Steve Waugh[1]. Playing league cricket in England in the summer of 1985, Waugh met a PBL representative and signed the contract. The future Australian captain later wrote: 'I did nothing over three years. Just collected the cheques.'

The remaining three of the nine rebels opted to go to South Africa. The biggest loss was Terry Alderman, an English-style swing and seam bowler who took 42 wickets in the 1981 series and was to take another 41 in 1989. The next biggest loss was the former captain. Having been promised selection for the tour and then left out, Hughes agreed to captain the unofficial Australian team. He never played for Australia again.

Fast bowlers Hogg and Rackemann also took the rand, and Australia arrived in England with virtually no experienced bowling. Another young quick bowler supplied by state cricket, Craig McDermott, took 30 wickets in the series but enjoyed little support. Four England batsmen averaged more than 50 and England exceeded 400 in the first innings in five out of the six games.

England had eked out a solid 2–1 victory against India in 1984/85 despite the absence of Ian Botham, but Bob Willis had retired and the 17 counties had produced only one new quick bowler, Graham Dilley, since the end of World Series Cricket. He joined Botham, who had already taken 300 wickets in his eight-year international career, and the Middlesex spin duo John Emburey and Phil Edmonds. These four bowlers were unable to establish command, and Australia went into the fifth game at Edgbaston with the series level at one apiece.

This match was England's highest point in Ashes cricket until 2005. After Australia made 335 in their first innings, England moved steadily in reply to 572 for three with a double century from David Gower. Allan Lamb was then caught off McDermott for 46 and Botham strode out to bat. Having hit over 50 sixes in first-class cricket in the season to date, Botham was in the batting form of his career. His first ball from McDermott was straight and full and was disappeared into the Edgbaston pavilion. Australia lost the game by an innings, the Oval Test by an innings, and the series 1–3.

## Warning signs

Botham opened the bowling with Dilley in this Ashes series. Temporarily upping his pace, he took 31 wickets at 28 runs apiece and was again much of the difference between the two sides. He ended the 1985 season with 343 Test wickets at an average of 26 and 4400 runs at 36 and his status as the world's premier cricketer secure. Aged just 29, Botham appeared to have four or five more good years left in him.

Despite this, England lost the next three series, 0–5 to the West Indies in 1985/86 and 0–2 to India and 0–1 to New Zealand at home in 1986. In the Caribbean, the West Indies had Marshall, Garner, Patrick Patterson, Walsh and Holding, and only Gower averaged over 30. For England, Botham, Richard Ellison, Greg Thomas and Neil Foster bought wickets at 42 while the batsmen gave them away at 20.

The Palmer inquiry reported in 1986, over a year after being commissioned. Entitled *The TCCB Enquiry into the Standards of Play of English Cricket in Test and First-Class County Cricket*, it blamed one-day cricket for a decline in standards and for England's poor performance and recommended a first-class programme of 16 three-day games and eight four-day games.

In December 1986, the TCCB decided on a three-year trial of six four-day games and 16 three-day games to start in 1988, effectively a compromise of a compromise on the four-day programme proposed by Bob Willis five years before. No change was made to the three county one-day tournaments, and county players continued to play nearly 100 of the 155 calendar days in the season.

Other commentators shared the concerns about one-day cricket. John Arlott suggested that it be given a new name and Vic Marks wrote in *Wisden*: 'The county cricket season has become one prolonged, frenetic dash around the highways and byways of the country.' But, because two-thirds of county attendances in 1985 were at one-day games, and commercial sponsorship naturally followed, nothing was done to reduce the number of games and tournaments despite the detrimental effect on the England side.

In Australia, a loss of $1 million on the Sheffield Shield tournament in 1985/86 was easily made up by profits from the national team, and there was no need to play more than a single state one-day tournament. As a result, Australian state cricketers played fewer than 50 days a season.

In 1986, the loss in the Caribbean was followed by two successive defeats in the first home series against India. David Gower was sacked as captain but his replacement, Mike Gatting, made no immediate difference as England fell apart against Richard Hadlee in the second series against New Zealand. In the summer, 24 players were used and only Gatting and Graham Gooch played in all six games. In the final game at the Oval, Gladstone Small became the 11th player to open the bowling for England in the past year. Spectators voted with their feet, with grounds barely half full.

Bob Willis blamed the county game for this poor performance, writing: 'The ridiculous domestic programme continues to take its toll on the development of our top players.' He forecast that 'Unless the counties will endorse a much better-balanced programme of matches, there is little chance of England's producing enough players with enough class to remain a potent force in world cricket.'

As the 1986 season wound down, Gower decided to miss the last three games that he was due to play for Leicestershire. He blamed fatigue.

## Coach

Down Under, the seasons 1985 and 1985/86 were the worst ever. Weakened by the absence of the South Africa rebels, Australia registered only two victories in 15 Tests and lost two series in the same season for the first time, their bowlers buying wickets at 46 against the 30 earned by the batsmen. Spectators voted with their feet here too. Only 283,000 people (10,000 per day) attended the six Tests at home in 1985/86.

The ACB decided to act. The first step was the appointment of a national coach. Bob Simpson, Australia's emergency captain during the first year of World Series Cricket, was asked to accompany the side on the trip to New Zealand in early 1986. Simpson had coached New South Wales to successive Sheffield Shield titles in 1984/85 and 1985/86 and immediately determined that the Australian side had no work ethic. He found a team management system in chaos, commenting later, 'When I first took over as Australia's coach in 1986, there were 44 players running around in the Sheffield Shield who had played some form of international cricket. A joke ... There has never been a period in history when Australia had 44 players good enough to play for their country.'

Simpson set about whittling the national squad down to those he felt had the right attitude towards representing their country. This would take time, so he decided to make immediate improvements in Australia's fitness and fielding. Limp fielding practices that club cricketers would recognise were replaced by sessions designed to simulate match conditions, with balls hit hard and in inconvenient directions. Steve Waugh, who had just made his debut, was on the New Zealand tour and said later, 'Basically his professional attitude was the biggest change in Australian cricket. And the way he trained. I don't think we trained properly before he came on to the scene.'

The ACB was aided by a state system which continued to produce an average of two international-class players per year. During these dark years, five players stepped forward to accompany Allan Border. David Boon and Craig McDermott started against the West Indies in the 1984/85 season and Geoff Marsh and Merv Hughes against India in 1985/86. Dean Jones, who first played on the tour to the West Indies in 1983/84, was the fifth. This gave Simpson and Australia a solid bedrock of six players.

## Three legends

These players themselves were fully on side with Simpson and Border's programme of rebuilding. Nowhere was this clearer than on the Australia tour to India in late 1986. At the First Test at a blisteringly hot and humid Madras in September 1986, Australia batted first, and at 48–1 Dean Jones went in. Having played his first two Tests on the disastrous tour to the West Indies in 1984, scored 65 in four innings, and not been picked since, he was determined to prove to his captain and the coach that he was mentally tough enough to play Test cricket.

In the four hours remaining on the first day, Jones made 56. On the second, he batted first with Ray Bright and then with Border, with whom he passed his first Test century. At lunch he was on 131 but the heat and humidity had given him stomach and leg cramps.

Back out in the middle after lunch, Jones vomited[2] several times and pissed himself twice. Unable to focus on the ball or move his feet, he started to slog and block. On 174, he felt unable to continue and told Border he was leaving the field, but Border kept him going with a taunt about strong Queenslanders (Border) and weak Victorians (Jones). Jones went into tea on 202 and was bundled into a shower by two team mates. Because the dehydrated batsman was unable to think straight, it fell to Border to make a decision about whether he would continue. The captain said, 'he's going out', and Jones made another eight before being bowled. He collapsed on his return to the pavilion and was taken to hospital where he fell asleep until midnight and was given seven bottles of saline drip. He lost a stone.

Bob Simpson called this one of the great innings of all time. Australia declared on 574–7, bowled India out and then set them 348 to win. On the last day, Greg Matthews bowled all day in tandem with Bright, each taking five wickets, and India were all out for 347. The match was tied.

In one game, Team Australia had created a team legend and an individual legend. It went on to create a third legend with draws in the remaining two games. This 0–0 result, only the second level series out of seven since the retirement of Greg Chappell, Rod Marsh and Dennis Lillee, was obtained in difficult conditions on a tough tour.

## Team Australia

The ACB recognised, too, that reform begins at home. In September 1986, Malcolm Gray was elected the Chairman of the ACB by the 14 state delegates. With David Richards as Chief Executive, Lawrie Sawle as head of the selectors, Simpson as coach and Border as captain, Australian cricket had a small executive team. According to Harte and Whimpress' *History of Australian Cricket*, the state delegates on the ACB had been removed from power by the effects of World Series Cricket and the deal with PBL. The *History* says: 'All the delegates really had to do was—after a lot of hot air—rubber-stamp the proposals put in front of them.' This limited non-executive interference in the business of Australian cricket.

In late 1987, Gray announced that all Australian player contracts would be for two years. Border was placed on a five-year contract at $50,000 a year, and players also benefited from contributions into a provident fund that would provide them a pension. According to the *History*, 'The result of this move was, for the first time in twenty years, a fully contented squad of players who were now being paid a fair amount of money with guaranteed minimums.' This stability and continuity was demonstrated by the granting of Australian Test caps to just 12 players between 1987 and 1991. During this period, England handed out 31.

This was not all. The Prime Minister, Bob Hawke, suggested that cricket be added to the roster at the Australian Institute of Sport (AIS). The ACB agreed, and the AIS / ACB Academy opened its doors at the Adelaide Oval in January 1988. Driven through by Graham Halbish, a future ACB Chief Executive, it offered 12-month scholarships to 15 cricketers aged 17–21 picked by the Test selectors. At the opening, Halbish said:

> It will set the pattern for the training and development of young players for a long time to come. The approach being taken is unique to cricket and the training will be uniquely Australian. We want to stress the importance of aggressive captaincy and positive play. All the outstanding features of Australian cricket will be built into the training programmes, and we will use the latest methods available in the world of cricket.

In 1986/87, Australia introduced a state Under-17 tournament to supplement the Under-19 tournament that had commenced in 1969/70. These two competitions, together with the new Academy, meant that Australian cricket had started systematically mining its population for elite young cricketers. Together, they constituted an elite youth conveyor belt that delivered the best 19-year-old players to the six states, and possibly the national team, complete with a track record and ready for induction into professional cricket.

The cumulative effect of these changes was substantial. In 1988, a small ACB executive group led the professional game. The elite youth conveyor belt began with the state Under-17 and Under-19 teams and continued with the national Academy, which then connected the best players into the state and national squads. Six states maintained a small reservoir of 100 players that made selection for the national side simple and reliable. A commercial firm, PBL, carried out the marketing and advertising & sponsorship work on behalf of the ACB, and Channel Nine did the television and ABC produced the radio. The national side, Team Australia, was contracted to the Board and a coach was employed to maintain peak performance by the players.

There have been virtually no changes in the Australian professional game since 1988. Apart from minor match-fixing and drugs problems in the late nineties and the occasional standoff over player remuneration, the management of Australian cricket has been relatively harmonious and free of controversy. In his 1996 autobiography, Bob Simpson wrote:

> I think the structure of cricket in Australia today is very nearly ideal – light years ahead of the rest of the world in most respects ... Very few players escape the net ... The grass-roots strength of Australian cricket is also its strength at the top.

## Second-tier logic

Simpson's statements incorporate some interesting logic governing the structure of the second tier in a cricket hierarchy. In any cricketing nation, this second tier is wedged between the national squad, which sits above, and the top level of the recreational game, which sits below. It also connects into the elite youth conveyor belt[3], which churns out a few players a year. Unless they are good enough to go straight into the national squad—few are—these new players go into the second tier and await the call.

From the point of view of those organising the national squad, the second tier has four main functions. The first is to sit at the end of the elite youth conveyor belt and train its products to international standard. The second is to maintain a reservoir of players ready for call-up. Third, the second tier must collect *all* of those coming off the elite youth conveyor belt as well as the few late-developers from club cricket. Fourthly, it provides a place for national players to go for refresher training should they be dropped or be returning from injury.

The optimum size and shape of the second tier is governed by the first three of these functions. International training requires the highest possible standard, but the greater the number of teams, the weaker the standard of each. Talent, therefore, must be concentrated into as few teams as possible. The reservoir function requires that the second tier provide sufficient cover for the eight key positions in cricket (captain, wicketkeeper, opening batsman, middle-order batsman, all rounder, quick bowler, seam / swing bowler, spinner). This, too, necessitates as high a standard as possible, but also demands a measure of volume. The collection function requires that teams in the second tier cover the whole country. Because sporting genius occurs at random, more or less, this last purpose is vital if the national team is not to miss players who come from distant or unfashionable places.

A second tier of just one team is useless because it has no opposition but tourists. It also provides insufficient cover. Two, three and four teams also provide too few games to keep the player reservoir fit and ready. Five teams, though, provides berths for 100 players (20 per squad), enough to provide at least five substitutes for each position in the national squad. It also provides enough games (eight home and away, versus the other four sides, in each form of the game, plus games against touring sides) to keep players ready. It concentrates talent to an acceptable degree, and it provides enough space for refresher training. Six teams, with 120 players, starts to offend against the requirement for concentration without adding any reservoir benefit. Any more than six teams dilutes talent and reduces standards.

The optimum size of the second tier from the point of view of the national team, therefore, is five or six teams, so long as those teams cover the whole country. The elite youth conveyor belt is then organised to feed into this second tier. Each second-tier organisation operates as many youth teams as are necessary to scoop up talent and identify the top players in each year-group in its patch.

They say that Australia is the lucky country. Its second tier consisted of five teams until 1977/78, when the need for more complete geographic coverage led to the admission of Tasmania to make a perfectly acceptable six. Whether or not the two best Tasmanian players in recent years—David Boon and Ricky Ponting—would have crossed Bass Strait to play for Victoria is a moot point. A useful by-product of this system for Australia is that all its second-tier grounds are used for international cricket.

The logic of the second tier starts at the top of the cricket pyramid and not at the middle. It holds for every cricket country regardless of the size of its population for the simple reason that every country has the same number of national men's first XIs. One.

## The last Ashes for 18 years

In England, the TCCB operated through a set of more than 10 committees composed of representatives from the 17 counties, the MCC, the two universities, Scotland and Ireland. A Chairman and a Secretary kept order in the style of the Secretary of State and the Permanent Under-Secretary of a government department, just as they had before World Series Cricket. This structure made reform along Australian lines subject to the approval of the counties and rendered unlikely any changes that were not in their interests.

One reform introduced by Australia did not conflict with those interests, however. A year after Bob Simpson started work with the ACB, the TCCB appointed Mickey Stewart as England's manager / coach.

In the mid-eighties (and possibly before), the conflict of interest between county and country that led to excessive one-day county cricket began to affect the players, especially England's two best quick bowlers, Ian Botham and Graham Dilley. Like all England professional cricketers, Botham and Dilley were county players who also played for the national side. Although England paid healthy fees, it did not offer player contracts, there was no coach and most selection was on the basis of county performance. In other words, there was no Team England. The only income that a player could rely on was his county salary, so England players turned out for their counties too.

In 1986 and 1987, the volume of England cricket increased to 80 days each year from an average of 60 in the previous three years. As many as 142 England days[4] were concentrated into a 21-month period between February 1986 and November 1987.

In the middle of this period, England went to Australia for the 1986/87 Ashes. This series was a battle between two sides at the bottom of their game that was played in competition with the second Australian rebel tour to South Africa. In the First Test, Border put England in—always a mistake at Brisbane—and England took a lead of 208 on first innings thanks to a thumping 138 by Botham and 5–68 by Dilley. England won by seven wickets. 4–79 from Dilley won England a 191 lead on first innings at the second game in Perth, but Australia escaped with a draw.

With the Third Test a high-score draw, the MCG Boxing Day Test was the crucial match. Botham delivered his last great bowling performance as he and Gladstone Small dismissed Australia for 141 on the first day in front of 58,000 people. 349 by England produced another first innings lead of 208, and Phil Edmonds and John Emburey spun England to victory on the third day to give them an unassailable 2–0 lead in the series.

Allan Border vowed that he would never again be associated with such abject failure, and the ACB took the unprecedented step of cancelling the 1988 tour to West Indies, telling the WICBC that it would have been a one-sided flop. But, for England, the warning signs had turned to danger. Their two main bowlers, Botham and Dilley, were in the middle of 142 days of England cricket on top of their county commitments. The two were on their last legs.

## Botham and Dilley

Dilley[5] did not go on the West Indies tour in spring 1986, but in the 15 months from May 1986 to August 1987 he played 165 days of cricket, equal to 35% of the calendar days. Of these days, 81 were with England and 84 with his county. He had two breaks, of four and 10 weeks respectively, and withdrew from four Tests because of injury, two of them on the morning of the game. His last game in the period was in August 1987, when he developed a side strain during a County Championship game against Glamorgan. Injury prevented him from going to the 1987 World Cup.

Botham did go on the West Indies tour in 1985/86. He played 215 days of cricket in 21 months, also equal to 35% of the time. Of these days, 118 were for England and 97 were for his county. He had four breaks totalling five months, one of which was a two-month ban by the TCCB in June and July 1986 for admitting to the use of cannabis in a newspaper. It may well be that this ban preserved Botham and helped England win the Ashes in 1986/87.

Botham was unfit for the MCC Bicentenary game against the Rest of the World in August 1987 but played the last few games for Worcestershire at the end of the 1987 season, most of them without bowling. He chose not to go to the 1987 World Cup. Instead, he spent the 1987/88 season with Queensland. In his autobiography, he wrote:

> The cricket turned out to be fantastic — tough and uncompromising — and I really believe we could learn a lot in this country from the way the game is structured in Australia. The top three states could easily live with any of the counties in this

*country, and when you think that the population of Australia is equivalent to that in Greater London, what they achieve from a much smaller base than us is remarkable.*

*As I see it, the biggest advantage the Aussies enjoy is that they don't play nearly as much cricket as us, and therefore there is little danger of succumbing to the disease most prevalent among English professionals, namely, burnout.*

In 1987 England came back from the Australia tour to meet Pakistan in a five-Test series. Neil Foster and Dilley did well, but with Small out injured, Botham performing poorly as third seamer, and neither Phil DeFreitas (56 at 26 in county cricket) nor Jonathan Agnew (101 at 24) getting the selectors' nod, England's spinners did not have much of a platform to build on. The 1987 summer ended at the Oval with England's bowlers on their knees as they were carted for 708, with Javed Miandad getting 260 and Botham and Dilley each bowling more than 45 overs in the innings. England could only hold out for a draw and concede a 0–1 series defeat, the first victory by Pakistan in England.

Botham announced in May 1988 that he needed an operation to fuse two vertebrae and he did not play again for England until 1989. In his last 23 Tests after the 1985 series against Australia, he took only 40 more wickets at 46 and hit 791 runs at 24. Apart from the two farewell performances against Australia in 1986/87 that helped secure England's last Ashes victory for 18 years, his career was essentially over in 1985.

Dilley played a full part in the 1987/88 trips to Pakistan and New Zealand, but he broke down with a knee injury during the Third Test against New Zealand in March 1988 and had surgery in June. He played six more Tests and then, aged 30, elected to go on the 1989 rebel tour to South Africa, ending his England career. In all, he played 11 more times for England after the Oval game in 1987.

David Gower had run into the wall for the second season in a row.

Under the headline 'Why I Need Time Off', Gower wrote towards the end of the 1987 season: 'I have reached the point at which the prospect of another winter's cricket does not inspire the enthusiasm that it should in someone aiming to represent his country.' Like Botham, he chose not to go to the 1987 World Cup.

## Collapse

With Botham effectively out of the picture, Dilley struggling to hold the bowling attack together, and players such as Gower (30), Gatting (30), Gooch (34), Emburey (35) and Edmonds (36) getting on, England needed to start replacing those who had sustained England through the Packer years and beyond. But county cricket had not obliged with new international-class bowlers and it knackered existing ones by playing them when they were off national duty.

In the two years from September 1987 to September 1989, England played 19 Tests, won one and lost nine, suffering successive 4–0 drubbings at home by West Indies and Australia and winning only against newcomers Sri Lanka. It used 40 players, of whom 15 were debutants and four were wicketkeepers. Only five of those 15 debutants—Jack Russell, Mike Atherton, Devon Malcolm, Robin Smith and Angus Fraser—went on to successful international careers. The selectors, evidently, were forced to use England games as trials because the county system did not tell them what they needed to know.

England also suffered from captaincy problems. An on-field row between England captain Mike Gatting and umpire Shakhoor Rana during a Test in Pakistan in 1987/88 sealed Gatting's fate. Pakistan won the series 1–0, with leg-spinner Abdul Qadir taking 30 wickets.

The West Indies then arrived in England for the 1988 season. England had no answer to Malcolm Marshall, Curtly Ambrose and Courtney Walsh except for Dilley, who took 15 wickets at 26 in four games. England drew the first game, but Gatting was sacked after tabloid allegations about his conduct with a barmaid. Despite nine wickets by Dilley in the second at Lord's, England lost by 134 runs under the captaincy of John Emburey. At the third game, England were slaughtered by an innings in spite of another four wickets from Dilley in the West Indies' only innings.

England made seven changes for the fourth game at Headingley, dropping Emburey altogether. Gatting withdrew from Test cricket indefinitely, having been referred to the TCCB disciplinary committee over revelations in his autobiography. Chris Cowdrey, the godson of the Chairman of Selectors, Peter May, was made captain, but when he arrived at the ground the day before the game the gateman did not recognise him and refused entry to the car park. Even worse, some West Indian players were racially abused by the crowd. On the field, the West Indies bowlers decimated England's batsmen, most of whom were fresh from county cricket, winning by 10 wickets in front of only 44,000 spectators.

The selectors dropped David Gower for the Fifth Test at the Oval and made Gooch the fourth captain of the summer in place of Cowdrey, who became the second captain in successive Tests to lose his place in the team. Only 53,000 turned up to watch England lose by eight wickets in four days. Cowdrey declared himself unavailable to tour India and never played Test cricket again. In the event, the tour was cancelled because the Indian government would not grant visas to eight of the selected players, including the latest captain, Graham Gooch, because of their South Africa links.

Had it gone ahead, England would probably have set a new world record of five different captains in seven games. As it was, Tony Cozier wrote in *Wisden*: 'The morale and reputation of English cricket has seldom been as severely bruised as it was during the 1988 Cornhill Insurance Test series against West Indies.' Editor Graeme Wright noted that a discernible gap had opened up between county and Test cricket.

At the end of the 1988 season the TCCB asked its Cricket Committee to produce 'special recommendations' to improve England cricket and to look closely at the fixture list, the quality of pitches and the influence of overseas players. In November 1988, though, Peter May explained the selection of so many players in *The Cricketer*, saying, 'We have more players of a certain standard than any other country. It's often easier to pick a team if you have fewer players to choose from.'

At the end of the year, the TCCB set up an England committee led by the new Chairman of Selectors, Ted Dexter, accompanied by the coach Mickey Stewart, the team captain—whoever that was—and the Chairman of the TCCB cricket committee, Ossie Wheatley. The first task of the committee was to choose the captain, but Wheatley vetoed Gatting and Dexter did not want Gooch. So England turned once again to Gower, despite having sacked him two years earlier and dropped him only months before.

## Australia builds

After the loss to England at home in the 1986/87 Ashes, Allan Border and Bob Simpson had four batsmen they could count on: Border himself, Jones, Boon and Marsh. They had two experienced bowlers in Lawson and Alderman and four relative youths in Rackemann, Hughes, McDermott and Bruce Reid. Rackemann and Alderman, though, were banned for going to South Africa and Reid, a tall, slightly-built man, could not withstand the physical wrench of fast-bowling. Border also had a young all-rounder, Steve Waugh, two spinners in Greg Matthews and Peter Taylor and a useful one-day all-rounder in Simon O'Donnell.

The West Indies tour having been cancelled, Australia played only thirteen Tests in the following two home seasons, winning three, losing three and drawing six. A better result at home against the West Indies, 1–3, was accompanied by victory in the 1987 World Cup in Calcutta.

In April 1989, Border was given a three-year contract worth $300,000 with the express intention of preventing his retirement. The upcoming 1989 Ashes series in England would be the first time since

1981 that both countries could pick from all their fit players and only the second out of eight series from 1977. Five of Australia's six best quick bowlers were fit to travel because, unlike England, the team did not have to play year-round. This meant that bowlers could rest in the northern summer between March and October if they were not touring England. The selectors decided to take Alderman, Lawson, Hughes and Rackemann, leaving McDermott at home because he had lost form for Queensland in the 1988/89 season. Reid's back problems had wrecked his 1988/89 season, and Australia left him behind too.

In the five seasons (three Australian and two English) before the 1989 Ashes series, McDermott played about 175 days, or 17% of the time. Hughes played 21% of the time, and Lawson 18%. When the latter two went to England in 1989, neither had played county cricket and the playing rate of Australia's bowlers was about half that of their counterparts in England.

## 1989 Ashes

When he arrived in England, Allan Border expected to lose the captaincy should Australia lose the series. Ian Chappell had told him, 'I can handle you losing to the West Indies, India and Pakistan, but for God's sake don't lose to the Poms'. But after the 1985 tour Chappell had said, 'AB, those blokes were beating the hell out of you but you were out there being their best mate for Christ's sake.'

Border and Simpson therefore decided to do what was required to win this series. They banned wives and girlfriends from the team hotel until late in the tour and decided to cold-shoulder the England side. Border told his opposite number, 'David, the last time we came here I was a nice guy who came last.'

When David Boon[6] arrived in England, he was slightly groggy from necking 52 cans of beer on the flight from Sydney to beat Rod Marsh's record by seven tins. Despite this, Boon played in the First Test at Leeds, although he only scored nine and 43. On the other hand, Botham, Dilley and Gatting did not play in this Test because they were injured. Foster, DeFreitas, Phil Newport and Derek Pringle constituted such a weak bowling side that Steve Waugh batted without a helmet, scoring 177 not out as Australia piled up 601 in their first innings. Alderman took 10 wickets in English conditions and Australia won by 210 runs.

The Second Test at Lord's was sold out in advance for the first four days, but England's injury problems caused muddle and chaos. Botham was still unfit, Gower had just had a shoulder operation but still played and Gatting was recovering from a broken thumb. Botham's replacement, David Capel, was also injured and Allan Lamb was injured on the Saturday before the match. Dilley came back after injury for Newport, who was injured. DeFreitas and Pringle were dropped and Paul Jarvis was brought in. Australia scored 528 in their first innings through another Waugh hundred, Alderman got another nine wickets and Hughes six and, despite a Gower century in the second innings, Australia won by six wickets.

For the Third Test, the selectors dropped the opening batsman, Chris Broad. With an average of 38 from 25 Tests and six hundreds, Broad was a mainstay of the England side. Instead, the selectors picked Chris Tavaré for his first game in five years (and last) and retained a county cricketer, Kim Barnett. Foster, who had played in the first two games, was injured, forcing the recall of Jarvis, who had been dropped. Botham came back and Angus Fraser was given his debut, meaning that none of the four bowlers who featured in the First Test played in the third. It made no difference. For the third time in succession Australia scored more than 400 in their first innings. Luckily for England, bad weather forced a draw.

Before the game, Ted Dexter handed a song-sheet to the players. On it was written five verses to be sung to the tune of *Onward Christian Soldiers*. The first verse ran:

*Onward Gower's cricketers, striving for a score.*
*With our bats uplifted, we want more and more*

*Alderman the master represents the foe*
*Forward into battle, down the pitch we go.*

On the first morning of the Fourth Test, Dilley pulled out unfit and Dexter handed Gower a list of 16 names instead of another song-sheet. Dilley's name was on it, alongside those of three others selected for this game – Foster, Emburey and Tim Robinson. Gatting, Cowdrey and Broad were there too, and Jarvis made up the quick bowlers. The players had agreed to undertake a second rebel tour of South Africa.

Paul Jarvis, at 24 a big loss to England cricket, noted that 'I would have to play in every Test at home and away for the next six years to earn as much as eighty thousand after tax.' In the match itself, Lawson demolished England's first innings and Australia scored 447. Alderman then took five wickets in England's second innings and Australia won back the Ashes on 1 August 1989.

Into this mess stepped a 21-year-old Mancunian named Mike Atherton. Newly-graduated from Cambridge University, and having a month earlier captained a strong Combined Universities (i.e. Cambridge and Oxford) against the Australians, Atherton had few first-class games[7] under his belt and was completely unprepared for the fray. When facing leg-spinner Trevor Hohns, he encountered a strange delivery that spun longitudinally rather than laterally. This was the flipper, and neither Atherton nor most of those watching had seen or heard of it before. In his first innings he was, like Mrs Thatcher in the famous graffito, out LBW bowled Alderman.

Gladstone Small was selected for the fifth game at Trent Bridge but dropped out injured on the eve of the match. No rebel was considered, so the new new-ball pairing was Devon Malcolm (0 Tests) and Fraser (2). After Australia won the toss, Geoff Marsh and Mark Taylor batted through the first day and put on 329 for the first wicket. According to Taylor, David Gower was so pleased at capturing the first Australian wicket on the second morning that he cracked open a bottle of champagne at lunch.

England were shot out in both innings for a combined total of 422, which Australia had passed in their only innings for one wicket down. When asked if he took any positives from the game, Dexter replied, 'Who could forget Malcolm Devon?' Malcolm had taken one for 166 in 44 overs, whereas Atherton top-scored in the second innings, just as he had done at Cambridge and would do frequently for England over the following decade.

Malcolm was injured for the Sixth Test and his replacement, DeFreitas, who had been dropped earlier in the series, pulled a hamstring. With Fraser injured, and Ricky Ellcock and Norman Cowans at Middlesex reporting unfit, there were two bowling positions open the day before the game. Pringle was brought back and Alan Igglesden was brought in, Mickey Stewart kindly announcing that he was the seventeenth choice. In a rain-affected game, Australia scored 468 in their first innings and set England a target of 402 to win, but the match was drawn.

## Reaction

When the series was over, the Australian team held a party at *The Grosvenor* in London to celebrate a 4–0 victory that could easily have been 6–0. After months of discipline and dedication the team let its hair down thoroughly and racked up a huge bill. It was paid by three Australian cricket fans of note: John Cornell, Austin Robertson and Paul Hogan.

Allan Border was cockahoop, saying, 'It's the highlight of my career. No question of it. I didn't want to give England any hope whatsoever.' Ian Botham wrote: 'AB was a different captain – a very, very charged and motivated captain who wanted those Ashes back and got them back. He had a good side, and a tough side, and really Australia hasn't looked back since. It's been forward, march, march on to greater achievements.'

Reaction by England officials was more muted. Dexter said, 'I am not aware of any errors that I have made,' and Gower said, 'As far as I know no lives have actually been lost yet.' He was sacked for the second time. On this occasion, Dexter wielded the knife but at least had the decency to lend Gower his Porsche for the weekend. Gooch was appointed captain with an instruction not to consider Gower or Botham for the West Indies tour the following spring, and Gatting and his rebels received a five-year ban.

Many writers again blamed one-day cricket, but one pundit posited a theoretical England bowling attack of DeFreitas, Malcolm, Small and Ellcock (all black British), with Nasser Hussain (half-Indian) getting an honourable mention. Others blamed pitches for providing an advantage to seam bowlers over spinners, the benefit system for filling county ranks with past-it players awaiting their chance to beg for a pension, and overseas players for denying slots to true-blue Englishmen.

John Arlott wrote that 'England has never been so impoverished in the development of outstanding players', and added presciently that 'At the moment it looks as if its recent bankruptcy in all but medium-pace seam bowling will probably betray it in international competition for many years to come.' In *Wisden*, Graeme Wright pointed out that county and England interests had diverged, writing:

> The TCCB ... selects the national team, it promotes cricket and it is also finding itself answerable to a lay membership whose interests are not necessarily those of the game itself. However, the TCCB does not own English cricket. It administers it on trust, and increasingly it is encumbered by a conflict of interests.

No pundit appears to have mentioned the superior Australian system as a reason for the wide gap that had opened up between the two countries.

## Financial disconnect

Despite two dreadful home seasons in 1988 and 1989 and one win in the previous 19 Tests, all was financially rosy in the English garden.

Total revenues rose to £16 million[8] in 1989 from £8 million in 1985, an increase of 13% per year on top of inflation. England ticket prices rose from an average of £7 to about £12 and the BBC paid £1.25 million a year for television rights in 1989, four times as much as in 1985. Sponsorship, though, had begun to level off.

Of this £16 million figure, about £7.5 million was earned by England, £7 million by the counties and the rest by the MCC. For the first time, therefore, revenues generated by the England team exceeded those of the county game. But, as before, England's profits were divided up amongst the counties on the basis that they provided the England players that earned the money. In 1989, the 17 counties each received £300,000 from the TCCB, with £5 million distributed in all. This helped meet a county salary bill of over £4 million, double that of 1985.

As a whole, the game continued to break even, although the loss-making 17-team county system was evidently failing to produce an England team that could compete successfully against old rivals Australia and West Indies and new rivals India, New Zealand and Pakistan.

After the 4–0 beatings by Australia and West Indies, the winter of 1989 would have been a good time for England cricket to compare the structure of Australia cricket with that at home. This might well have led to a redirection of England profits towards contracts for the England team and a National Academy. But, unusually for a professional sport, on-field failure by England was not reflected in poor financial performance – quite the opposite in fact. This disconnect between finance and success removed the main incentive for the TCCB and its controlling member counties to change their modus operandi.

Instead, in December 1989, the TCCB and its 17-man Cricket Committee decided to defer further consideration of a wholly four-day championship to allow a consultation of the counties. Once this was done, the TCCB rejected the idea by 14–4. In *Wisden Cricket*

Michael Holding at the Oval in 1976 after taking 8 for 92 in the second innings. No aspect of this scene would be likely today.
(Photo by Keystone/Hulton Archive/Getty Images)

Bob Willis in 1980. Since retiring in 1984, Willis has led calls for radical change in England cricket.
(Photo by Allsport UK/Allsport/Getty Images)

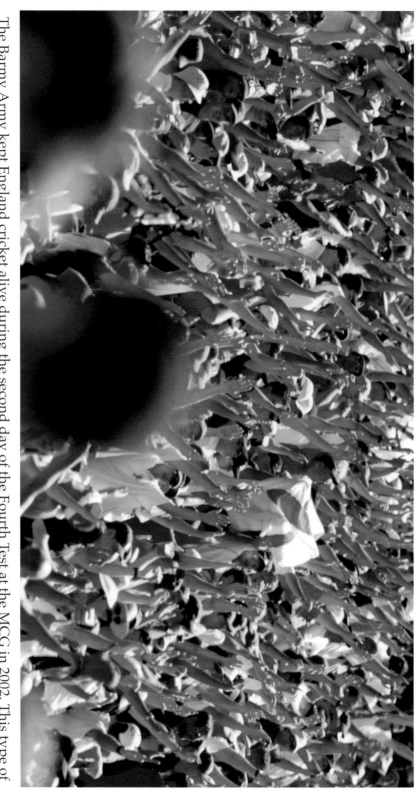

The Barmy Army kept England cricket alive during the second day of the Fourth Test at the MCG in 2002. This type of crowd is only seen on the fifth day of Tests played in England, when tickets are relatively easy to come by.

(Photo by Sean Garnsworthy/Getty Images)

Winning matches and friends. Justin Langer humours England fans at the MCG in December 2002.

(Photo by Hamish Blair / Getty Images)

Steve Waugh leads a lap of honour at the Sydney Cricket Ground in January 2003 after Australia's 4-1 defeat of England.

(Photo by Nick Wilson / Getty Images)

The Melbourne Cricket Ground on 29 November 2005.
(Photo by Sean Garnsworthy / Getty Images)

The MCG on 26 December 2005, the first day of the Boxing Day Test against South Africa.
(Photo by Kristian Dowling / Getty Images)

The MCG on 25 March 2006 during the 2006 Commonwealth Games.
(Photo by Ryan Pierse/Getty Images)

Tessa Jowell and Ken Livingstone inspect the initial design of London's
2012 Olympic Stadium during a press conference in July 2005.
(Photo by Saeed Khan/Getty Images)

The conclusions to the Fifth Tests in 2005 and 2006/7. Australia won the two series 6-2. It won previous home-and-away pairs of series by 8-2, 6-3, 7-2 and 7-0, respectively.

(Photo by Adrian Dennis / AFP / Getty Images)

(Photo by Cameron Spencer / Getty Images)

Tony Greig in London during the Packer case in September 1977.

A World Series Cricket day / night game at the SCG in February 1979. Packer people are proud of having invented day / night cricket.

Kerry Packer in 2005, aged 67. The best thing that ever happened to cricket, according to Don Bradman. (Photo by Patrick Riviere/ Getty Images)

A scene from the state memorial service for Packer at the Sydney Opera House in February 2006. (Photo by Greg Wood/Getty Images)

*Monthly*, Yorkshire Chairman Tony Vann pointed out that a 27% reduction in first-class games (from 22 to 16) would mean only one every three weeks for his members to enjoy.

Durham made an application to become the 18th first-class county and was accepted in 1990. The TCCB also signed deals to put a county one-day competition on one satellite channel (BSB) and the Sunday League on another (Sky). The rebel tour to South Africa finally persuaded the TCCB to offer contracts to England players, but these were designed to keep the top players out of South Africa rather than to create any Team England.

## Continuing divergence

Australia continued to improve, and 1989 turned out to have been the bottom of the cycle for England, too. In between the 1989 and 1993 Ashes series, England played 33 Tests, winning nine and losing 13. It lost away to the West Indies 1–2 and held them to a 2–2 draw at home in 1991. Australia also played 33, winning 13 and losing 6, with home and away losses to the West Indies by 1–2 on each occasion. The difference between the two sides was a 3–0 victory by Australia in the 1990/91 Ashes.

These four closer results against the West Indies signalled that nearly 20 years of West Indian dominance of the international game were drawing to a close. Malcolm Marshall retired after the Oval Test in 1991 and Patrick Patterson's last game was at Brisbane in 1991/92. This left 'just' Ambrose and Walsh, with Bishop in support, but he had serious back problems. In any case, they did not represent the menace of any combination of four selected from Roberts, Holding, Daniel, Croft, Garner and Marshall.

The Australian elite youth conveyor belt and second tier continued to outperform the English equivalents in player production. Australia gave debuts to just eight players between the 1989 and 1993 Ashes, five of whom (Mark Waugh, Shane Warne, Damien Martyn, Justin Langer and Paul Reiffel) became mainstays of the team.

England gave debuts to 17 players, of whom only Hussain and Stewart went on to long Test careers. Five others (Chris Lewis, Phil Tufnell, Graeme Hick, Ian Salisbury and Mark Ramprakash) had spasmodic careers but the remaining 10 made little impression on the international game. England therefore continued to rely on and off on four daddies of the eighties, Botham, Gower, Gooch and Gatting, all of whom had played during the Packer years. Down Under, only Border remained of that cohort, and Australia had long since got over that particular hump.

England and Australia embarked on divergent paths off the field too. All administrative questions had been settled in Australia, and the next major development came in 1990 when comedian Billy Birmingham released the CD *Twelfth Man Again*. Featuring a picture of Merv Hughes on the front cover, the album lampooned, among other things, the names of Sri Lankan and Pakistani players. It reached number one in the Australian charts. In April of that year, British politician Norman Tebbit introduced his cricket Test concerning the loyalty of immigrants to the UK, saying, 'It's a question of which way a chap cheers. Is it for the country he leaves or the country of his adoption?' If there was any lampoonery in that comment, it escaped most.

While Birmingham affectionately mimicked the Channel Nine commentators, Sky put together a similar team featuring Tony Greig, Michael Holding and Geoff Boycott to cover the 1989/90 England tour to the West Indies, the first overseas England series to be covered live by television. When the England team returned home having lost the series 1–2, Frank Chamberlain, the new TCCB Chairman, said, 'But I really think both cricket and finance are cyclical. ... We've struggled on the international scene recently, but the side in West Indies this winter has been well-trained, well-disciplined and fit, and we've seen the improvement.'

Chamberlain's comment was focused on the effect—England's cyclical performance—rather than its causes. It seems that he had not considered the possibility that the West Indies had declined more than England had improved. He had also, apparently, not looked closely at what the Australians had been doing to produce and maintain a competitive national side.

## 1990/91 Ashes

England set off for the 1990/91 Ashes tour with a reasonable bowling side containing Malcolm, Fraser, Martin Bicknell, Small, Lewis, Eddie Hemmings and Tufnell. It could have been stronger, but Jarvis, Foster and Dilley were banned. The Australian coach, Bob Simpson, had coached Leicestershire and said in *The Times* in September 1990 that 'I have not seen anything over here that makes me think Australia will not win.'

Events bore out his view as Australia put England away 3–0. Two oldies, Gooch and Gower, both scored 400 runs in the series but England lost the First Test in three days and then the second and the fifth. The Australian attack of Hughes, McDermott, Alderman and Reid, three of whom had played in the 4–0 rout of England in 1989, collectively averaged under 27. Of the two other fast bowlers in the Australian stable, Rackemann got one game and Geoff Lawson was not selected. For England, Tufnell did reasonably with nine wickets at 38, but only Malcolm played all five games, and he was carted. Injuries again cost England with Fraser out for two games and Lewis returning home after the First Test.

Those in England watching the Melbourne game courtesy of Sky could see a vast hole in the side of the Melbourne Cricket Ground caused by the construction of the 48,000-seat Great Southern Stand for the 1992 World Cup. On the field, England also lost to South Australia and New South Wales and narrowly escaped defeats against Victoria and Western Australia with defensive actions in the fourth innings. The states put out full sides, and Victoria (Hughes, O'Donnell and Paul Reiffel), Western Australia (Reid and Alderman) and Queensland (McDermott, Rackemann, Hohns and Michael Kasprowicz) all had bowling attacks of international calibre.

Bob Willis' thinking leapt ahead as a result of this second successive Ashes defeat. In *Wisden Cricket Monthly* he wrote: 'Australia have as few as 26 professional cricketers, yet have managed to build over a period of time an efficient, exciting but by no means brilliant Test team.' The reason, he said, 'is because their Sheffield Shield competition is a highly competitive league playing cricket as close to those conditions found in the Test arena as possible. We do not.' Ian Chappell added that 'Some players found it a shock – the type of cricket played here, the standard, the approach, the attitude.'

*Wisden* editor Graeme Wright went further, writing: 'Yet this summer, eighteen professional counties will attempt to keep the show on the road and off the breadline. Why? Because it has always been thus? Because it is part of the fabric of British life? Or because no-one will stand back and say the time has come to overhaul the professional game?' Wright then predicted that:

> *Such changes would almost certainly bring about the demise of some counties.*

Minor reforms continued, however. In May 1991, the TCCB accepted coloured clothing and the white ball in the Sunday League, nearly 14 years after World Series Cricket. Sunday play in Tests was agreed for 1992, 15 years after WSC. Later in 1991, the TCCB set up another review into the question of four-day county cricket, this one named the Murray Working Party. But, six years after the other MCC had accepted women members, England's MCC voted in 1991 against such a move. In response, Matthew Engel launched another attack in *Wisden Cricket Monthly*, saying, 'The MCC is a private club. That is the problem: at the heart of English cricket is an organisation that is nothing to do with the rest of it.'

England staged a short-lived mini-revival in 1991 and 1991/92, holding their own against the West Indies for the first time since 1973/74 despite 48 wickets at 21 for Ambrose and Marshall in the five games. Stalwart batting from Gooch and Smith kept England going in one of the rare series where a much better bowling team failed to win. Although England picked seven pace bowlers, 22 wickets from DeFreitas at 21 and a single good performance each from four others enabled England to nick a 2–2 draw. In New Zealand, England doled out a 2–0 defeat to a weak side that had just lost Richard Hadlee to retirement.

## More collapse

David Gower and Ian Botham both retired from international cricket in 1992, finally bringing to an end England's long history of extremely talented cricketers who played for fun and who lived as they played. Botham, for instance, pulled off the single-best performance in Test history, consisting of 13 wickets and a century in his only innings, against India in February 1980 despite drinking a hard-boiled journalist on the *Daily Mirror*, Chris Lander, under the table on the second night. In the morning, Lander woke up and switched on the curry-coated television only to see Botham take a wicket with the first ball of the day.

Gower famously hit his first ball in Test cricket in 1977 for four and buzzed an England tour match in a Tiger Moth during the 1990/91 trip to Australia, having scored two centuries in the previous two Tests. When the authorities tried to discipline him, he told them that they had over-reacted and left the room. There are no surveys to back up this contention but, when Botham and Gower left the game, hundreds of thousands of fans went with them.

Mike Gatting followed in 1993. Then, lacking enough new talent, England embarked on a precipitous collapse that was even sharper and deeper than in 1988 and 1989. In the five seasons between 1992 and 1994/5, they played 20, won three, lost 13 and drew four. A total of 37 players was picked, including a staggering 16 pace bowlers, as many as took part in all Australian first-class cricket. Only two of the 16, Malcolm and Martin McCague[9], were genuinely quick. The latter learned his cricket in Australia, attending the Academy in Adelaide and making his debut for Victoria in the same game as Shane Warne.

The first loss was by 1–2 to Pakistan in the five-Test series of 1992. Once again, only one pace bowler played all five games: Chris Lewis. Wasim Akram (four games) and Waqar Younis (five games) both took over 20 wickets in the series, with back-up from Mushtaq Ahmed, the leg-spinning successor to Abdul Qadir. Top of the England bowling averages was Graham Gooch, with five wickets at 19. The best serious bowler was Neil Mallender, with 10 wickets at 22 in the last two Tests. He never played for England again.

In the September 1992 edition of *Wisden Cricket Monthly*, David Gower asked for less cricket and 'enough gaps in the fixture list to allow players to recover from the demands of persistent cricket, without having to play seven days a week.' Remarkably, he confessed that 'over the 1991 season I had become so disenchanted with the Sunday slog (in both senses) that I had played so consistently badly on the Sabbath as to persuade my employers that somebody else might be more usefully selected on the day.'

This was the third time in six years that Gower had complained of fatigue. On 6 September, he opened *The Mail on Sunday* to read that he had been omitted from the tour party to India, despite averaging exactly 50 in his three games in the summer. Like Mallender, Gower never played again for England.

In May 1992, the Murray report recommended a first-class programme of four-day games to start in 1993, 12 years after Bob Willis proposed it in his book and 101 years after first-class cricket began in Australia with timeless inter-state games.

In the winter of 1992/93, England lost 0–3 in India and then lost a Test for the first time to Sri Lanka. Against India in the First Test at Calcutta, England fielded a four-seamer attack, leaving out Emburey and Tufnell and, according to *Wisden*, were beaten 'physically, mentally, technically and tactically.' India's leg-spinner Anil Kumble took 21 wickets and Graeme Hick took eight at 25, but England's seamers all averaged over 40. In Sri Lanka, England conceded a first-innings lead of 89 despite scoring 380. A collapse in the second innings led to a Sri Lanka victory by five wickets, with Sanath Jayasuriya belting Tufnell for six to win the game.

Back in England in March 1993, Chairman of Selectors Ted Dexter's main comment about the debacle in the sub-continent was that 'we will be looking at the whole question of people's facial hair.' Bob Willis, on the other hand, delivered another volley of bouncers at the English system:

> *In our professional game we have far too many players who are mediocre in the extreme … To have around 400 professional players is a joke. Australia has about two dozen! … The plethora of so-called all-rounders who bowl a brand of medium-pace negative rubbish and slog in the middle order of county cricket are the bane of our beloved game and must be hounded out at the earliest opportunity.*

Willis recommended fewer domestic teams and fewer matches, although he thought that '… none of this will ever happen, so let's find our scapegoat instead.' An invention by his former captain, Tony Greig, was adopted, however. In March 1993, 15 years after World Series Cricket, TCCB members approved the use of the fielding circle in the Sunday League.

## Leg-spin

In the previous two seasons, England had faced two leg-spinners from the sub-continent in Mushtaq Ahmed and Anil Kumble. Although they had one leg-spinner, Ian Salisbury of Sussex, he was not an international cricketer. For their part, Australia had lacked a world-beating spinner since the end of World Series Cricket but had recently put two candidates under intensive development. One, Shane Warne, had been selected for the Academy in 1990 and the other, Stuart MacGill, went a year later. Australia brought Warne with them for the 1993 series.

Leg-spin in England had effectively been dead since the retirement of Doug Wright and Eric Hollies in the early fifties. Hollies took 5–131 against Australia at the Oval in 1948, including his famous dismissal of Bradman for a duck with a googly, and Wright had achieved the last five-wicket haul by an England leg-spinner in 1950/51. After that, Robin Hobbs played seven Tests from the late sixties, followed by Ian Salisbury two decades later.

Leg-spin never died in Pakistan and Australia. For Pakistan, Abdul Qadir carried the baton from 1977 until 1990, playing 67 games with 236 wickets, and Mushtaq Ahmed played 30 One-Day Internationals before Warne started his career. With Danish Kaneria today, Pakistan has had a leg-spinner continuously since the seventies.

In Australia, four leg-spinners provided continuity after the retirement of Richie Benaud in 1964, each playing a dozen seasons or more. Terry Jenner played in state cricket until the mid-seventies, with nine Tests, assisted by Peter Philpott with eight. Kerry O'Keeffe started slightly later, playing 24 Tests before the end of the seventies, and Trevor Hohns played from the early seventies until 1990/91, with seven Tests. On Ian Chappell's recommendation, Jenner was employed to pass on the leg-spinner's craft to a new generation at the Australian Cricket Academy.

Once unearthed, Warne was thrust straight into the national side after four first-class games for Victoria, making his Test debut in January 1992 at the age of 22. It would be fair to say that in the early nineties the new Australian elite youth development system was looking for examples of this exotic species.

## Mr Marsh's pies

The problems of selection and the inadequacy of domestic cricket recurred during the 1993 series. England picked 24 players, of whom only Gooch, Atherton and Alec Stewart played all six games, whereas Australia used just 13. In the bowling department, 13 players represented England, including 10 quicks, none of whom was successful as Australia averaged nearly 450 in their first innings, with two scores over 600 and six batsmen averaging at least 50. All four Aussie bowlers (Warne, Hughes, Reiffel and Peter May) took their wickets at well under 30.

The one England bowling success, with 16 wickets at 34, was off-spinner Peter Such. Strangely, after playing five games in this series, he played only six more Tests in his career. Even more remarkably, England gave debuts to seven players, initiated a new captain and used a debutant, Andy Caddick, to deliver the first ball of the series.

The first game belonged to the spinners. Such took eight for 145 on his debut and Warne eight for 137, including the scalp of Mike Gatting with his first ball in Ashes Tests. Merv Hughes was the only seamer to make any contribution and Australia won by five wickets. At Lord's, Australia swatted England's attack away with 632–4 in the first innings. Another eight wickets for Warne and six for Tim May secured an innings victory.

Afterwards, the head coach at the Australian Cricket Academy, Rod Marsh, launched a sustained verbal assault on England professional cricket. Marsh blamed England's 0–2 position in the series on 'county cricket and the fact that it's not a good competition'. He went on:

> You see blokes in county games scoring hundreds and taking bags of wickets who you know wouldn't have a hope of playing first-class cricket in Australia, and would struggle to make it in a first-grade side. Take Michael Slater's innings of 152 at Lord's – sure it was a good knock, but there's a lot of blokes in this country who would have given their right arms to bat against that attack. Michael will probably admit he's made better 30s or 40s in Sheffield Shield domestic state level cricket than the 152 he made against England.

Marsh said he hoped Shane Warne would reject offers to play in county cricket because it would harm his development as a cricketer. Australian cricketers would be better off playing the southern winter in Darwin than going to England because:

*They go over there and face bowlers that are really just pie throwers, and they are not going to learn anything about the game.*

For the third game, the England selectors decided to play four debutants, only one of whom (Thorpe) subsequently made a mark. England's attack consisted of four bowlers with a total of four caps between them – Andy Caddick (2 Tests), McCague (0), Such (2) and Mark Ilott (0). A good performance by a strong batting side consisting of Gooch, Atherton, Hussain, Thorpe, Stewart and Smith produced innings of 321 and 422–6 that enabled England to draw the match.

The Fourth Test was a repeat of the second. England dropped Such, despite 12 wickets in three games, and selected a bowling attack with five caps in total that contained another debutant (Martin Bicknell). During the Australian first innings of 653–4, McCague went off injured with what turned out to be a stress fracture of the back. Despite more strong batting, England went down by an innings, taking only four Australian wickets in the match for the second time in the series.

Gooch resigned as England captain and Atherton, aged 25, was appointed as his replacement ahead of Stewart. At the press conference, Dexter let slip that 'We were unanimous, except for Dad.' According to Ian Botham, selector Mickey Stewart was forced to ring Atherton and explain himself.

Atherton took charge at Edgbaston with England 0–3 down after four. For his first game as captain, the selectors picked an attack of Bicknell, Ilott, Such and Tufnell and packed the team with batting. Atherton top-scored with 100 in his two innings but Warne and May ensured another Australia victory.

This was England's ninth defeat in 10 games and Dexter resigned as England's Chairman of Selectors to applause around the ground. At the press conference afterwards, Atherton promised a fresh start. England would, he said, 'identify young players with two things, talent and temperament, and then show faith in them.' These were the same three items that Allan Border and Bob Simpson had emphasised during Australia's re-building phase seven years earlier.

Despite a victory in the last game at the Oval to register a 1–4 series defeat, England ended the 1993 season in free fall, with a young and inexperienced captain, no Gower and Botham, no Chairman of Selectors, a weak bowling attack and little sign of any replacements. In the county averages for 1993, nine of the first 16 bowling places were taken by non-England players, with Pakistani Wasim Akram at the top.

As in 1989, the failure of the county system to produce and sustain a competitive England team was there for all to see. Rod Marsh's former captain, Ian Chappell, added some telling insights in a seminal *Wisden* article entitled *Why We Beat The Poms*. He asserted that 'England's ability to over-theorise and complicate the game of cricket is legendary' and dispensed with the backward-looking arguments about pitches and one-day cricket that had bogged England commentators down for a decade. He then wrote:

> *England are on the right track with four-day first-class games. I think they should go a step further and reduce the number of teams to make it more competitive, as there are players in the county system who are not up to first-class standard. Any system that protects incompetence needs changing.*

## Grumpy

Allan Border retired at the end of the following Australian season having completed the turnaround of Australian cricket that he and Bob Simpson had begun in 1986. Missing only one of the 157 Tests played during his 15-year career with Australia, he led them to victory in three successive Ashes series and established supremacy over all other Test teams except the West Indies. That was his only failure, and he bequeathed his three successors[10] a solid platform that they have exploited well.

During his career, Border earned the sobriquet Captain Grumpy for his unsmiling grimace during hard times on the field. Towards the end of his career, England produced Mike Atherton, a cricketer with the same obduracy and toughness in the face of adversity. Like Border, Atherton started in international cricket and became national captain with his team at a low point. His wicket became the most prized, and he would also come to earn the title Captain Grumpy. Fittingly, the captaincy record between them is one game apiece.

Despite the prognostications of Bob Willis, England wasted the decade and a half after World Series Cricket arguing about the merits of one-day, three-day and four-day cricket, the standard of county pitches and the question of overseas players. The result was a widening gap between county and country and a poor national side made worse by a plague of injuries to its leading bowlers. Slowly but surely, as the finances of the England side improved and those of the county system grew worse, conflict arose between county and country regarding the use of the top players and the increasing profits generated by the England team.

Unlike Border, Atherton was not backed up by like-minded administrators determined to do whatever was necessary to re-build England's performance. As a result, England's slump had many years yet to run.

# CHAPTER 5

# EVOLUTION

*The county system seems to have stuffed up badly. The over-riding priority in English cricket is the welfare of the counties and while that is understandable it is, in the interests of the overall game, a selfish, introverted view.*

Bob Simpson, 1996

## Changes in the game

The era of politics came to an end in the early nineties, providing the basis for a massive expansion of the game. The ICC went from seven full members to nine with the readmission of South Africa and the admission of Zimbabwe in 1992, and then to 10 with Bangladesh in 2000. The latest pair struggled to obtain fixtures, so in 2001 members agreed a ten-year international programme in which each member was obliged to play the other nine both home and away in the following five years, and then again in the five years after that.

These changes increased the volume of international cricket from about 180 days per year in the early nineties to 375 per year in the early 2000s. During 2000 to 2002, seven teams played 80–90 days per year, New Zealand and Zimbabwe 70 and Bangladesh 40. A schedule of 80–90 days required about 250 days on the road, depending on how tightly governing bodies could pack it. This prompted New Zealand Chairman of Selectors Richard Hadlee to say in 2002, 'So what break is there in 12 months? Probably two months. To keep your intensity, your fitness and your mental game going ... boy, you have to be a special player to stay on top of your game.' Darren Gough said in the same year, 'If young guys play every Test and One-Day International, they're not going to last more than four years. Their bodies will give in.'

This expansion steadily turned the international game into a big business. The 1999 World Cup in England, for example, was watched by 2.3 billion people in 129 countries, and the ICC made a profit of £30 million. The ICC then sold eight years of World Cup and Champions Trophy television rights, including the 2003 and 2007 World Cups, for US$550 million plus a profit share. New television deals in England and Australia in the late nineties brought riches to the game and became the single biggest source of revenues in both countries.

The increasing volume of international cricket meant that few international players had the time or energy to play domestic cricket, even in England, despite salaries denominated in pounds sterling, a hard western currency. England players, though, continued to have no choice but to play for their counties all the way through to 2000.

The ratio of one-day games to Tests stabilised at 2.5-to-one in the late eighties and has remained at that level ever since. England increased its ratio steadily through the nineties from about one-to-one at the beginning to 1.5-to-one in 2000–2002, still well below its main competitors. Its great fear in the eighties that the Test match would fall by the wayside did not come to pass, but the country deserves great credit for its commitment to the longer form of the game.

The West Indies, with only Curtly Ambrose and Courtney Walsh left of the rich seam of fast bowlers, fell back. For India, Anil Kumble and the unheralded Javagal Srinath formed the basis of the bowling, while Sachin Tendulkar and latterly Rahul Dravid and V.V.S. Laxman led the batting. The side won more games than it lost and beat Australia twice at home. Sri Lanka also came on strong, winning the 1996 World Cup and beating England away in 1998 for the first time. For Pakistan, Waqar Younis, Wasim Akram and Mushtaq Ahmed bowled through to 2002, joined by Saqlain

Mushtaq in 1995 and Shoaib Akhtar in 1997. They helped Pakistan become the second-best Test team at the turn of the century.

## England and Australia

Figure 7 shows the form of England and Australia in the years 1993 to 2002. During this period, England's form never once remotely matched that of Australia.

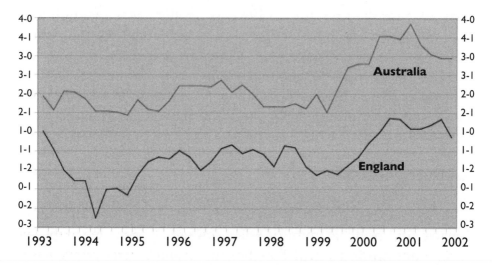

FIGURE 7: ENGLAND AND AUSTRALIA FORM DECEMBER 1992
TO SEPTEMBER 2002

In 18 games between spring 1992 and spring 1994, England recorded two victories and 13 losses and fell to its lowest point in all cricket history. Continued poor performance led to a series of vitriolic attacks on the management of the game so that, by 1996, the counties that controlled the TCCB realised that something had to give. Between 1997 and 2002, under the leadership of Ian MacLaurin, a series of reforms was instituted that collectively added up to Team England. These, and the arrival of Duncan Fletcher as coach in autumn 1999, brought an immediate improvement in performance.

Each of these reforms took a long time to agree and implement. By 2002, though, England was close in terms of team management to where Australia had been in 1988. The changes were paid for by further increases in the price of access to England games for fans and an increase in the number of England home games from 2000 onwards. The approach was evolutionary rather than revolutionary and the business model of England cricket remained intact throughout.

Team Australia put in a consistently strong on-field performance, and became the world's best team when it beat the West Indies in early 1995 for the first time in 19 years. In 1999, Steve Waugh took over as captain and John Buchanan was appointed coach, and the side began an ascent from good to excellent that led to complete domination of the international game. From September 1999 to September 2001, it reached a peak that few other professional sports teams can have attained. Of 26 Tests, it won 20 and lost four, compiling a sequence of 16 successive victories in the process.

## Recovery dashed

With Ted Dexter out of the picture as a result of the 1993 Ashes debacle and no Chairman of Selectors yet appointed to replace him, Atherton and Keith Fletcher, who had started as coach / manager at the beginning of 1993, were able to engineer a development team for the West Indies for the spring 1994 tour. Only three players were aged over 30, the average number of caps was only 15, and there was no Gooch, Gower, Gatting or Botham. Unusually for England in recent years, 13 of the 17 players would go on to have significant Test careers and the first-choice bowling combination of Malcolm, Fraser, Lewis, Caddick and Tufnell was selected and then fit to go.

The West Indies won the first three games and took the series 3–1, Ambrose, Walsh and Kenny Benjamin capturing their wickets at 26 or under. In the Third Test, Ambrose and Walsh bowled England out for 46 in only 19 overs, and in the fifth Brian Lara hit 375 to register the highest score by an individual batsman in Test history. As was the case with Australia in the mid-eighties, only four

England players performed. Fraser took 16 wickets at 28 and Caddick 18 at 30, and Atherton and Stewart both averaged over 50.

An away loss against this opposition by a young team was no disgrace. The signs of a recovery were particularly evident when England won the fourth game, in Barbados, by 208 runs in front of 6,000 England fans thanks to two centuries from Stewart, 8–75 by Fraser and 5–63 from Caddick.

In March 1994, former England captain Raymond Illingworth was appointed as the new Chairman of Selectors. At 61, Illingworth was 35 years older than Mike Atherton and had played his last Test in 1973, when Atherton was five. He immediately made a poor start. When asked by *The Cricketer* how many current England players he admired, his answer was: none.

Illingworth brought in two other selectors of a similar ilk to himself: Brian Bolus (aged 60) and Fred Titmus (61). They ditched Atherton's re-building approach in favour of a policy of picking on county form that paid no heed to the Australian Team concept based on faith, talent and temperament. Instead, the new selection team embarked on a systematic trawl through the counties, watching 63 players by the end of May 1994. Only five of the squad that had been to the West Indies played in the first game of the summer.

England recovered a little through a victory against New Zealand and a draw against South Africa which featured the Atherton dirt-in-pocket saga and Devon Malcolm's 9–57 at the Oval. That game was Malcolm's first of the summer and was the sixth in a series of seven Tests that he played where each game was against a different country from the one before.

Overall, Malcolm played 40 Tests for England in 14 separate blocks, meaning that he was injured or dropped 13 times. The only fast bowler produced in England in this era, described by Steve Waugh as 'a difficult assignment ... a match-winner', could never really be said to have been part of the England setup. Instead, according to

Waugh, 'Australia, as a team, breathed a sigh of relief whenever a steady medium-pacer was picked in front of him.'

Regardless of this, England cricket hit a bonanza in August 1994 when the TCCB announced a new television deal for 1995 to 1998. After a three-way competition, the BBC and BSkyB won with bids totalling £58.5 million over the four years, an average annual value triple that of the previous deal and 12 times the one in place in 1989. The BBC would cover the Tests and the county Nat West Trophy, and Sky the Texaco Trophy One-Day Internationals and the county B&H Cup.

Suddenly, the game had more money than it could handle. But when the TCCB set up a Working Party to decide what to do with the cash, the outcome became inevitable.

## War of words

In the 1994/95 tour to Australia, England squandered the momentum Atherton and Fletcher had created in the West Indies six months earlier. To start with, Fraser was left out of the tour party despite being the leading England bowler with 85 wickets at 28. Then, Atherton's youth policy was further reversed with the selection of Gooch, Gatting and an inexperienced 33-year old bowler, Joey Benjamin. Fraser's father was so disgusted that he wrote to *The Daily Telegraph*. Fraser himself wrote that 'It was an enormous shock. I was angry and hurt because no-one had taken the trouble to tell me I had been left out.'

In the event, injuries took their toll of the tourists and Fraser was called up. In all, six players were forced out of the tour, including two of the three quickest bowlers, Martin McCague and Darren Gough. A grand total of 22 England players went to Australia and, once again, no England bowler played all five games.

When the trip began in October, Atherton and Illingworth commenced a low-level war of words through the media. It seems to have started when Atherton hinted to journalists that he had wanted Fraser in his squad. Just before the First Test, Illingworth claimed at a sports writers' lunch back in England that his intervention in the dirt-in-pocket affair the summer before had saved Atherton's neck. This claim was based on the fact that Illingworth had quickly fined Atherton for his misdemeanour and perhaps drawn the sting out of any further official sanction. Illingworth also said that the tourists had too many days off and criticised Atherton for not phoning him for advice. One can only guess at what Atherton, out in Australia, thought about Illingworth's comments.

The first ball of the First Test at Brisbane was bowled by Phil DeFreitas and hit for four by Michael Slater in what Richie Benaud called 'one of the best and most calculated attacking ploys in recent years of Test cricket'. Slater and new captain Mark Taylor took 26 off the first four overs and reduced, says Benaud, 'England's bowling and general out-cricket on the opening day into a shambles.' This ploy of turning up at the ground and attacking from the start represented an extension of the Ashes from the physical domain into the psychological. In the years since, Australia has made this second domain its own so that, as Steve Waugh comments, 'Under the blowtorch they seemed to buckle while we held firm.'

At Brisbane, an Australian first-innings lead of 250 was converted into a win by 184 thanks to 8–71 from Warne in the second innings. In between the First and Second Tests, the Australian Cricket Academy beat England in successive one-day games, prompting Christopher Martin-Jenkins to write: 'All the qualities of Australian cricket—above all their instinctive aggression and well-trained athleticism—were shown in stark relief against the jaded complacency of their professional opponents.' During the series, in fact, Academy graduate Glenn McGrath made his Ashes debut for Australia and another graduate, Slater, was Australia's most successful batsman with 620 runs at 62. Overall, the Academy had helped develop 11 Test players and 53 first-class players in its first seven years.

England were destroyed by McDermott and Warne in the Second Test at the MCG, scoring only 304 runs in their two innings. For the Third Test, though, England fielded its strongest bowling attack for many years in Fraser, Malcolm, Gough and Tufnell. Australia, set 449 to win, went for it and reached 344–7 at the close, but the draw meant that Australia retained the Ashes.

Afterwards, Atherton said in the *Sydney Morning Herald* that 'The England situation is very much analogous with Australia's situation in the mid-eighties. Australia identified a group of players with sufficient talent and temperament, and they stuck by them through some poor times.' Another strong attack, with Lewis in for an injured Gough, enabled England to win the fourth game to keep the series alive, but Australia turned it on in the last game to win by 329 runs and take the series 3–1.

During the trip, Atherton invited Ian Chappell out to dinner. He later told an interviewer what happened. 'I never really sat down and talked about [captaincy] with anyone, till Ian Chappell,' Atherton said. 'It was fascinating, and the first time I'd done that. He has great clarity, and he talks forcefully, so he carries you along with him. He's very straight. I suppose he's the typical Aussie, his background would be to take the game to the opposition, take it by the scruff of the neck, aggression, aggression, aggression. Which is very different from how you'd be told to play the game in England. Refreshing.'

In a press conference at the end of the Fifth Test at Perth, Atherton produced a prepared speech. He repeated his wish for a young team with character and desire and then said, 'What we require are selectors who are more in touch with the dynamics of the modern game, ideally former recently retired Test players who are able to communicate with current players more effectively because they have played the same game and talked the same language.' Soon afterwards, Illingworth got his own back, saying of Atherton, 'He has been to Cambridge and never been out to work in his life. It's hard for him to gee them up.'

The one-day tournament in early 1995 was contested by Australia, Zimbabwe, England and Australia A. England managed to lose one of its games to Zimbabwe and one to Australia A and so, at the SCG and the MCG in January 1995, crowds totalling 90,000 watched two fine Australian sides contest the best-of-three finals.

## Reaction

In March 1995, the TCCB sacked Keith Fletcher halfway through his five-year contract and appointed Illingworth as his replacement, thereby handing virtually complete control of the England operation to one man. Looking back in his autobiography, Fletcher reflected on the absence of Team England. Players, he said, turned up on the Tuesday of a home Test and had a net and a dinner. Sometimes, they hardly knew each other. Worse, he commented that 'the coach of England should not have to teach his players how to play slow bowling' and 'I think I was the first person to organise fielding drills at England practices'.

*Wisden* commented that 'The longer the tour lasted, the more obvious it became that in the small print of the game—fielding, running between wickets, practice techniques, plus attitude to practice—England were running second not only to Australia, but to state and colts teams too.' Richie Benaud blamed 'the type of cricket played at county level where there is less of an accent on playing hard cricket'. Like Michael Holding before him, Malcolm Marshall blamed county cricket for over-bowling young quicks.

Former TCCB Chairman Raman Subba Row wrote a letter to *The Times* complaining that vested interests blocked progressive thinking and complaining that 'more and more cash is being distributed to fund more and more mediocrity'. Saying that 'expanding revenue from commercial sources is only exacerbating the problem', Subba Row called for a 'drastic structural reorganisation, resulting in the parent running the subsidiaries and not vice versa as at present.' But, he carried on, 'ailing organisations don't mend themselves', so 'Someone must break into this vicious circle of mismanagement and create a new accountable structure.'

Paul Sheldon, the Chief Executive of Surrey, agreed that 'The issue in cricket is not remotely about money. In fact, you could argue that the new money will merely obfuscate the issue.' However, even this senior cricket executive despaired of change. 'What we need is the right structure,' he continued. 'Unfortunately, the TCCB is too unwieldy to bring it about. The member counties vote for their own parochial interests and few are able to make decisions in the best interests of the game.'

Perhaps tired of bashing his head against a brick wall, Bob Willis designed a new England-centric professional structure in which 24 players would be contracted by England and the 18 counties would be divided into three leagues of six. This, he said, would create a smoother pyramid, close the gap between county and international cricket and reduce the playing commitment of each second-tier professional.

Nothing came of these proposals, and cash continued to haemorrhage. Warwickshire recruited Brian Lara on a base salary of £100,000, more than England players made. In May 1995, the players' union, the Cricketers' Association, asked for a minimum wage for capped county players of £20,000, citing the television deal with the BBC and BSkyB. The union eventually secured £18,500, an increase of 28%. To help fund this, the TCCB more than doubled its payments to each county from the £327,000 distributed in 1991 to about £750,000 in 1995.

## Australia

Player payments also became an issue in Australia. In March 1994, the contract between PBL and the ACB expired after 15 years and the television rights came up for grabs. The new deal negotiated with Channel Nine by ACB Chief Executive Graham Halbish more than quintupled the payment from $2 million a year to an average of $11 million for the five years from 1994.

The Australian players wanted some of this and let it be known that they were considering their alternatives. This led to a new agreement, negotiated for the players by Austin Robertson and John Cornell, which provided for two-year contracts for 20 players and a four-year guarantee for the captain Mark Taylor. Between 1992 and 1997, these payments doubled and Australian players started to make serious money. Taylor, in particular, was in a dramatically better contractual and financial position than his counterpart in England, who was employed by his county club and reappointed by England for each series. Whereas Taylor had a proper job, Mike Atherton was, to all intents and purposes, a temp.

Immediately after England departed, Australia set off for a four-Test series against the West Indies, whom they had not beaten since 1975/76 in either official or Test series cricket. Facing them were Ambrose, Walsh and two Benjamins, who appeared to outgun McDermott, Reiffel, McGrath and Warne. When McDermott fell off a sea wall and went home with torn ankle ligaments, things seemed bad. However, a rough, competitive and tight series went down to the last game. Steve Waugh hit a double century, one of the great Australian innings, to enable Australia to win the series 2–1 and collect another tickertape parade on its return home.

Since then, Australia has lost only five out of the 42 series it has played, all of them away. Three were to India, one to Sri Lanka and one to England. Australia is unbeaten at home since 1992/93.

## Coins in a spin-dryer

Darren Gough and Dominic Cork made their England debuts in 1994 and 1995 respectively, giving England a first-choice attack in the mid-nineties of five out of Malcolm, Fraser, Gough, Caddick, Cork and Tufnell, depending on conditions. Atherton, Stewart, Hick, Smith, Thorpe and Hussain made a decent batting line-up. In the bowling reserve, England had DeFreitas and Alan Mullally, and Lewis was straight into the all-rounder slot if he could improve his batting. With John Crawley and Jack Russell also pushing for a place, England had a strong squad of 17 players with good cover for all positions except spinner. However, the first-choice side (excluding Malcolm) never played together because of an endless succession of bowler injuries and some further peculiar selection.

In the early 2000s, medical research[1] in Australia established the factors that make fast bowlers injury-prone. A two-year survey of 90 bowlers in over 5,000 sessions of grade, state and international cricket found that bowlers who average fewer than two days between bowling sessions are 2.4 times more likely to be injured than those averaging between three and four days between sessions. On the other hand, bowlers averaging over five days between sessions were found to be 1.8 times as likely to be injured as those averaging between three and four days, suggesting that there is a minimum activity level as well as a maximum.

The survey concluded that 'Fast bowlers should bowl with a session frequency of 2–5 days, and bowl in 2–3 sessions per week.' The implication of this is a fortnightly schedule, for a fast bowler, of one four-day or five-day game and two one-day games. This would require five or six bowling sessions and would place the bowler in the middle of the recommended range.

During the nineties, leading England fast bowlers continued to be battered, like Ian Botham and Graham Dilley before them, by the demand that they bowl over 80 times in the 22-week, 155-day home season. The average mid-season weekly schedule of one four-day game and one one-day game required a quick bowler to produce four or five bowling sessions, week after week. This was a much greater frequency than was subsequently found to be advisable.

At the end of each season, players had just a little respite before overseas tours that were only marginally less intensive. Despite pleas from some quarters for a reduction in the volume of cricket and plenty of anecdotal evidence that the overuse of bowlers was weakening the England side, the authorities did nothing.

By the late nineties the evidence became overwhelming. Justin Langer related in his diary of the 1998 Middlesex season, *From Outback to Outfield*, how the workload wore him and his team-mates down. Noting that Middlesex played five times as much one-day cricket as Australia's state sides, Langer worried about the burden on quickie Richard Johnson. For 22 May, he wrote: 'I don't know how he can possibly make it through the season at this rate. This workload is incomprehensible.' On 3 June, he encountered a 19-year-old Steve Harmison for the first time, writing: 'This boy was quick, and I mean really quick ... The big question is will his body be able to survive the constant demands of county cricket?' After playing 14 days out of 16, he said on 8 June, 'I am starting to agree with the popular consensus that English cricketers play far too much cricket.' About another Middlesex bowler, he said, 'It seems absurd that Angus Fraser, just selected for the Fourth Test against South Africa commencing on Thursday [two days hence], today played his sixth day straight.'

Ian Botham himself provided the most telling insight into the plight of the England fast bowler. In his 1997 book, *The Botham Report*, he discussed the thorny subject of injuries and pharmaceutical drugs, particularly non-steroidal anti-inflammatory pills. Botham estimated that 90% of county pace bowlers in 1993 were taking great quantities of these drugs. He went on:

> *The amount of anti-inflammatory drugs I took during my career would be inconceivable to the man in the street. They were rattling round me like coins in a spin-dryer. But for me and countless other bowlers they were just a fact of life.*

Botham reported that Dilley took so many pills that he developed an abnormal liver function which was detected when he went in for some surgery. Then, in 1999, both BBC *Radio Five Live* and *The Mail on Sunday* reported that up to 90% of county fast bowlers were on painkillers by mid-season. Angus Fraser said, 'I tend to take one most evenings, because I know that the following morning I am going to be up for the job in hand.' Elsewhere, Darren Gough said the same: 'Ninety per cent of bowlers are on painkillers.'

Botham quoted two England physios in support of his arguments. Dave Roberts told him that 'as a pace bowler, if you play the amount of cricket our international players do … I don't care how fit you are, you are going to be physically and mentally knackered most of the time … the demand made on our top international bowlers by our county clubs mean that, from time to time, almost all of them have been operating in Test matches with their bootlaces tied together.' Wayne Morton told him: 'Basically, most of the problems of burn out and injury in young bowlers stem from the fact that we have been approaching a professional game in a far too amateur fashion for far too long.'

Botham concluded:

> *Such a gruelling workload and the almost non-stop travelling that went with it is simply absurd.*

## Explaining mediocrity

The effects on England fast bowlers were disastrous for the performance of the team. From 1994 to 1998, when Fraser played his last Test, the careers of Caddick (England's eighth-highest wicket-taker in Tests), Gough (ninth) and Fraser (15th) overlapped for 53 games. But this trio never played a single Test together. In half of the 53 games, two of them played. In a bit under half, one played. In seven, none played.

England won 13 of these 53 Tests and lost 19. Had all three players been fit, firing and selected for most of these games, then England might well have won, say, 24 and lost 14. This would have been close to Australia's record during the same period of 25 won and 13 lost out of 49 games, part of which was achieved against England teams lacking these very bowlers.

In reality, Fraser turned up to a Test in 1994 and Illingworth commented, 'The bugger looks shagged out already, and we haven't even tossed up yet.' Botham has described Fraser arriving at the

Third Test in 1995 completely knackered. Gough pulled out of the West Indies tour in 1997/98 and Caddick missed the first half of the 1994 season and all of 1995 with shin problems, reporting that he had two operations that left long scars up both of his legs. He said, 'I was in a wheelchair for two weeks and on crutches for another two. I had to crawl, on all fours, to the toilet.' In 2000, Caddick was 31 but had only played 30 Tests.

Gough, in a 1998 interview, gave details of the incentives operating on players that were no different from those experienced by Botham and Dilley 10 years before: '… I don't see how players can sign ECB contracts because it would affect their futures with their counties. We've got some good young bowlers here at Yorkshire and if they get established while I basically disappear for a couple of years playing for England and resting in between, how could I then come strolling back to Yorkshire and expect a place in the team?'

In 2006, their contemporary Chris Lewis looked back on his career in *The Wisden Cricketer*. This marvellous sportsman, perhaps the most talented player in the barren years between Ian Botham and Andrew Flintoff, had this to say:

> Basically you were the main man at your county; they would flog the horse before you played Test cricket. You'd finish that, report for Test cricket with no break, then they'd flog the horse. When that was done it was back to your county where they would flog you again. It was hard to be 100%. Tiredness did not get you a day off. Even if injuries meant you could not bowl, you were still fit to field or bat.

Lewis' captain, Mike Atherton, played most of his England career while suffering from a non-cricket-related condition, ankylosing spondylitis. On many occasions, he was severely affected by spasms in his lower back and was in considerable pain while fielding. This player frequently stood alone for England when barely able to stand at all.

Without the support structure of a Team England, Atherton was left to deal with these problems by himself. He has since written that 'It was not exactly a professional or caring system', and in his autobiography he laments the failure of the authorities to look after him with the single word 'disgraceful'.

England, the fans, Atherton and his bowlers were short-changed by the unresolved conflict between county and country which festered through the eighties and nineties. Atherton's view, spiced up with some choice Packer-Chappell terminology, applies to the whole of England professional cricket at that time.

## Foreigners

In the six series between the 1994/95 and 1997 Ashes, England clambered back up from the low point of spring 1994 and the away loss to Australia in 1994/95. The team registered five wins and five losses in 22 games, winning two series, losing two, drawing two and steadily regaining the mediocrity of old.

The first of these series was a visit by West Indies in 1995. Illingworth further asserted himself by warning Atherton not to criticise selection of sides again, and the simmering row came to a head in April when the two met during a county one-day game. After they had traded accusations, England selector David Graveney asked them whether they could work together. Both said 'yes'. Illingworth then left Fraser out for the First Test despite his successful efforts in Australia.

Against a tired West Indian team with disciplinary and captaincy problems, England achieved a 2–2 draw despite picking 21 players, of whom only Atherton and Thorpe played all six games. Caddick was injured for most of the summer and Tufnell was not selected, but Cork took 7–43 on his debut at Lord's to win the game. Gough, though, succumbed to injury after the Third Test, so England only fielded a strong attack twice. Again, no England bowler played all the games whereas, for the West Indies, Bishop and Walsh managed all six and Ambrose five.

Dennis Silk, the Chairman of the TCCB, admitted that 'There are many things wrong with our cricket, and we need a firmness of purpose if we are not to remain a third-world power, which is what we have become.' However, in July, a nasty row broke with the publication of an article entitled 'Is it in the blood?' in *Wisden Cricket Monthly*. The article contained the following observations:

*An Asian or Negro raised in England will, according to the liberal, feel exactly the same pride and identification with the place as a white man. The reality is somewhat different.*

*For 30 years or more those with authority in education, assisted by politicians and those in the mass media, have conspired — in the sociological sense of creating a climate of opinion — to produce a public ideology designed to remove any sense of pride or sense of place in the hearts of those who are unequivocally English. It has not been entirely successful, but it has had a profound effect on the national self-confidence of many Englishmen.*

The writer suggested that 'foreign' players were playing for themselves rather than for England and that this caused 'real' Englishmen to lose pride in their team. These 'foreign' players did try, apparently, but it was not 'instinctive'. Malcolm, Lewis, DeFreitas and Mark Ramprakash were mentioned, court action followed, and apologies and damages were extracted.

This extraordinary article inadvertently epitomised a tendency to load the blame for England's relative decline since World Series Cricket on outsiders. First up was Kerry Packer and his obsession with money. Then came the West Indians and their brutal bowling that supposedly contravened the spirit of the game. Then there was one-day cricket. Finally, 16 years after World Series Cricket was over, England's continuing struggles suddenly became the fault of 'foreigners' unable to try hard enough.

This blame-outsiders reflex obscured the simple fact that England usually fielded only two or three of its six front-line bowlers during this era because of poor personnel management, over-use and the absence of Team England. By substituting little-England arrogance for a more worldly humility, it blinded English cricket to its many deficiencies and delayed the development of the consensus required to overcome the control of the TCCB by the counties.

No surveys are available that reveal how non-white Britons perceived the England cricket team in the nineties. But, in 1995, the MCC still excluded women—white, black or brown, Prime Minister or cleaner—from its membership. The combination of Norman Tebbit, the MCC and this article might well have made the England team even less attractive, post Gower and Botham, to those Britons in the fortunate position of being able to chose their cricketing allegiance in an era when India had Tendulkar and Kumble, Pakistan had Waqar, Wasim and Inzamam-ul-Haq and the West Indies still had players of the calibre of Ambrose, Walsh and Lara.

## Financial disconnect

The TCCB lived in a world far removed from this problem. Finance, the England team's poor performance and county cricket dominated its agenda. The task of reaching out to female and non-white fans, if it featured at all, was even more difficult for the TCCB than the yet-to-start construction of Team England.

The television deal with BSkyB and the BBC in 1994 enabled cricket's finances to continue to grow quickly. In 1995, the game's revenues hit £41 million[2], representing growth of 12% per year since 1989 after allowing for inflation. As well as a 10-fold increase in television money between 1989 and 1995, when £12 million was received, both the Cornhill sponsorship and England ticket receipts doubled.

Overall, the England team generated about £27 million in 1995. The counties made £12 million from their games, about 40% of the revenues earned by England. In 1989, though, the two had still been neck and neck. In the six years, England had forged ahead while the counties had stagnated.

These finances reflected audience interest. In the nineties, domestic second-tier cricket attracted an annual ground attendance of between 1 million and 1.5 million, but although county one-day games enjoyed good television coverage the audiences were small. England, by contrast, attracted a continuous average television audience of 1.5 million for Test matches. With about 30 days of England cricket most years, the national side generated many more viewing hours than the 18 counties put together.

The lack of interest in county cricket was pithily summarised by John Holmes, at various times agent to Mike Atherton and David Gower, who said, 'When is the last time anyone heard the County Championship being discussed in the pub?' The low audiences meant that the TCCB had to pay £750,000 to each county from England team profits—over £13 million in total—to allow the county game to break even.

The effect of this change in the financial balance between England and the counties was to turn Atherton's unsuccessful side into a cash cow to be milked for the money needed to fund an uneconomic and increasingly pointless county circuit. In return, the counties provided Atherton with a bowling attack wracked by injury and fatigue and also failed to look after him.

The need for fundamental reform of the game's business model was even clearer in 1995 than it had been in 1989. Despite this, payments to each county increased to £850,000 in 1996 and £1 million in 1997.

## Almost a chinning

The England party to South Africa for the first post-apartheid trip in 1995/96 included Malcolm, Cork, Fraser and Gough, but Caddick was again injured and Tufnell not selected. The batting was strong, with all the first-choice players except Hussain on the plane. But, the day before the team departed, the first of a three-part interview of Illingworth by Geoff Boycott was published in *The Sun* under the headline 'Atherton is so stubborn, inflexible and narrow-minded'.

Atherton, because of a TCCB ban on press articles, could not reply to the comments of a man who was both his coach and his Chairman of Selectors.

At the first game four-day game in Soweto, Malcolm was greeted by Nelson Mandela, who remembered his 9–57 against South Africa in 2004 and who told him, 'I recognise you, you're the destroyer.' On the third morning, however, Malcolm was ordered down to the nets for some surgery on his bowling action with Peter Lever, who was then quoted, 'He has just one asset – pace. That apart he is a nonentity in cricketing terms.' Atherton told a journalist, 'I hope when they write that the management has washed their hands of Devon they don't mean me. I'm on his side.'

Rain wrecked the first and third games in the five-Test series. In the second, the South Africans set England 479 to win in the fourth innings in five sessions. Atherton batted nearly eleven hours for 185 not out, scoring only 129 runs with Jack Russell (29 not out) in the last four and a half hours. Illingworth, perhaps now appreciating Atherton's stubbornness, called it 'one of the greatest innings of all time'.

When the fourth game was drawn everything then depended on the fifth. England scored 153 in the first innings and, with South Africa 171–9, the game was level. But Malcolm bowled poorly and South Africa crept to a lead of 91. England were then all out in the second innings for 157, gaining a lead of only 66. In the changing room, Illingworth told Malcolm, 'You bowled crap and probably cost us the Test match.'

Both Ian Botham, whose second career as a commentator with Sky was well underway, and Atherton have subsequently written that Illingworth was lucky to escape a chinning. England lost the game and the series and Illingworth then told a journalist the names of six players he was unhappy with. Three of them—Stewart, Fraser and Malcolm—were among England's finest. Botham reported that he had to talk another, Robin Smith, out of quitting altogether.

During the tour, again according to Ian Botham, Atherton lamented during dinner with Mark Nicholas that ex-players went into the media rather than into cricket administration. In his report to the TCCB, Atherton recommended central contracts and asked for good preparation time and annual rests for his players. Like Ian Chappell's complaint to the ACB in 1976 and Bill Lawry's original request in 1968, his suggestions produced no action.

England was more or less broken, losing the one-day series 1–6, with Botham commenting that he could see the emptiness in the players' eyes. In the World Cup which followed, England narrowly made it through the group stage by beating the UAE and Holland, despite losing to three main teams. In the quarter-finals, they ran up against eventual winners Sri Lanka and their new tactic, pinch-hitting. Chasing 235, Sri Lanka reached 113–1 in the 13th over, with DeFreitas going for 32 in 12 balls at one stage. England were overwhelmed and, for the umpteenth time, a notable innovation in the game had been deployed to good effect by a team other than England.

The next day, 10 March 1996, the headlines were grim. The *News of the World* said, 'We must get rid of Lord's losers'. 'Hapless, hopeless, humiliated' was the *Independent on Sunday*'s verdict. A few weeks later, Christopher Martin-Jenkins noted in *The Daily Telegraph* that 'The England team and the system which produced it is a heavy lorry in the slow lane being passed by a succession of sports cars.'

Dennis Silk said, 'If we don't change ... our game will die. All we'll have left will be village cricket.' But the scale of the problems facing the game was illustrated by the Chief Executive of Northamptonshire County Cricket Club, Steve Coverdale, who said in January 1996, 'We are a members' club, and if I took a poll asking "Would you like Northants to win or England to win", 9–1 would say Northants.'

In contrast, Ian Chappell gave a British journalist at the World Cup final an insight into how far Australia had moved ahead. 'If our selectors reckon there could be a shortage of a certain type of player in a few years' time, they tell Rod [Marsh], and he sends the word out,' said Chappell. 'Our cricket used to go in cycles. I reckon we can now make sure, by producing a constant supply of good players, that we don't have any more downs – even if we can't guarantee that we'll have those ups.'

## England first

The South Africa trip and the dismissal from the 1996 World Cup seem to have been a turning point in the history of the England game. Criticism of its structure and management and of the performance of the England team reached an all-time high in summer 1996 when, for the first time, players and officials started to lambast the system that cited cyclicality as an excuse for inaction in the face of perpetual mediocrity.

Dennis Silk said, 'We can carry on having a cosy game amongst ourselves in domestic cricket, which might please some. But it is not going to do us any good at all in terms of international cricket.' Players added their insights. Kim Barnett said, 'The development of the game is hampered by the conservatism and flawed thinking of an amateurish and self-serving bureaucracy.' Graeme Hick complained that 'I was not mentally prepared after seven years playing for Worcestershire. It is a big step upwards and it takes time to adjust to it mentally.'

Chris Broad added his pennyworth in *Wisden*. 'I am sad though,' he wrote, 'that all the beneficial changes to cricket seem to be coming from the whizz-kids in the southern hemisphere. Why can't England, the so-called home of cricket, move with the times and come up with some progressive ideas? At Lord's they just seem to sit back, rake in the money and don't develop a radical enough approach to preserve the game.'

Major reform towards an England-first approach was widely understood to be urgent, and the jostling for position began. The formation of Team England on the Australian model would require central contracts, an Academy and stronger team management. Above all, the counties would lose control over the leading English players and county cricket, already in rapid commercial decline in relation to England, would be devalued yet further.

The TCCB set up the Acfield Review to look at the management of the England team. Illingworth was replaced as manager-coach by David Lloyd but kept his Chairman of Selectors position despite interest from co-selector David Graveney, who pushed the Team England concept, and despite being reprimanded by the TCCB for comments about Malcolm in a book.

## The class structure

First on the agenda was a national academy. Ostensibly, this was one of the easiest components of Team England. But, in fact, an academy was politically sensitive because of its location in the elite youth conveyor belt. Traditionally, counties had produced and then owned the country's leading players, but a successful England Academy would by definition intercept and divert the best young players to England.

The former Australian leg-spinner Peter Philpott was asked to be the academy manager in June 1995, the counties approved it 16–2 in August, and Mark Nicholas was offered the chairmanship by Dennis Silk in October. But in November 1995 Philpott received a fax from the TCCB saying that the plan was on hold. He exploded with rage, saying, 'Surely, of all countries, England needs a concerted plan to develop its cricket standards … Geographically, England has great advantages, but the egocentricity of county cricket is destructive to the game. And crowds will not flock to watch a Test team whose performances are poor.'

Philpott ended his tirade with the questions: 'Who does rule? Is there an overall plan? Or is it simply a selfish in-fight?' In 1996, Somerset opened a cricket academy and other counties got on with building theirs.

The England team crisis also forced open a fundamental division within the TCCB between six members—the MCC, Surrey, Warwickshire, Lancashire, Nottinghamshire and Yorkshire—which owned Test grounds and the other 13 first-class counties that did not. With second-tier logic stipulating that a national side needs five or six professional teams underneath it, the idea of reducing the second tier to the five big-ground clubs required only a short intellectual leap.

The MCC and the first-class and minor counties formed a hierarchy of five interest groups according to the ownership, or not, of a ground used by England and the ownership, or not, of a first-class team. Table 3 shows this structure, in descending order.

TABLE 3: INTEREST GROUPS IN ENGLAND PROFESSIONAL CRICKET

| Collective term | Members | Test ground | First-class |
|---|---|---|---|
| MCC | MCC | Yes | No |
| Major major counties | Five first-class counties | Yes | Yes |
| Minor major counties | 13 first-class counties | No | Yes |
| Major minor counties | 19 minor counties | No | No |
| Minor minor county | Huntingdonshire | No | No team at all |

This setup, which continues to the present day, mirrored the class structure of English society. At the top sat the MCC, owner of Lord's Cricket Ground and The Laws of Cricket, which did not condescend to participate in something so vulgar as professional cricket. Next came the five major major counties, serious professional operations based in the four biggest urban centres in England & Wales (London, Birmingham, Manchester and Leeds) plus Nottingham.

The bottom two positions were occupied by the 20 dispossessed counties which, by accidents of geography and luck, had not made the first-class cut in the nineteenth century. These minor counties divided into the 19 which ran a team and the one which did not. This county, Huntingdonshire, was so minor that it did not have a cricket team of its own. A relic of another age that was abolished by local government reform in 1965 and merged into Cambridgeshire (a minor county) in 1974, it was in effect a minor minor county.

Wedged into the middle of this hierarchy sat the 13 remaining first-class counties. Based in the larger market towns and smaller industrial cities, they combined the characteristics of the major county in that they ran a first-class team and of the minor county in that they had no England games. Both hopeful of promotion and fearful of relegation, they formed the middle class of English professional cricket.

To climb the hierarchy, these middle counties had to get England games allocated to their grounds. To avoid falling into the lower classes, they had to use their share of England profits to sustain a first-class team that could compete with those put out by the major majors. This made imperative the maintenance and expansion of those profits and the use of bureaucratic devices to prevent the major majors developing into an elite that would allow them to break out on their own.

There was a sixth class, with one member, whose job was to cater to the counties like a Lord Lieutenant's servant. This outfit had no ground because, strictly speaking, it wasn't even a proper county. It ran a mediocre, scratch team staffed with players borrowed from real counties, to which it handed all its profits. These players were over-worked, badly-paid and frequently injured. Whenever it came up against the Australians, this team was annihilated.

Like Milo Minderbinder Enterprises in *Catch-22*, England cricket was bombing its own airfield.

## Politics

Inevitably, this five-part structure led to some fractious politics. In the mid-nineties, a group named the Test Match Grounds

Committee formed under the leadership of Tony Cross, an executive at Warwickshire. It produced a report criticising 'a system of county cricket which perpetuates mediocrity and has not produced enough players of sufficient calibre to create an English team which is an international force.' The report proposed a two-divisional County Championship and the inclusion of the minor counties in a sharper, more coherent pyramid below international level. It also suggested more voting power on the TCCB for the major majors.

This was seen by the 13 minor major counties as an attempt by the MCC and the major majors to seize power at the TCCB and squeeze them out of first-class cricket. But the big clubs only had six votes versus the 13 enjoyed by the minor majors, so this strategy had little chance of success. Moreover, the minor majors learned, if they did not already know, that the six big boys considered them a waste of space.

At the TCCB a vacancy opened up with the retirement of its Chief Executive, Alan Smith. In May 1996, Mark Nicholas agreed to interview for the job. He proposed two divisions in domestic cricket, an academy, a 25-over tournament, five regional teams to play the tourists and a Team England with full coaching and medical backup and central contracts. He also demanded that the Chief Executive have 'absolute power' to make decision about the game that cut across the interests of the counties if necessary.

During the interview process, Nicholas got into a row with Doug Insole, the Chairman of one of the TCCB committees and scion of a minor major county, Essex. Sneering at Nicholas' agenda, Insole asserted that success in the international game was cyclical and that England's turn would eventually come round again. Nicholas withdrew, telling Ian Botham, 'Cricket is our national summer game, but it is run selfishly as if it is a private recreation. It's such a shame … The counties and their members control cricket. It is a ridiculous state of affairs and hopeless for the future of our game.'

Cricket carried on despite all this manoeuvring. In summer 1996, England played three-Test series against both India and Pakistan, winning the first 1–0 and losing the second 0–2. Tufnell, Gough and Fraser did not feature at all, despite playing full county seasons. Instead, the bowling was led by Lewis, Mullally and Cork. One-Test-Wonder Simon Brown got a game against Pakistan, and was then dropped. For Pakistan, Waqar Younis, Wasim Akram and Mushtaq Ahmed constituted a formidable trio, just as they had in the previous series in 1992. After Pakistan completed its series victory at the Oval, captain Wasim added his voice to those of countless others: 'They say Dominic Cork is burnt out already. You play far too much cricket. Your players know about it; we talk about it on the circuit.'

In July 1996, David Acfield published his report. Not before time, it focused on the excessive use of England's leading cricketers. According to the report, Shane Warne played or toured for 127 days between April 1995 and April 1996 compared with 239 by Cork. In that time, Cork played 71 days of domestic cricket and Warne 13. To counter this, the report said the Chairman of Selectors should have the right to withdraw players from county matches to protect them from over-use and injury. Then, confirming counties' fears of a separate conveyor belt, it stated that an England Second XI should play home internationals and that it and the England Under-19 team should take precedence over county cricket.

The main recommendation was a new management structure for the England team, but the report fudged the critical issue of central contracts. At a TCCB meeting in August, the 18 counties rejected the idea that players could be removed from county cricket. The Second XI and Under-19 proposals simply disappeared.

The principal effect of the Acfield Review, therefore, was a new management structure and the creation of several new jobs. Later in 1996, the West Indies Board offered year-round contracts to 20 players.

## The England & Wales Cricket Board

In September 1996 the TCCB published another report. This one, named the Morgan report, recommended the formation of a new body to represent the interests of the professional and amateur games. It was to be called the England & Wales Cricket Board[3] and its members would be the 18 first-class counties, the 20 minor counties and the MCC, reduced after 210 years to a single vote out of 39. The list of minor counties included England cricket's nearest equivalent to a rotten borough, Huntingdonshire.

A parallel body named the First Class Forum (FCF) was also set up. Composed of the MCC and the 18 major counties—the *MCC & Counties*—it would have the right of approval over key ECB proposals and would also nominate a majority of the ECB's 14-person Management Board.

This convoluted three-part structure was a long way from the demands of Mark Nicholas for executive independence. Essentially a political compromise, it forced ECB officials to secure the agreement of the MCC & Counties for anything significant. Ian MacLaurin[4], a former minor county cricketer and one of the UK's most accomplished business executives, was recruited as Chairman. Tim Lamb, the ex-Northamptonshire bowler and formerly TCCB Secretary, was recruited as Chief Executive. Absurdly, Lamb could go to meetings of the Management Board and speak, but he had no vote. He was Chief Executive in name, but a more apt title would have been his old one: 'Secretary'.

Cricket fan and television personality Michael Parkinson commented in *The Daily Telegraph* that 'The Test and County Cricket Board has become the England and Wales Cricket Board. This is a bit like replacing a ventriloquist's doll with a glove puppet. The manipulating hand still belongs to the counties.' Parkinson continued, 'What we need is positive action. What we have are working parties, committees and, God help us, management courses. Oh my Tony and my Kerry of not so long ago.'

On the field, England reached another low point in winter 1996 when they went to Zimbabwe. Starting with a loss in a three-day game against Mashonaland, they went on to draw both Tests and lose the one-day series 0–3. After the First Test was drawn with scores level, coach David Lloyd told the press that 'We flippin' murdered them.' Lamb and MacLaurin arrived immediately afterwards and were disturbed to see that England players were sharing hotel rooms. When MacLaurin asked Atherton about his game plan, Atherton replied, 'Chairman, you are the first person who has ever talked to me about it.'

Carlsberg-Tetley dumped its sponsorship of England and the team found itself seventh out of nine in the unofficial table operated by *Wisden Cricket Monthly*. In New Zealand, though, England won 2–0 in a three-Test series, picking the same team in successive Tests for the first time in three years. Tufnell, Caddick, Gough and Cork played in both these games, the only occasions when four of England's top five bowlers of this era were on the park together. In the series, Gough and Caddick bowled in tandem, taking 27 wickets at under 20.

David Graveney was appointed Chairman of Selectors to replace Illingworth, a position he has occupied since. In Australia, Bob Simpson left the ACB in 1996 and promptly wrote a book. In one chapter, he gave his views on the present and future of the English game:

> *With their resources and tradition they should be producing far better players than they are ... As there are so many counties looking for players, the pool of talent is stretched thin ... In my opinion, a large part of the future of English cricket at the international level depends on how the counties are allowed to use their TV windfall: If they simply give mediocre players more money they will not lift standards and there will be precious little investment in the years to come.*

Like Ian Chappell, Simpson knew the Pommies better than they knew themselves.

# Marching on

With the ECB in place, Ian Botham got his suggestions in fast via his book *The Botham Report*. Perhaps influenced by Simpson's view that his own performances had for many years covered the deficiencies in England cricket, Botham launched a gigantic assault. Describing the 10 years from 1987 as 'cosy suicide', he tore into the counties:

> *We do produce some talented young cricketers, but by the time they have been put through the process of playing uncompetitive county cricket for two or three seasons, their mental edge is dulled.*

To remedy this he proposed most of the Nicholas combination: a two-division County Championship, central contracts for England players, a national academy, one 50-over league and a Chief Executive with the power to run the game. He concluded:

> *Adapt or die. That is the stark and only choice facing English cricket today. For too long the counties have existed on a diet of complacency and romanticism. The complacency was founded on the mistaken belief that ... fortunes in cricket were cyclical ... The romanticism existed in the sincere but misguided conviction that the traditions of the game and its history by themselves would enable the game to survive and prosper.*

For his part, MacLaurin moved quickly to make the national side his top priority, writing in *Wisden*: 'We've got to get it right at the top level, so all the other levels can thrive.' In *The Mail on Sunday* in October 1996, he said, 'There are those who persist in claiming that success in cricket is cyclical, that if you wait long enough it'll all come right of its own accord. I simply don't believe that's true. You wouldn't last very long in my business if you just said "everything is cyclical"'.

MacLaurin and Lamb quickly set about creating Team England. Through 1997, a press officer, a fitness consultant, an international teams director, an analyst and some specialist coaches were recruited to join coach David Lloyd. There was a team-building exercise, and 'The England Players' Handbook' was issued. David Graveney introduced the practice of personally informing players of their selection or omission.

In the middle of this belated little burst of change, Australia arrived for another Ashes contest. A 3–0 whitewash by England in the one-day games and a victory in the First Test by nine wickets apparently heralded another new dawn, made brighter when MacLaurin sent each player a bottle of champagne. But, after a draw at Lord's, Australia won the next three games to clinch the series 3–1 with one remaining.

The series was dominated by the ball. England picked nine bowlers overall, with no bowler playing all six, yet again. Cork's season ended with an injury while playing for Derbyshire in April and Fraser was again not picked although he played another 90-day season for Middlesex. Tufnell was picked only for the last game at the Oval, where he took 11 wickets. For the Fourth Test, a player named Mike Smith was preferred over Caddick (11 wickets in three games) on the basis of a successful county season for Gloucestershire. His career lasted one game. Caddick returned with eight wickets as England won at the Oval to finish at 2–3.

For Australia, McGrath and Warne played all six games, taking 60 wickets between them, and Mike Kasprowicz, Jason Gillespie and Paul Reiffel shared two spots as Australia opted to play only four bowlers.

Justin Langer and Adam Gilchrist were unable to break into the side and Stuart Law, who was not on the tour but had led Queensland to victory in the Sheffield Shield, described playing in the County Championship as 'like having a net'. Ian MacLaurin described England cricket as 'woeful in the extreme'.

In July, the first Sunday League game under lights took place between Warwickshire and Somerset in front of 15,000 spectators.

They saw English cricket emulate the innovation introduced in 1977 by World Series Cricket.

In August, the ECB published MacLaurin's blueprint for the English game. Called *Raising The Standard*, it proposed a three-group championship in which the six members of each group played the twelve members of the other two groups once, to give 12 games per county. This was immediately dismissed in the press as overly sophisticated, and the First Class Forum rejected it the following month. In 2007, an official told me that the three-group system was invented to reduce the volume of cricket without getting rid of any of the counties. He admitted that the whole idea was a compromise.

Although the major majors were in favour of two divisions, the minor majors feared being marginalised, and they had 13 of the 18 votes on the FCF. But the existing 90-day program was widely accepted to be excessive, so the new ECB executive was stuck. In a scathing review of this political muddle, *The Economist* said, 'The counties deserve a large raspberry.' Reasoning that county audiences would remain small anyway, the magazine argued that the only point of county cricket was to produce better players for England. The piece ended with the memorable phrase:

*Meanwhile, the Aussies march on.*

Ian Botham, like his team-mate Bob Willis before him, was incensed. 'It's a terrible day for English cricket,' he wrote, 'I think we're in the biggest mess we've been in. We've had the chance to put it right, but these people live in their little ivory towers.' Then, in one sentence, Botham defined the fundamental purpose of the professional game in general and the England team in particular:

*The biggest problem is that they think the game is for members. It's not. It's for the whole country.'*

# Still no contracts

After the Ashes in 1997, England lost five of the next six series, including a second-ever home loss to New Zealand and a first-ever to Sri Lanka. For the West Indies tour in 1997/98, Fraser and Tufnell were picked despite having played only one Test between them in 1997, but Gough was out injured and Cork did not make the touring party either after playing little at Derbyshire in the 1997 season. In the event, Ambrose and Walsh took 52 wickets and Fraser was England's choice bowler with 27 wickets at 18 apiece. England went down 1–3 and Mike Atherton resigned the captaincy of England. The poisoned chalice was handed instead to Alec Stewart.

During the tour, Graham Thorpe begged for central contracts, saying, 'I don't think our structure allows us to prepare properly. You're trying to perform for county and country. You're kidding yourself if you think you can maintain form for 10 months. It's very frustrating.' On bowlers, Thorpe added: 'We're always compromised, especially the fast bowlers, which is why so many get injured.' Then he demanded: 'The burden needs to be reduced. We need those contracts now.'

The 1998 summer was another mixed season for England. South Africa were seen off 2–1 but the team suffered its first home loss to Sri Lanka at the Oval thanks to 16 wickets by Muttiah Muralitharan. In the South Africa series, Fraser and Cork both played five games and Gough four, and the three bowlers took 59 wickets between them to help England to their first major series victory for 12 years and show what three good quick bowlers in the same side could do. Strangely, like Fraser the year before, Caddick was not selected despite taking 105 wickets at under 20 for Somerset.

The South Africa series featured two highlights. The first was an epic confrontation between Atherton and Allan Donald when Atherton refused to walk after clearly being caught behind off a glove. The second occurred at the end of the Fifth Test at Headingley. With the series at one game apiece, a tight, bowlers' match was won on the fifth day when local boy Darren Gough had Makhaya Ntini LBW. In a foretaste of what was to come seven years later, 10,000 spectators turned up to watch the last day even though South Africa were eight wickets down at the start.

The summer featured a third highlight. After voting marginally in favour of women members in April but failing to reach the required two-thirds majority, the MCC came under fire in the press and from Sports Minister Tony Banks, who said that he would willingly join a women's march on Lord's. In September, the MCC finally voted nine to four in favour and the measure was passed. Banks was ecstatic, saying, 'What it really means is that the MCC has taken cricket into the twentieth century. For so long it's been in the nineteenth.'

However, the 20-year wait for membership means that any significant influx of females cannot occur until 2017. And that will only happen if a respectable number ignored the Lord's Effect and applied for membership. By 2004, the number of female members had reached 23.

## Two more compromises

Suddenly, after years of failure and criticism, things started to shift a little and the ECB era got going. In October 1998, the First Class Forum agreed a grand compromise with the ECB executive under which an increase in England's home schedule to seven Tests and 10 One-Day Internationals per year would generate more revenue with which to fund county cricket's burgeoning losses. In exchange, England's leading players would be contracted to the ECB and there would be two divisions in the County Championship from 2000 onwards.

However, this compromise neither incorporated second-tier logic nor even reduced the volume of county cricket. And, with three up and three down each year and England profits still divided up equally among the 18 major counties rather than on the basis of performance, this reform did not create an elite nine-team premier league to close the gap between county and country. Indeed, as England players disappeared from domestic cricket, that gap became still wider. For all its faults, though, this compromise still operates today.

At the end of summer 1998, the television deal with the BBC and BSkyB expired. During the lifetime of this deal a new Broadcasting Act had introduced a subtle change in regulations[5] regarding the list of events that had to be on free-to-air television. Now, all of an event on List A and the highlights of an event on List B had to be on a free-to-air channel. England's home Test matches were placed on List A and BSkyB was thereby eliminated from the bidding to show these games live.

ITV had never shown much interest in Test cricket and nor had Channel 4. So, the removal of BSkyB left the BBC unopposed in the auction for Test match rights from 1999 onwards, allowing it to drop its bid at will. If this happened, where would the 18 sets of £1 million for the counties come from?

At the time that the Act was under discussion in Parliament in 1995, the TCCB tried and failed to get cricket off List A and on to List B. In 1998, the ECB tried again. Ian MacLaurin told Culture Secretary Chris Smith that cricket was not a rich sport and that it was difficult to negotiate a decent deal with only one interested party. The ECB also argued that the length of a Test match made it hard for traditional single-channel broadcasters to cover the game uninterrupted.

In July 1998, a compromise was agreed. The government placed Test cricket on List B subject to a 'Gentlemen's Agreement' between Smith and MacLaurin under which MacLaurin said he would keep Test cricket on free-to-air television. This agreement had no legal force and did not bind either man's successors, so this apparent compromise was little more than a sham.

BSkyB was henceforth free to bid for Test cricket as well as for one-day matches, although the ECB was in the interesting position of having promised the UK government to keep Test cricket on free-to-air. Despite fears of a lone bidder, Channel 4 unexpectedly entered the race for the 1999–2002 rights and in October 1998 the ECB announced that Channel 4 would pay £53 million for 21 Tests over four years and BSkyB £51 million for one Test per summer and all the One-Day Internationals. The combined fee of £26 million a year represented a 70% increase on the previous deal.

Channel 4 was a great success. Advertisements between overs appeared, 22 years after World Series Cricket, and viewers did not seem to mind. Channel 4 also introduced the 'Snickometer', the Analyst, the Red Zone and Hawkeye, the six-camera ball-tracking system based on military technology. All of these innovations except the Analyst have since been adopted by Channel Nine.

The television rights saga had two related implications. The first was that the counties had their money and England's business model could survive for another four years. The second implication did not become clear until December 2004. Mike Atherton, no longer England captain and even freer to speak his mind, wrote: 'The conversion to Channel 4 is good because it seems at long last the ECB has recognised the need for change. Notions of tradition and loyalty are precisely the ones holding back the development of cricket in our country.' Atherton then joined the Chappell, Wright and Willis camp with the comment:

> The professional game is an anachronism; the presence of 18 counties is damaging to the development of high-class first-class cricket.

## More failure

In Australia, the ACB struck a new seven-year deal with Channel Nine that brought in $25 million per year, an increase of $10 million on the previous deal similar to the 70% achieved in England. The Sheffield Shield, though, lost $6 million a year compared with the £20 million or so (about $50 million) lost by England's 18 major counties, meaning that there was more money available to pay the national players and to fund recreational cricket.

Flush with cash, the ACB decided to professionalise state cricket. Each state was given $240,000 with which to contract a squad of players at between $5,000 and $40,000 each, far below the level of remuneration available to players in English county cricket. To this day, state player salaries in Australia are negotiated and agreed by the governing body, preventing the states bidding salaries up and wasting national resources.

Australia hosted England to an Ashes series in 1998/99. England omitted both Tufnell and Caddick, the latter despite 105 wickets in 1998. Ian Botham described these omissions as 'ludicrous' and Bob Willis stated on Sky that 360 of the 400 county cricketers were mediocre.

For the first four games, Australia were without Warne, but Stuart MacGill capably filled the hole with 27 wickets at 18 in support of 24 at 21 from McGrath. For England, Dean Headley took 19 wickets at 22 but Fraser failed to produce, Cork fell out of favour with captain Stewart and tour manager Gooch, and Gough took 21 expensive wickets. In the final Test, Australia's two leg-spinners bowled in tandem and took 14 wickets between them to clinch the series 3–1.

Angus Fraser's Test career ended at the Melbourne Cricket Ground with two wickets in the first innings but an economy rate of four an over in the match. During his nine-year career, Fraser took part in only 46 of 103 Tests and finished with 177 wickets at 27. Only 18% of the balls he bowled were for his country. Craig McDermott, who was also born in 1965, took 291 Test wickets. He bowled 52% of his balls for Australia.

It is anybody's guess how many Tests Fraser would have played and how many wickets he would have taken had a Team England structure permitted him the luxury of bowling one in two of his deliveries in international cricket. The same goes for Gough, Cork and Caddick, who averaged about 25% of their bowling for England. Glenn McGrath, born in 1970, the same year as Gough, bowled 73% of his deliveries in international cricket and continued to perform at a high level through to the 2007 World Cup.

At home in 1999, the World Cup took over the grounds of England. Shortly after a poor opening ceremony and heavy criticism of inadequate arrangements for British Asians, England lost to India in their final group match and went out of the tournament. The Super Six stage went ahead without the hosts and Australia thrashed Pakistan in the final to take the trophy.

Alec Stewart was replaced as captain by Nasser Hussain and David Lloyd as coach by Duncan Fletcher, to start at the end of the summer. In another bowlers' series, against New Zealand, no batsman averaged above 37 and only three centuries were scored, none by England. Gough was injured for most of the season, but Caddick and Tufnell came back into favour suddenly and took 34 cheap wickets between them.

Despite this, England registered its second-ever home defeat by New Zealand, to general opprobrium. On the first morning of the Fourth Test at the Oval, Cornhill announced that it was reviewing its sponsorship. On the last day, the team was booed off the pitch after losing by 83 runs, and captain Nasser Hussain was jeered as he collected the losers' cheque. England was the worst Test team in the ICC, ninth out nine in the *Wisden World Championship* table.

## I'm just an Aussie

Two selectors were sacked, and the pundits piled in. The first page of *The Sun* was a picture of burning bails with the headline reading 'English cricket 1744–1999. Official: death of our national game'. Ian Botham tore into the authorities again, saying that 'the complacency, self-interest and indolence of some of the men running English cricket in the past decade meant that such an outcome was merely a matter of time.'

Graham Gooch, one of the sacked selectors, complained that 'The Australians have never respected us—they think the cricket here is weak and the attitude is not what it should be—and I hate to hear them joke about how nothing will ever change.' Bob Willis wrote a letter to *The Times*. Claiming that 'The clubs have an ongoing conflict of interest with international cricket', he called for the Sports Minister, Kate Hoey, to appoint an interim board of directors to take control of the game from a 'self-interested and parochial county-led administration'. Even the new England captain took a jaundiced view of the system that supplied his players when he said of the 21-year-old Andrew Flintoff, 'The more he plays just in county cricket, the more he will get dragged down into it.'

Stuart Law said, 'Let's face it: out of 66 players in Australia you could pick three teams that would beat England.' When asked what he thought of the idea of two divisions, he responded:

> *Mate, who am I to say, I'm just an Aussie. There are pros and cons for this system. What they really need to do is just cut down the number of county cricket teams.*

ECB Chief Executive Tim Lamb rejected the idea that fewer counties would increase standards. Just after the Oval defeat, he said, 'People say there are too many counties. We have 18, while there are only six states competing in the Sheffield Shield. But our population is three times that of Australia.'

By that logic, India should have had nearly 400 first-class sides and New Zealand one. In fact, India had 27 and New Zealand had, like its big neighbour, six. In a professional sport, if the second tier loses bucket-loads of money, then its only purpose is to support the national team. At that point, cold second-tier logic comes into play. It says: less is more, population size is irrelevant, and five or six domestic teams are sufficient.

# Evolution

In 1999, Ian MacLaurin published his autobiography *Tiger by the Tail*. After telling the story of his election to the Chairmanship of the ECB in 1996, MacLaurin hinted that he had a bigger agenda for the game than delivering Team England and two-divisional county cricket. After quoting with approval Botham's comment about 'the whole country' owning the game rather than 'the members', his last words in the section on cricket were:

> *Disraeli was right – revolutions are not to be evaded.*

Despite this statement of intent by the ECB Chairman, the business model remained *in situ* and the politics associated with it went round in circles. In 1999, the payout from the ECB rose to £1.2 million for each county, 40% up from three years before. The Test Match Grounds Consortium renewed its demands for a greater share, objecting to having to hand the bulk of their England ticket receipts over to the ECB only for them to be wasted by the minor majors. After lengthy negotiations, it was agreed that more of the ticket revenue would be kept by those hosting England games, so long as it was spent on ground improvements rather than on producing better teams.

Hampshire recruited Warne in 2000 for a reported £150,000 and Worcestershire recruited McGrath for a reported £120,000. With players like these, the ground improvement agreement, three up and three down in the County Championship, and rules preventing the free transfer of players, the minor majors prevented the concentration of talent in the first division that could have lead to an elite.

Meanwhile, MacLaurin and Lamb completed the first stage of their programme. In May 1999, the First Class Forum confirmed central contracting, 22 years after Kerry Packer used three-year contracts to secure the world's best players for World Series Cricket. In August the FCF set aside £1 million for 16 players for 2000 and in December it decided to set up a National Cricket Academy in late 2000, 12 years after Australia. But after 23 years Cornhill decided not to renew its sponsorship of home Test matches in England.

## Immediate improvement

Like 1989 and 1994, the summer of 1999 turned out to be the bottom of the England cycle. In the two-year period starting with that summer, England played 22, won 9, lost six and again achieved mediocrity. By scoring away victories against Sri Lanka and Pakistan in 2000/01, England went one better. For the first time since the heyday of Botham and Gower in the first half of the eighties, they became pretty good.

The first batch of 12 central contracts started in March 2000. This new arrangement was another compromise, however, because the contracts covered only the summer and England cricketers were also contracted to their counties. The other half of the bargain with the counties was a programme of seven Tests and 10 One-Day Internationals. In 2000, Zimbabwe arrived first and played two Tests. Then the West Indies came for a triangular one-day series, followed by England versus West Indies in a five-Test series. This format strongly resembled World Series Cricket's schedule in 1977/78.

The new contracts were an instant success as England kept Caddick, Gough and Cork fit all summer. Caddick and Gough played all seven Tests, just three County Championship games apiece and took 64 Test wickets. Cork played the last four Tests against the West Indies, with 20 wickets, and 10 County Championship games (he was not centrally contracted). The trio collectively averaged under 18 and England won the series 1–0 and 3–1 respectively.

During the seven years in which the careers of these three bowlers overlapped, England played 86 Tests. But the trio played together on only nine occasions, winning six and losing two. Four of those games occurred in 2000 and showed, again, what might have been.

For the last games of the summer at Headingley and the Oval, England fielded the same side, its strongest for many years and its first-choice too, and beat the West Indies in both games. On the last day at the Oval, an excited full house of 18,500, with thousands turned away, saw England complete a victory by 158 runs in Ambrose and Walsh's last game in England. The number *158* was thereby written into Oval history five years ahead of time.

County cricket made no progress, however. In December, PPP Healthcare withdrew its County Championship sponsorship early, Australian players were employed at 12 counties, and six Aussies featured in the top 12 in the 2000 batting averages alongside only three England-qualified players. Only four England-qualified players featured in the top 10 bowlers.

As a result, players continued to assail the county system. Dean Headley told an interviewer: 'It all comes back to the fact that the game needs to be restructured and if they don't do it soon then it's going to be in trouble.' Justin Langer, the Middlesex captain, wrote: 'As long as the same number of players are being paid to play mediocre cricket, two divisions will not automatically help the state of English cricket. Not now and not in the future.'

The newly-fresh bowlers performed well on tours the following winter to Pakistan and Sri Lanka. England won the three-Test series against Pakistan 1–0 with Ashley Giles and Gough taking 27 at 25 and the second series 2–1 with Gough and Caddick 23 wickets at 22. In both series, England picked just 12 players and in the second against Sri Lanka 10,000 England spectators saw their team win its fourth series in succession.

## The clangers

Central contracting and the other Team England reforms were working, but in the spring and early summer of 2001, Ian MacLaurin dropped two mighty clangers. The first came in March when he told a journalist what he thought of the setup he found in

1996. 'I came in cold from business,' he said, 'and I was pretty alarmed by what I found. I was surprised by how selfish it all was. The counties were primarily interested in themselves. England was not high on their agendas. I went to one county whose Chairman told me he would rather win the Championship than see England beat Australia.'

England drew its first home series, a two-match affair against Pakistan, one game apiece. Just before the Second Test, MacLaurin was asked by another journalist whether he would like to reduce the number of counties. He replied, 'I think we would probably be better off with 12, but that is not my brief, and quite clearly not the brief of the ECB, which in its Articles of Association states that 18 first-class counties, plus the MCC, are sacrosanct.'

MacLaurin's intention was probably to cut the costs of the county system and reduce the volume of cricket and hence player fatigue. In 2001, cricket's revenues were £71 million[6], of which the England team generated about £48 million from broadcasting rights, sponsorship & advertisements and tickets. But the 18 counties generated only about £20 million from county cricket. Losses in the £25 million range were almost all made up by the ECB disbursement from England's profits. As always, the whole game roughly broke even.

Although the number 12 is unlikely to have been derived from second-tier logic, which suggests five or six teams, it stuck in the minds of the 13 minor major counties, each of whom had about a 50% chance of survival should the reduction envisaged by MacLaurin have proceeded. For each, the incentive to get England games and join the major major class became even stronger than it already was.

## The English disease

Despite recent successes, business as usual resumed when the Australians arrived for the 2001 Ashes. Gough and Caddick played all five games but took their 32 wickets at well over 40 each. Cork was injured for most of the summer and England used 19 players.

The Australian first innings in the series averaged 450 and the team used just four bowlers.

For Mike Atherton, it was also business as usual. When Nasser Hussain broke a finger during the First Test, Atherton took over as captain for two games, losing them both to end his captaincy career at 0–3 against Australia. This was the same state of play against the same opposition when he made his debut in 1989 and when he took over the captaincy in 1993.

During the series, John Buchanan was ridiculed in the UK press for referring to the writings of Sun Tzu, a Chinese military strategist and philosopher in the fifth century BCE, in team memoranda that were leaked. *The Daily Telegraph* commented that the references were 'likely to strengthen the argument that he is a harmless crackpot riding on the coat-tails of the Steve Waugh's mighty Australia team.' However, Australia caned England 4–1, winning the Third Test and the Ashes with a no-ball from Caddick after only 11 days of cricket.

Both coaches made scathing comments about domestic cricket in England. Duncan Fletcher called for fewer county matches, saying 'We must get away from the same daily monotonous routines which do not lead to new visions, new ideas and new techniques.' Buchanan noted the academy and two divisions but said, 'Undermining these initiatives, though, is an archaic playing system, a true servant of mediocrity.'

Graeme Wright, back as *Wisden* editor, wrote in the 2002 edition: 'And however loath I am to say it, I believe the county system runs counter to a positive future for English cricket at the highest level … The system survives on a confederacy of mediocrity.' Wright suggested that the ECB let counties go to the wall and proposed that county teams be replaced by city teams.

Justin Langer suggested mergers as a way to reduce the number of teams and increase standards, saying, 'During my time at Middlesex

I often thought about merging with Surrey.' Michael Parkinson took a more revolutionary view. Advocating eight teams, each with an England ground, he fantasised, 'Ideally what English cricket needs now is a rich dictator like Kerry Packer to revolutionise the game as he did once before. Too many committees, too many working groups, too many bosses. That is the English disease.'

Australia's dominance of England extended even further. In 2001, seven Australians featured in the top eight batsmen in the averages. Four of them were with the touring side, but Darren Lehmann, Mike Hussey and Law plundered nearly 5000 runs between them in county cricket at an average of just under 80. Sensibly, no Australian bowlers played county cricket.

The ECB ignored all this and set up another review, named the Domestic Structure Working Party. To lead it, the Board selected a man whose 1996 review the TCCB had completely ignored: David Acfield.

In July, Rod Marsh was appointed as the first director of England's new Academy. He set as his primary goals the production of one 10-year Test player each year and the improvement of the standard immediately below international level to fill the vast gap between the counties and England. In an Australian newspaper, Ian Chappell wished his former wicketkeeper 'Good luck, yer Pommy bastard.'

## Waste

In the summer, the ECB negotiated an extension of the television contract with BSkyB and Channel 4 to cover the years 2003 to 2005. The channels agreed a 75% increase in annual fees from £26 million to £45 million, with BSkyB doubling its payment for one Test and all the One-Day Internationals to £25 million per year, and Channel 4 increasing its payment by 50% to £20 million.

Needing stars, the counties decided to allow themselves two overseas players in any match from 2003, with four permitted in any one summer. And, fed by England money, county salaries continued to increase. Angus Fraser wrote in *Wisden Cricket Monthly* that the increased competition caused by a two-division championship had driven up player salaries. Then, citing the example of an overseas player without international experience being paid £65,000 by a county, Fraser called for a wages ceiling.

At the end of 2001, the ECB decided to allocate a Test to a new ground for the first time in a century. Durham's Chester-le-Street became England's seventh Test venue in June 2003 when it hosted Zimbabwe against England. At the same time, the ECB also conferred 'international status' on an eighth ground, Hampshire's new Rose Bowl. In 2007, when asked about this expansion of the number of England grounds in defiance of the second law of stadiums, an official told me, 'Six Test Match grounds is too many. If I had a blank sheet of paper, I wouldn't start with 18 first-class counties either. But you have to start with what you've got.'

Australia did not waste its resources on overseas players or on building more small grounds. In the same month, for example, the Melbourne Cricket Ground embarked on a facelift for the 2006 Commonwealth Games. At a cost of $400 million, a new 55,000-seat Grandstand was to augment the Great Southern Stand and raise the capacity of the ground to 100,000.

The story about another precious commodity, former national captains, was the same. After his retirement, Allan Border became an Australian selector and was subsequently elected to the Queensland Cricket Board (2001) and appointed a director of Cricket Australia (2002). But when the other Captain Grumpy, Mike Atherton, retired from international cricket after the Oval Test against Australia in 2001 he did not enjoy a similar succession of appointments

Like Bob Willis two decades earlier, Atherton had already marked out his media territory. After the 1999 defeat to New Zealand, he said of England's professional game, 'If it changed, if the game were put in the hands of a small competent management team then, like many others, I would be interested. But there is no chance of that.' In

2000, he went over the top on *Radio Five Live* with: 'County cricket in its present form fulfils no useful purpose whatsoever. Very few people turn up to watch, it doesn't prepare people for a higher level of cricket and it doesn't attract television deals or sponsorship. It is living on borrowed time.'

Atherton was slapped down by the ECB Chief Executive, Tim Lamb, who said this was 'commercially naïve' and 'completely inappropriate'. Atherton then elaborated the point in his 2002 autobiography, *Opening Up*. Citing 'mind-numbing repetitiveness', he confessed that he could barely remember any Championship matches. He concluded:

> *The structure of our domestic game is an anachronism, bound by history and tradition ...Its justification could be in the entertainment it provides for a large number of people ... or in the fact that it is financially self-sufficient ... or that it fulfils a role as a strong breeding ground for the national team. ... It is clear that County Championship cricket fits none of the above criteria.*

Atherton's opinions on the England system have drastically reduced the chances of his following Border into an executive role in England cricket. So, despite his remark to Mark Nicholas during the 1995/96 tour, he inevitably followed his rebellious predecessors Bob Willis and Tony Greig into the media. Unless he starts to toe the line, or a tolerant administration brings him into the England operation, he is likely to remain on the outside indefinitely.

Not content with wasting scarce resources on pointless county grounds and teams, England cricket also seems determined to waste the considerable talents of its most experienced and capable ex-captain.

## Warning signs

In 14 months from February 2001, England visited Sri Lanka, India, Zimbabwe and New Zealand and played a full summer at home. This schedule totalled 16 Tests, 25 One-Day Internationals and 30 days of tour matches, equal to just under 30% of the calendar days. Opening batsman Marcus Trescothick played in all the Tests and One-Day Internationals, enjoying only three short breaks from the game of between three and four weeks each.

Having participated in most of the cricket since the expansion of the schedule in 2000, Darren Gough dropped out of the autumn 2001 tour to India in order to get a rest. Two inexperienced replacements with only 11 Tests between them, Matthew Hoggard and Andrew Flintoff, did reasonably well but without a third successful bowler England lost the three-Test series 0–1.

During the series, Thorpe flew home for personal reasons. Gough then joined the squad for the one-day series after Christmas and told a newspaper in January 2002 that 'This game was the first in years I've played without needing painkillers to get me through my bowling spells.' The next month, Hussain wrote in his newspaper column: 'Something has to give with this hectic schedule, whether it be mind, body or family life.'

In New Zealand in March and April 2002, Hoggard and Andy Caddick took 36 wickets between them at 22 to help England draw 1–1. Trescothick, though, complained about burn-out during a match against Otago. But, having played an average of 73 days from 1999 to 2001, England increased its schedule to 94 international days for 2002 and 90 for 2003.

Meanwhile, the ECB Working Party under David Acfield beavered away. There were leaks, and in March 2002 a newspaper quoted the report: 'It was suggested that the first division might gradually evolve into a Premiership and deliver a higher standard of competition for all the best players. The Working Party believes that this would be a method of delivering a stronger feeder system into the international game.' But, it concluded that 'The Working Party is aware that the majority of counties would strongly resist these measures and they do not form part of this report's recommendations.'

In 2002 England easily disposed of a weak Sri Lankan side but in the main series against India reverted to type, playing 17 players with only Hoggard playing all four. In what amounted to a generational changeover, six quick bowlers represented England in three groups: Caddick and Cork the old guard, Flintoff and Hoggard the new guard, and debutants Simon Jones and Steve Harmison.

England lost Gough to injury all summer and Flintoff also succumbed. Before the Second Test, Jones and Alex Tudor, neither of whom had a central contract, also fell to injury. Hussain said, 'It's time someone looked at why all these young bowlers are getting injured. The amount of cricket they're playing can't be good for them. These guys just aren't going to be able to bowl with raw pace for 10 years because eventually something will have to give.'

India had virtually no pace bowling and relied on spinners Harbhajan Singh and Anil Kumble, so the series was drawn 1–1. For the Third Test, England played an injured Flintoff. He took just one wicket, scored a pair and underwent a hernia operation soon afterwards. At the Oval, Dominic Cork completed his England career at the age of 31. With 131 wickets in just 37 games, Cork bowled only 16% of his professional deliveries for England.

## Money-eating monster

During the summer, the First Class Forum agreed to increase the number of contracted players from 11 to 20, allowing a strong England reserve and squad rotation. The FCF also agreed to introduce annual ECB-only contracts that completely removed players from county control. But, towards the end of his third two-year term in charge, Ian MacLaurin wrote to the 18 major counties to propose that the next stage of evolution be independence for the executive team from the counties, as proposed by Mark Nicholas in 1996. MacLaurin commented: 'Someone asked me recently whether I thought I had finished the job. My answer was an unequivocal "no"'.

MacLaurin received only five replies to his letter and resigned. David Morgan, the former Chairman of Glamorgan, was voted in as the new Chairman of the ECB on a manifesto of consolidation, saying, 'Although Team England will be my priority, joint top will be to ensure that the counties prosper again.'

Like others, MacLaurin saw that county cricket had turned into a monster that devoured England's cash and always demanded more. He and his Commercial Director, Terry Blake, had negotiated an extra £19 million for each of the years 2003 to 2005 from BSkyB and Channel 4 and had increased England's schedule to a bowler-breaking 45 days per home summer, with a similar increase in the overseas schedule under reciprocal agreements with other full ICC members. This extra money bought the ECB a further three years to do what MacLaurin himself had failed to do: get the monster under control.

In a parting shot in August 2002, MacLaurin issued a stern warning about the financial situation and virtually begged his successor to reform county cricket before it was too late. 'Financially, the game is in good health at present,' he said. 'That is partly because of the extension to the television deal we negotiated a year ago ... But how these [monies] are used is of the utmost significance. If they go simply to player wages and keeping them employed then I can tell you we will be talking about a very different game in the near future ... Over the next two years the number of professional players, now in excess of 400, must be drastically reduced to something around 200.'

These comments suggest MacLaurin was assuming that his successors would keep to the Gentlemen's Agreement that he had made with Chris Smith. It also appears that after six years of running an evolutionary regime that had managed finally to deliver Team England while further increasing the flow of cash to the counties, MacLaurin had decided that the time for compromise was over.

David Morgan had different ideas, however, and set about giving the counties 'joint top' priority. Before his first term as ECB Chairman was up at the end of 2004, England's cricket fans would see for themselves exactly what this meant in practice.

# SECTION 3

# Today

## CHAPTER 6

# CYCLE

*When I took this on I thought England could be a very good team and I liked the challenge, but I really didn't know how much talent there was here. Speaking as an Australian, I found the depth of talent frightening.*

Rod Marsh, 2005

## Changes in the game

The ICC has admitted no new full members since 2002, perhaps calculating that any more would be the straw that broke the camel's back. Consequently, total international days have remained in the 350–400 range, with most countries continuing to average 80–90 days per year, New Zealand 50–60 and Bangladesh the minimum of about 50 days generated by the ICC fixtures cycle.

Cricket has become an ever bigger business. In 2006, the ICC relocated from Lord's to Dubai and loosened the cycle to six years. But it added a Twenty20 competition and continued to allow members to add fixtures as they saw fit. The three financial superpowers of world cricket, England, Australia and India, promptly announced a four-year cycle of their own. The ICC television deal for the period 2007 to 2015 is reported to be worth about twice the amount of the previous deal, or US$ 1.1 billion. In both England and Australia, also, the value of television rights nearly doubled between 2000 and 2007.

Player burn-out has reached a critical level. Tim May, the Chief Executive of the Federation of International Cricketers' Associations, said in 2006, 'More than ever we are seeing the game's top players being forced to retire … as a result of the constant and unrelenting schedule. On top of this, injuries and forced absences to the world's blue-ribbon fast bowlers are becoming more pronounced, and some teams are forced to apply rotational systems to ensure players are not flattened by these congested playing schedules.' In 2007, Richard Bevan, the Chief Executive of England's Professional Cricketers' Association (PCA), mooted the possibility of disruption at the 2008 ICC Champions' Trophy tournament.

International cricket has developed into a circuit entirely separate from the domestic professional game underneath. Today, about 200 players shuttle between 50 venues around the world, accompanied by large retinues of support staff and the cricket commentariat. With their extreme fitness, their own patois and a uniform sun-drenched sheen, international cricketers have evolved into a different species. The batting branch of this species is better able than the bowling branch to survive a schedule of 80–90 days per year.

The UK's geographic position means that England is the only team to play year-round and not enjoy a four-month break from May to August. Its natural break between seasons, September and October, is increasingly used by the ICC for its annual competition (Champions Trophy in 2004 and 2006, Twenty20 in 2007), probably because every country other than England has just had a long rest. Poor scheduling has not helped either. Three times in a row, England has undertaken its two most important and difficult engagements in the cycle—away to Australia and the World Cup— in quick succession, getting precisely nowhere on all six occasions.

Many non-England-qualified players continue to be attracted to county cricket, but the only country with a domestic game strong enough to provide international-standard training is Australia. In an attempt to save the county game from complete financial oblivion, England introduced Twenty20 cricket in 2003. This was immediately successful and was adopted by Australian states two years later. The first international game was Australia versus New Zealand in February 2005, and the first major tournament took place in September 2007.

# England and Australia

Figure 8 shows the recent form of England and Australia.

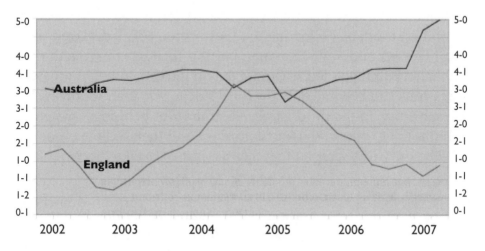

**FIGURE 8: ENGLAND AND AUSTRALIA FORM
MARCH 2002–DECEMBER 2007**

The completion of the Team England structure in 2002 notwithstanding, England continued its usual cyclical performance between 2002 and 2007, reaching a nine-month peak in 2004 and 2005 before falling back rapidly as its leading players went down with injuries and burn-out and the county system again failed to produce adequate replacements. The decline continued into the 2007 home season with injuries to the leading four pace bowlers.

Australia has dominated the international game since 1999, winning three World Cups in succession and sustaining a consistently excellent performance in Test cricket. Since the 1999/2000 season, Australia has played 94 Tests, won 73, drawn 11 and lost only 10. In the 30 complete Test series, it won all the games on 18 occasions, including five-match series against West Indies in 2000/01 and England in 2006/2007, and all but one of the games on a further six occasions. Its only two series defeats were both away and both thrillingly close. Indeed, much of the best cricket between 1999 and 2007 has involved Australia handing out a beating or being run close by a side at the top of its game.

Five examples stand out. In the 2000/01 series away to India, Australia won the first game. In the second, India conceded a lead of 274 on first innings. Following on, they scored 657–7 declared with Rahul Dravid and V.V.S. Laxman batting through the fourth day. Harbhajan Singh bowled Australia out on the fifth to help India win by 171 runs and become only the third side to win after following on in Test history. In the third game, Australia was behind all match. It set India 155 to win in the fourth innings and then reduced them to 135–7 before India scraped together the last 20 to take the series 2–1.

The series against England in 2005 was even closer and more exciting than this, also ending at 2–1 against Australia. In one-day cricket, the semi-final encounter with South Africa in the 1999 World Cup is generally accepted to have been the best-ever game in this format. After Australia came back from the dead to get to scores-level on the final delivery, Damien Fleming rolled the ball to Adam Gilchrist to run out Allan Donald and take the match. Australia then rolled Pakistan in the final to win by eight wickets, using only 20 overs in their innings.

In the 2003 final, Australia carted India's bowlers for 359 for two in their 50 overs to put the game beyond India by half-time. In the 2007 tournament, the Aussie batsmen scored their runs at six an over and averaged 63 per wicket. In turn, the bowlers ceded runs at 4.5 per over and took wickets at 20. In the final, Australia blitzed Sri Lanka from the outset to reach 172–0 in the 23$^{rd}$ over and kill the game in less than two hours. At the end of that game, Glenn McGrath noted with some satisfaction in a TV interview that his team had continuously improved over the eight years.

Australia played that tournament without Shane Warne and the injured Brett Lee, did not pick Stuart MacGill and played Stuart Clark just once. Those four would make up four-fifths of a world-class one-day attack. Mike Hussey, the world's top one-day batsman after Kevin Pietersen, was required to bat in only six out of the 11 matches and contributed a total of 87 runs.

## Machine

World Series Cricket from 1977 to 1979, Allan Border and Bob Simpson's revival from 1986 onwards, the luck of having six domestic teams, the completion of the Team Australia structure by 1988 and the comprehensive elite youth conveyor belt together led to a consistently good Australian performance through the nineties. In 1999, Geoff Marsh was replaced as coach by John Buchanan and Steve Waugh took over as captain from Mark Taylor. Together, the new coach and captain added new elements to the mix that produced the step change from good to excellent.

Buchanan's fascination with Sun Tzu suggests this step change arose, at least in part, from insights derived from this quarter. Sun emphasised the informational ('know your enemy') and psychological ('break the enemy's resistance without fighting') aspects of one-on-one engagements rather than the more prosaic question of capability, which Australia had in any case already solved. Predictions of 5–0 victories, the practice of mental disintegration, the targeting of opposition batsmen by Warne and others, and the use of lap-tops and databases, together formed a pattern that is consistent with Sun Tzu's approach.

Buchanan and Waugh created a team that could turn up at a ground and blast from the word go and which could quickly replace a malfunctioning limb. This outfit developed a will to win rarely seen in sport and performed at a high level on almost every occasion. The overall effect was that, sometime around the turn of the century, the Australian cricket team mutated into a machine.

So total was Australia's superiority in 2007 that Ian Chappell issued a warning in that year's *Wisden*. After repeating his point that Australia's system for producing international players is better than anyone else's, Chappell called Australia's dominance 'unhealthy' and reminded readers that the retirement of Shane Warne, Glenn McGrath and Justin Langer gave other teams an opportunity to catch up. But, he concluded:

> *If the rest of the world doesn't take advantage, it could also be judgement day for cricket.*

## 2002/03 Ashes

Without a similar platform of capability and consistency, England has put in a cyclical, inconsistent and fragmented performance. *Excellence, continuous improvement* and *will* remained abstract management concepts the practicality of which usually fell victim to one political, financial, selection or performance crisis after another.

For the 2002/03 Ashes, England selected a strong side containing two young pace bowlers in Steve Harmison and Simon Jones, experience in Darren Gough and Andy Caddick, accuracy in Matthew Hoggard and a bowling all-rounder in Andrew Flintoff. The batting was solid if unspectacular, with Michael Vaughan, Graham Thorpe, Nasser Hussain, Alec Stewart, John Crawley, Mark Butcher and Marcus Trescothick. To compete in the series and continue the revival in fortunes over the previous two years, England needed both Gough and Caddick to bowl at their peak, one of the new boys to come through, and Flintoff to start to realise his potential. And, with four left-handers out of seven, there was at least a chance that the threat of Warne could be countered.

For three months this team was booted from one end of Australia to another, playing 24 matches, losing 16 and winning just four. Thorpe withdrew from the tour for personal reasons before it started, Gough pulled out injured, Jones sustained a ghastly injury during the first day of the First Test and Flintoff was unfit most of the time, probably because he had bowled with a hernia at home in 2002. England used 31 players in all during the trip and only avoided a 0–5 Test defeat because Hussain won the toss at the Fifth Test in Sydney and Australia, without Warne and McGrath, batted last on a deteriorating pitch.

Caddick and Ashley Giles performed reasonably well with 26 wickets at 33 but Hoggard and Harmison (16 Tests between them before the tour) were mashed up. England was forced again to reach into the county system, digging out Chris Silverwood. Opening the bowling with Alex Tudor in the crucial Third Test at Perth, Silverwood was clubbed for 29 off four overs by Matthew Hayden and Langer. His ankle then gave way and that was it for him. The ECB put out a press release saying, 'This is a new injury and not related to the joint inflammation in the same ankle at the end of the English season'. *Wisden* added: 'Which convinced nobody.' England lost that match in three days and the series in 11.

In the VB one-day series, England lost all four first-round games to Australia but won three against Sri Lanka to go through to the best-of-three finals. The first game lasted only 53.2 overs. In 41 of them England were bowled out for 117. In the other 12.2 overs, Hayden and Langer smacked 118. *Wisden* reported that 'It hardly mattered that Australia were without McGrath, Gillespie and Watson; they displayed awesome strength against a battered side.' In the second game, the people of Melbourne voted with their feet: only 23,000 turned up to watch a closer game inevitably won by Australia.

A few weeks later, 26,000 went to the Sydney Olympic Stadium to watch New South Wales and South Australia inaugurate this new cricket ground in a one-day ING Cup match.

## Reaction

England's Chairman of Selectors, David Graveney, told the Australian press: 'Every match that England has played, whether it is the state teams, Australia A or even the Prime Minister's XI, you guys have fielded the strongest possible side to support your national team … in England there would not be that collective responsibility. We would not even be allowed to select an England A side or Second XI to play Australia because the counties would not release their players.' Graveney did not mention that the English counties were also in the habit of fielding insultingly weak teams against tourists in order to preserve their players for the County Championship.

Mike Atherton commented, 'We keep saying we're not good enough to beat Australia but nothing changes. Those in the firing line have to say let's change the system. Twenty-five million pounds goes into county cricket every year and what do we get out of it?' His former boss, Ian MacLaurin, repeated his idea of 12 counties to counter the 'mass of mediocrity', adding, '... we've got to look ahead at the likelihood of less revenue in two years' time. If Channel 4 don't bid for the Tests and the rights go to the BBC, it's possible we'll get £50 million and not £65 million per year. If the handout falls below £1 million, you could see half a dozen counties go out of business.'

David Morgan disagreed, saying, 'We need to focus on the county game in a way that we've failed to over the six years of ECB. I think the county game is an essential ingredient in the on-going success of cricket in England and Wales and an essential ingredient of the continued success of the England team.' On the question of the number of teams, Morgan uttered England cricket's fatal canard[1]: 'I think 18 centres of excellence in a country the size of England and Wales is about right ... If you look at Australia the population is a lot smaller and they have five or six state sides.'

A month later, in March, the 2003 World Cup began in South Africa and Zimbabwe. After various machinations involving the players, the ECB and the ICC, England ended up not playing its group match against Zimbabwe and went out before the Super Six stage for the second time in succession. Bob Willis castigated the 'total mishandling' of the Zimbabwe problem and called for a Packer-style revolution in English cricket.

The ECB annual report for 2003 defined the ECB's vision that 'England becomes and remains the most successful and respected cricket nation in the world.' In response, Atherton wrote that England could in theory be top dog by 2007 but asked:

*Is the ECB really serious about being No 1? If the essence of our professional game is still in place in five years, the answer is no.*

The main recommendation eventually produced by an ECB review of this series involved the provision of medical care to England players. Then, the loss of £4 million revenue due to the Zimbabwe World Cup boycott led to a reduction in the number of central contracts for 2003 back to 11, the same number as in 2002, although the counties still received £1.4 million each from the ECB. In 2003, the last three major counties opened an academy, completing the full set of 18 before the ECB opened the National Academy at Loughborough at the end of 2003.

The battle lines were drawn between the old pro-England regime led by MacLaurin and the new pro-county regime led by Morgan. This would have been a good time for MacLaurin to assemble the organisation and finance required to follow up the Packer suggestion made by Willis and Michael Parkinson. However, those who insisted that 'the county game is an essential ingredient in the on-going success of cricket in England and Wales' were, unfortunately, spared a Packer-style meat mangler on this occasion.

## Takeoff

Following the failures in Australia and at the World Cup in 2002/03, England bounced back up again to enjoy a two-year, five-season golden era. Of the following 10 series, it won eight, drew one and lost one, winning 22 Tests and losing only five out of 35 played. In December 2004, for the first time in 17 years, England's form over the previous two years was better than that of Australia.

This performance was entirely built on the fast-bowling quartet of Harmison, Hoggard, Flintoff and Jones. Protected by central contracts, they each played an average of four County Championship matches per year. As a result, Flintoff managed 31 of the 35 Tests, scoring 2,000 runs at 43 and taking 110 wickets at 28, becoming by 2005 the most valuable player in world cricket.

Harmison managed 30 Tests, Hoggard 28, and Jones put together a run of 16 out of the last 23.

The revival began at the 2003 Oval Test against South Africa after England had produced a fairly ragged performance in the first four games to go 1–2. This included the sudden resignation of Nasser Hussain after the First Test and a poor showing in the Fourth at Headingley. With the first innings approximately level in that game, England had South Africa 219–6 in the second but then conceded 146 for the last four wickets. Set 401, England folded for 209.

At the Oval in the first week of September, South Africa batted first and scored 484. In reply, Trescothick and the returning Thorpe put on 268 for the third wicket and the third day ended with England 502 for seven with Flintoff 10 not out. On the Sunday morning, Flintoff hit a rapid 95 to give England a lead of 120. Harmison and Martin Bicknell took eight wickets as South Africa crumbled to 229 all out, and England rattled up the required 110 off only 22 overs.

Despite this success, new England captain Michael Vaughan blasted the second-tier system, saying, 'You only have to watch county cricket to see the enthusiasm levels drained out of the players. I heard from Jon Lewis, of Gloucestershire, after the Headingley Test that he had played 21 out of 24 days – that simply can't be right.' After collecting stick from some county chairmen, he clarified his position, saying, '… unless we change our domestic structure the England team will go on as it has for years. We win some games and from time to time we nudge up a notch in the rankings but there will be no clear upward curve, which is what we need.'

In June, the ECB decided to adopt *Jerusalem* as the official song for the England side, 25 years after Australian crowds first sang *C'mon Aussie C'mon*. It also decided to appoint as an England selector one of the players mentioned in that song: Rod Marsh.

# The Cricket Reform Group

In summer 2003, two of the sternest critics of England cricket, Bob Willis and Mike Atherton, joined forces and formed the Cricket Reform Group (CRG) together with David Willis[2], Michael Parkinson and the sports and property entrepreneur Nigel Wray. The background, according to David Willis, was a rumour that the BBC would not bid for the next set of television rights. With BSkyB apparently disqualified from Test cricket, this left Channel 4 as the only bidder. This could have meant a 'financial holocaust' along the lines described by Ian MacLaurin.

During the Oval Test, Atherton and Willis issued a press release advocating a complete re-organisation of England professional cricket. Then, referring to South Africa's decision to cull its second tier down to six sides in order to support the national team, Atherton wrote in *The Sunday Telegraph*: 'Whereas South African cricket, overnight, makes tough but necessary decisions, there is a good chance English cricket will still be debating in 50 years' time. We are world leaders in inertia ... We support 450 professional cricketers, more than any other country in the world. Yet when I talk to the selectors on any morning of a Test, they bemoan the lack of options.'

Parkinson asked, 'How can it be a system employing more than 400 professional cricketers is regularly thrashed by a country with barely 50 full-time pros?' He then came out with a one-sentence summary of England cricket:

> *We are bogged down in a mire of complacency and a quicksand of self-interest masquerading as tradition.*

The CRG launched its manifesto in the autumn. Written by Atherton and Bob Willis, it asserted that the county programme employed too many cricketers and was ramshackle. It left, they claimed, a big gap between county and international cricket that hindered the production of England players. The two laid the blame at the door of the First Class Forum, whose members, they said, were accountable only to their 100,000 members for the £20 million plus that they received from the ECB each year.

The two ex-captains proposed 24 contracted England players and 18 cricket associations covering England & Wales, based on the existing counties and subsuming the minor counties. A six-team national Premier League and two North / South leagues would play first-class cricket, with more ECB money going to the Premier teams. Each team would play about 60 days and full-time professionals would be cut to 250. Finally, all power at the ECB would be delegated to a four-person management team, exactly as specified by Ian MacLaurin.

The CRG sent this plan to the 39 members of the ECB but received zero replies, five fewer than had been received by MacLaurin the year before. As press reports hinted that MacLaurin was the guiding hand behind the CRG, this cannot have been too surprising. The former ECB Chairman said in the autumn that, without an overhaul, cricket in England risked becoming 'a former sport of the summer ... like croquet'.

The defence was led by Morgan and Giles Clarke[3], the Chairman of Somerset, one of the minor majors most at risk of being marginalised. Morgan reiterated his view that England needed 18 'centres of excellence', again conflating the necessarily small, concentrated second tier with the necessarily large, dispersed elite youth conveyor belt. Clarke was more direct, telling *The Daily Telegraph* that 'Any change of structure would be fiercely resisted in every area. If football hasn't had to do it, I don't see why cricket should.'

Clarke seems to have missed the point that professional football clubs in England are economically viable businesses that attract vast audiences, whereas the county cricket clubs in England are not. The prospect of a wealthy Russian oligarch buying Somerset County Cricket Club, or even Surrey, seems correspondingly remote.

The CRG went to see the ECB at Lord's to discuss its proposals. In his *Sunday Telegraph* column in November, Atherton wrote: 'The meeting was just about like every other meeting I've ever been to at Lord's. You come away with the impression that the administrators are very decent people, but then you hear that the proposals will go to the 'domestic structural review group' and you know, deep down, that nothing will ever happen.'

Six years earlier, Ian Botham had said that the game belongs to the whole country and not the members of county clubs. Here, Atherton went one step further, writing: 'If, at the end of it all, the CRG could achieve one thing it would be to change the balance of power so that the game is not simply in the hands of a small number of private members' clubs that are answerable only to a tiny proportion of people.'

Atherton was right about decent people doing nothing. One official[4] on the other side of this discussion 'agreed with the diagnostics' and said Atherton & Co talked 'lots of sense'. Regional cricket, said the official, 'was discussed time and again ... it gives a better pyramid. But the counties wouldn't wear it, it was the thin end of the wedge.' Had ECB executives pushed for regional cricket then they 'would have been out'. The official complained, 'It was very easy for Atherton, he didn't have the politics to deal with ... it's all about *realpolitik* ... the ECB is a representative body of its constituents ... politics is the art of the possible.' In conclusion, said the official, 'We are where we are'.

The CRG upped the stakes with a visit to Sport England, the UK government body responsible for channelling public and National Lottery cash to sport. In December, its Chief Executive Roger Draper told the press: 'We want to see slicker decision-making and the right decisions being made, but what we don't want to see are changes being stopped by vested interests. That's why we are looking at some of the recommendations of the Cricket Reform Group.'

A little after this flurry, Nasser Hussain published his biography, *Playing with Fire*. 'The whole system is about the preservation of the status quo,' he wrote, 'and that's why there is so much negativity in our county setup. In Australia everything is geared towards aiding the national team.' Hussain was the third successive England captain to make these points.

The Cricket Reform Group, though, failed to make any immediate progress. David Willis told me, 'We predicted then that 18 counties are unsustainable. In 10 years time, that will turn out to have been true. But we keep coming back to the absolute stumbling block: 18 county chairmen own and run this game for their own ends.'

## Twenty20

With Team England in place and the new ECB regime focused on the county game, it was apt that 2003 was the first year for the new domestic 20-over format, Twenty20. Mentioned by Mark Nicholas in his 1996 manifesto and subsequently recommended by an ECB committee, the concept was developed through an extensive programme of market research[5]. The 18 major counties, with attendances down from 650,000 (1,060 per day) in the County Championship in 1994 to 506,000 (880 per day) in 2002, voted to accept the proposals for three divisions of six produced by the ECB marketing and cricket departments.

At the launch, ECB Marketing Manager Stuart Robertson said, 'The audience profile for [county] cricket is disastrous: middle-aged, middle-class and white. Kids think it's for oldies and women think it's for men. Twenty20 cricket is about addressing these structural barriers and the research says it's women and kids who want this sort of cricket.' Tim Lamb added, 'This competition has the potential to give a real boost to county cricket, to increase attendances, to widen cricket's spectator base and to produce some thrilling matches.'

The launch year was wildly successful, garnering an average attendance of 5,300 for a total of 250,000. The key targets were reached: 62% of the audience was under 34 and 23% was female, compared with about 15% for each of these groups at County

Championship matches. In 2005, Twenty20 increased from five first-round games to eight and audience numbers leapt to 545,000 (7,600 per day), exceeding the 470,000 (820 per day) in the County Championship that year.

Like the John Player League in 1963, Twenty20 has injected some limited new life into the county system. An inevitable further rise to 10 games, allowing a full set of home and away fixtures in the three leagues of six, was announced in September 2007.

## New development system

England played three series during the 2003/04 season, winning the first against Bangladesh and losing the second to Sri Lanka and Muttiah Muralitharan's new doosra. The third series, against the West Indies in March and April 2004, featured the first appearance of the new bowling quartet. Harmison achieved Ambrose-like figures of 23 wickets at 15 and the quartet together took 58 wickets at 23. England won the series 3–0, using only 13 players, and a great team was born. Only a quadruple-century by Brian Lara prevented a 4–0 result.

England won all seven home Tests in 2004 against New Zealand and the West Indies, with Harmison, Hoggard and Flintoff taking 87 wickets at 28 and Giles chipping in with 31 at 26. England's batsmen exploited the bowling platform well, averaging 400 in the first innings with three totals above 500 and a low of 319. Flintoff put in a stupendous performance, averaging 60 with the bat and 25 with the ball. During a thunderous century at Edgbaston against West Indies, he somehow managed to hit a six right into the hands of his father in the stand at long-on, who dropped it.

For the first match of the summer, Vaughan was injured and England gave a debut to a 27-year-old county player, Andrew Strauss. He was an immediate success, scoring a hundred in his first innings and 83 (run out by Hussain) in his second. Hussain promptly retired to make room for the newcomer, who repaid the compliment with nearly 600 Test runs in the summer at an average of 45.

Press comment focused on the rarity of a county player breaking in to the England side. By 2004, the England elite youth conveyor belt included the 18 county academies, the England academy, the England Under-19 team and the England Second XI, known as England 'A'. The best young cricketers could expect to be involved with all four. The result was that Team England had floated free of the county structure underneath to the point where England rarely picked an established county player.

Ian Bell also made his debut in 2004, aged 22, and was far more typical of England's new players than Strauss. By the time he was awarded his first central contract in 2006, Bell had been on three Under-19 trips, done a winter at the Academy, gone on an England 'A' tour and been called up as a replacement for a full tour. He played four seasons of county cricket for Warwickshire.

Alastair Cook made his debut in 2006, aged 21. He had played for England Under- 15, 17 and 19, attended the National Academy for two years and been on one England 'A' tour. He has played only 31 four-day county matches and, even more than Bell, is the new model England cricketer.

Of England's 10 principal bowling debutants since 1999 (the quartet plus Sajid Mahmood, James Anderson, Liam Plunkett, Chris Tremlett, Ryan Sidebottom and Monty Panesar), two were aged 20 when they played their first game, one 21, five 23, one 24, and one 25. The oldest of these at debut, Tremlett, lost nearly two years to injury before finally playing a Test, against India in 2007. All but Tremlett and Sidebottom were picked up by David Graveney and Duncan Fletcher before they spent too long in county cricket.

Four gaps remained in 2004 compared with the Australia system that was completed in 1988. Both England 'A' and England Under-19 played away games only because the counties would not release players during the English summer. There was no county Under-19 tournament, and there were only 12 contracted England players, against the 25 in Australia. In 2005, the ECB closed three of these gaps. England 'A' and Under-19 now play home matches during the summer, and an England Development Squad of 25 players is now controlled by the England coach.

One important gap remains in the England conveyor belt. When Nathan Bracken made his debut for Australia in 2003/04, he was the 100th out of 139 debutants since 1969/70 to have played in the state Under-19 tournament. England decided in 2002 to phase out county Under-19 cricket and to move to a new structure featuring Under-21 and Under-17 teams. The following year, after the ICC withheld part of England's World Cup fee because of its refusal to play in Zimbabwe, these competitions were among the ECB activities to be cut. There is today no national youth tournament in England & Wales for players above 17.

In any case, Team England finally had 25 players under its control in 2005. And, 17 years after Australia, it finally had a comprehensive system for producing a pool of talent for the national side. This system involves a county team only for the period between the national academy and the award of a central contract.

If the purpose of England domestic cricket is to support the national side, then over 400 professional players are being employed to turn a few elite young cricketers a year into proto-England players and to keep a reserve pool of at most 30 additional players fit and ready. But these functions require only five or six teams and a professional cadre of 100–125 players. Likewise the job of finding and training the few late-developers with potential to play for England, such as Andrew Strauss (2004) and Ryan Sidebottom (2007), who are missed by the elite youth conveyor belt.

## ECB goes for six

Despite the successful trip to the West Indies and seven straight victories at home, 2004 was a disastrous year for England cricket. Already under assault by the Cricket Reform Group on the question of success and its former Chairman on the question of finance, the ECB was hit by six crises in quick succession.

The first was about Zimbabwe and the second was a continuation of the long-running saga of the structure of domestic cricket. In the summer, three top ECB executives resigned. In the autumn, television rights for England's home matches were awarded to BSkyB, and Sport England again waded in. Lastly, throughout 2004, the issue of non-England qualified cricketers in the domestic game became more pressing.

England had agreed to tour Zimbabwe in late 2004 but came under renewed political pressure not to give succour to the Mugabe regime. ICC rules stipulated that a governing body could only withdraw from a tour if its national government instructed it to do so, and the ECB was caught in a nasty trap in March 2004 when Richard Caborn, the UK Sports Minister, declared his opposition to the trip but said that the government did not have the power to stop it. Facing suspension from the ICC and the possibility of a catastrophic loss of revenues, the ECB was caught between the counties (money), the players (safety and ethics), the ICC (politics), the government (politics) and the public (ethics and politics). In the end, England went, playing and winning four One-Day Internationals in November and December. But the ECB lost a member of its Management Board, Des Wilson, in the process.

Because television rights and sponsorships were coming up for renewal, the ECB had to finalise the county and international programme that it would be offering. To this end, David Acfield was asked to convene another Domestic Structure Review Group (the same group to which the CRG proposals were referred). In April, the press got hold of the report. Acfield proposed to reduce first-class county cricket from 16 matches per team to 12 and also suggested that talent be concentrated in the first division. Both of these were anathema to the minor majors, and the number *12* probably reminded county officials of Ian MacLaurin's comments three years before. The First Class Forum set up a rival Interim Review Group to review the review, as in *Yes, Minister*.

The *Financial Times* commented: 'The outcome illustrates the difficulty in aligning the desire of the counties to safeguard or improve their own financial and operational circumstances and those seeking to improve cricket from the top down by producing a successful England side.' Peter Anderson, the Chief Executive of Somerset and therefore a colleague of Giles Clarke, told a local paper that 'We suspect that reform is not the real agenda. The demise of six counties is. Without support for the stance we are taking and trust in our position, Somerset could be one of those.'

Publicly undermined by his own members, Tim Lamb resigned as ECB Chief Executive, telling a journalist: 'My personal view is that the Chief Executive should be given more authority and more accountability. Give them delegated authority to get on with the business.' Mark Sibley, the Commercial Director, and John Read, the Director of Corporate Affairs, also resigned. Read told the press that 'Parochial self-interest and local power cliques should not be allowed to intrude on the development of the game at national level.'

Long-standing Commercial Director Terry Blake, who negotiated all the sponsorship and television deals since 1989, and Twenty20 man Stuart Robertson had both left the ECB in 2003. These six departures[6] marked the final end of the MacLaurin regime and left the ECB rudderless. Into the commercial breach as Chairman of the ECB Marketing Committee, a post directly appointed by the First Class Forum, stepped Giles Clarke.

In December 2004, during this interregnum, the ECB hit England cricket fans with a bombshell when it announced that all England's home games for 2006 to 2009 inclusive would be shown exclusively by BSkyB. This required fans without a dish to purchase a subscription for about £400 per year. At the time, Sky had between seven and eight million subscribers out of a total television market of 25 million, not all of whom subscribed to Sky Sports. About 80% of the audience for Test matches would be cut off at a stroke.

The lead negotiator was reported to have been Giles Clarke, assisted by an external consultant, the former Commercial Director Mark Sibley, who had previously worked at BSkyB. During the negotiations, the ECB was presented with a clear choice between two alternatives. One was BSkyB's exclusive bid worth £208 million for the four years. The other, worth about £126 million, was that Channel 4 and BSkyB share the rights on much the same basis as before. Under this arrangement, Channel 4 would cover the second Test series of each home summer and Sky would do all the other games.

This second alternative opens up an important set of questions about the ECB's negotiating strategy. The BSkyB component, £72 million, was equivalent to under half the amount, per day of England cricket, that it was paying[7] for the 2003–2005 rights. BSkyB had heavily reduced the value of its sharing bid, which suggests that it was trying to drive the ECB towards its exclusive bid.

There was nothing wrong with that. But, in response, did the ECB attempt to negotiate BSkyB's sharing bid back up to the daily rate that it was already paying? Had it successfully done so, then the value of the sharing alternative would have jumped from £126 million to £208 million, the same (strangely) as BSkyB's exclusive bid. In which case, free-to-air television could have been saved. On the other hand, did the ECB simply plump for the exclusive BSkyB bid and not bother with a little game of chicken?

Regardless of this nuance, BSkyB won the auction with its exclusive bid for £208 million. Reaction to the news was hostile, with several commentators aghast. The Editor of *Wisden*, Matthew Engel, said, 'This is the absolute pits. The game is in shock. I can't see how cricket can promote itself if it deliberately takes itself out of the grasp of the uncommitted follower of the game. What's the point of the money if you can't fulfil the most essential function and sell the game to people?' The former Sports Minister, Kate Hoey, said, 'The sell-off of cricket to the highest bidder is shameful and is a reflection of the short-sighted people running the game.' A spokesman for BSkyB, echoing Kerry Packer's statement 27 years earlier, pointed out: 'We didn't steal it. They gave it away.'

Two ex-England captains cited the *Inspiration Effect* of free-to-air access. Mike Gatting said, 'The ECB has a responsibility, and a duty, to keep the game on mainstream television, otherwise children are going to grow up without adopting Freddie Flintoff, Steve Harmison or Michael Vaughan as role models.' Alec Stewart said, 'My big heroes were Jim Laker and Richie Benaud and my dad, brother and I would sit down together and watch them on TV. It'll be a big mistake if the ECB restrict terrestrial coverage.'

A third ex-captain, Tony Greig, said, 'The cornerstone of Australia's success is the partnership Cricket Australia has with free-to-air television. At the expense of a few extra bucks for the counties, the ECB should ensure that free-to-air [TV firms] have live coverage of Tests and One-Day Internationals.' Earlier in the year, in fact, the Australian government had renewed its 'anti-siphoning' list of events for 2006 to 2010. This regulation prevents subscription- or pay- television firms buying monopoly rights unless free-to-air television firms have declined them. The list includes each Test and One-Day International involving Australia, played in Australia or the UK, and each World Cup one-day game. In 2005, Cricket Australia announced that it had struck a deal with Channel Nine for the years 2006 to 2013 that nearly doubled the fee from $25 million to $45 million a year.

Some minor major counties were pleased. Sussex chairman David Green told his local paper that the BSkyB deal saved county cricket, saying, 'If they hadn't signed it would have changed the face of cricket as we know it. The substantial difference would have questioned the viability of a lot of weaker clubs. They could easily have gone out of business. It was that critical.' Worcestershire Chief Executive Mark Newton said on the day of the announcement, 'There was a distinct possibility, in the present television climate, that central funding could have gone down but this deal will see the present level continue and rise in line with inflation.'

The fifth crisis came in May when Roger Draper of Sport England told the press that 'We want to see a streamlined management structure and an end to the toing and froing in decision making.' Later in the year he said, '... there are issues with the counties, where the feeling at the moment is that the annual hand-outs from the ECB disappear into a black hole rather than being distributed to community clubs or put towards the development of young English cricketers. This nonsense has to stop if we want to be the number one team in the world.'

With the best England players contracted to the ECB and revenues from domestic cricket falling further behind those generated by England, the 18 major counties resorted to ever more desperate attempts to improve the audience appeal of their product. In 2004, 26 Australian Test and state cricketers played in the County Championship, out of a total of 96 non-England qualified players that year. Of these, 59 were overseas players permitted under the existing agreements, 34 were EU-qualified, and three were Kolpaks[8].

Bob Willis, whose Cricket Reform Group proposals had got nowhere, delivered another rising delivery at the English game, writing in December: 'English cricket is like a sandwich. The English team is on top and the recreational game ... is at the bottom, disenfranchised. In the middle, the soft filling, are the counties, like Northants, Leicestershire, Derbyshire, employing 450 full-time professionals and hiring all the Kolpak and EU players they want. It's absolutely pathetic.'

However, the ECB at least managed to fill the vacant post of Chief Executive at the end of the year with the recruitment of David

Collier. As Nottinghamshire Chief Executive, Collier had given his view on who controlled the game to *Wisden* six years earlier. He said:

*We own the rights to cricket.*

## They'll be back

England had a relatively relaxed cricketing winter in 2004/05: a single trip to South Africa and Zimbabwe included five Tests and 11 one-day games. For the third season in succession, the quartet of quick bowlers delivered, taking 73 wickets between them. Three of the four played all five Tests, and Jones four. Strauss chipped in heavily with the bat, and England beat South Africa 2–1.

Kevin Pietersen, a South Africa-born player who had recently completed his four-year residency qualification, played in all seven of the one-day games against South Africa, scoring 450 runs at an average of 150, with three centuries. By May 2005, he would be hailed by both his captain and coach as a genius and would appear in national advertising for the 2005 Ashes series alongside Shane Warne, all before he had played a single Test.

Australia had busy 2004/05 and 2005 seasons. In all, during the year from 13 September 2004 through to 12 September 2005, it played 17 Tests and 28 One-Day Internationals, for a total of 113 days[9] out of 365. This is equal to 30% of the calendar days in that period, compared with the 75 days (21%) played by England.

Australia had eight weeks off before travelling to England for a five-Test and 10-ODI tour. On arrival, the mantle of invincibility slipped as four games were lost in one week, to Somerset, Bangladesh and England twice. Then, with the one-day triangular out of the way, the Test series began on 21 July.

England had an immensely strong team, built over six years by Duncan Fletcher and David Graveney on the Team England system introduced by Ian MacLaurin and Tim Lamb. England nearly fielded its first-choice team throughout the series, using just 12 players, with Paul Collingwood replacing Simon Jones for the last game at the Oval. The quartet took 75 wickets at 27 in the five games. In return, McGrath and Warne took 59 at 21, but Australia's support bowlers were shredded. The difference between the two teams lay in Australia's lack of effective support bowling, McGrath's injury, reverse swing and the wildcard Pietersen.

This series followed an ancient plot-line—the plucky mortal versus the indestructible alien—used in myths and stories since the year dot and to best recent effect in *The Terminator*. The series started with a straightforward piece of assault and battery, although England did land a couple of blows that forced the machine to descend to the mortal plane. Then, in a series of three close-run encounters, England cannily used guerrilla tactics to deplete Australia's strength and go 2–1 ahead. But during the denouement at a park in south central London the machine steadily worked its way into a position to strike the fatal blow so that by 1.40 on the last day England was cornered and facing a nasty four-hour execution. At exactly the right moment England deployed its secret weapon and the Aussies were battered into submission in front of an audience of screaming millions. The weapon was the exploding batsman, Kevin Pietersen.

## Under the Northern Lights I stand

For a few weeks afterwards the light went out on Australian cricket. Dennis Lillee called the series 'an ambush' and Cricket Australia convened a review in October 2005. The committee, including Allan Border, Mark Taylor and Cricket Australia Chief Executive James Sutherland, reported back in December. In early 2006 Trevor Hohns departed as Chairman of Selectors, Australia recruited more specialist coaches and obtained the services of England's bowling coach, Troy Cooley. These repairs made and reprogramming completed, the Aussie machine picked itself up off the floor and returned to operating mode. In the two years since, it has played 20 Tests, won 19 and drawn one and won the 2007 World Cup hands-down.

Clive Lloyd harked back to 1976 and richly complimented Pietersen with 'He must have some West Indian blood in him.' Mike Atherton wrote: 'The England team has become a team, in the truest sense of the word, rather than a disparate bunch of individuals who occasionally come together for a match.' John Buchanan said later, 'We were playing an England side that wasn't typically English: they wanted to be in our face, they wanted to be like Australia, they wanted to be aggressive. They took it to us and in the end we just didn't respond.'

To beat your enemy, you must become him.

At the end of the season, Rod Marsh finished with England after helping 16 Test and 21 One-Day International players over four years. Before he left, he told an Australian newspaper that England had so much talent it was frightening.

Another former Australian wicketkeeper, Steve Rixon, left his job as coach of Surrey with a 'dim view of English cricket.' Referring to the vacancy in England's ranks for the Oval game, Rixon said, 'You should have had people busting to replace Simon Jones at the Oval but all we had was a lot of tired fast bowlers.' Calling county cricket a 'cesspit of mediocrity', Rixon provided an explanation for England's post-2005 decline before it happened. 'Flintoff is the world's best player', he said, 'but depth is what's needed. And that's not going to happen under this system.'

One of the many Australian county players, Darren Lehmann, said, '... having fewer teams means talent is concentrated and the competition is much more tough and intense. But to get rid of county teams is going to be hard work.'

## Popular

Tickets for these Ashes games were scarce and expensive. For its game at the Oval, Surrey offered seats at between £40 and £66 and was sold out by March. Somewhere between 20,000 and 60,000 unsuccessful applications (reports vary) for this game alone were received by June, representing at least another 50,000 seats. In the early summer, an advertisement for debenture seats appeared in the *Financial Times*. For £2,000, the punter could obtain the right to buy a ticket for the same seat for eight years. The actual seat price was excluded, and this offer effectively priced Oval seats at over £100 per day.

In the event, a seat price of £1,200 was reported for the last day of the series and a flat with a view over the ground was priced at £3,500 per day.

The same was true elsewhere. The game at Trent Bridge sold out in two days flat and in June a representative of the MCC wrote to *The Wisden Cricketer* to say that seats at Lord's for the first Ashes Test could have been sold five times over.

Viewing statistics astonished those who had succumbed to the Lord's Effect and who did not know that throughout England's dark decade in the nineties a continuous average of 1.5 million viewers had tuned in to home Tests. A little under 30 million people in the UK saw some of the series, and the audience peaked at 8.4 million between 6.16pm and 6.30pm on the Sunday of the Fourth Test when England, chasing 129 to go 2–1 ahead, had fallen to 116–7. Next best was 7.7 million for the climax of the Third Test, when McGrath and Lee managed to bat out for a draw. The DVD of the series sold over 630,000 copies and Flintoff's autobiography over 250,000. *Wisden* reprinted its 2006 edition for the first time since 1982, the edition that covered Botham's Ashes.

The ECB Marketing Manager, Tom Harrison, repeated what PBL Chief Executive Lynton Taylor said after the end of World Series Cricket in 1979. 'We've found that we've managed to attract a whole new audience with no specific demographic,' said Harrison. 'It's enormously diverse: from housewives to kids to ethnic minorities. People who weren't previously cricket fans who are now taking a huge interest in the game and in the performance of the team. The job for us is to keep hold of these people and also get them to watch domestic games.'

But the ECB had a different strategy for access to the national side than PBL did in 1979. Given this, an 'instead' at the end of Harrison's last sentence would have been more apt than the 'also' in the middle.

## Assault on BSkyB deal

During the Ashes series, discontent with the new television deal grew as fans and pundits remembered that the Oval match would be the last to be screened on free-to-air television until 2010 at the earliest. The former director of strategy at Channel 4, David Brook, who had been instrumental in bringing cricket to Channel 4 in 1998, formed *Keep Cricket Free* to lobby for continued free access. Andy Duncan, the Chief Executive, said in August, 'It's a huge mistake [the ECB] have made. They've gone for the money and will probably spend that money on building county clubs or in paying overseas players ... They've got more money, but in a few years cricket won't be seen.'

In October, Labour MP John Grogan tabled an early day motion in the House of Commons calling for the restoration of Test matches to free-to-air television. In November, David Brook wrote that 'more than half of the money to be paid by Sky will go to the counties.' Brook went on: 'When you consider that the deal was negotiated by a county chairman, the argument that it is in the best financial interests of the game looks a little tenuous.'

An investigation by the House of Commons Select Committee for Culture, Media and Sport followed in November and December 2005. To understand this investigation, it is necessary to get into a little of the detail of the constitution, finances and strategy of England cricket in 2005, the year that Test cricket disappeared off most fans' television screens.

## Constitution and strategy

After the six crises in 2004, a hurricane of change blew through the ECB. In May 2005, a new set of articles[10] gave the MCC & Counties direct control of their organisation and the indirect control mechanism provided by the First Class Forum, no longer needed, was abolished. The ECB executive was finally granted the independence sought by Tim Lamb, Mark Nicholas, Mike Atherton and others, but the MCC & Counties effectively controlled[11] appointments to this executive and so the prospect of anyone who thinks like Atherton & Co working for the ECB dropped to almost nil. Furthermore, various protective clauses[12] prevented the major majors from moving on the minor majors.

Next came a new ECB strategy for the period 2005 to 2009, called *Building Partnerships*. In cricketing terms, the most important changes were the England 'A' home games and 25-person Development Squad. The earlier target for England to be the number one cricketing nation was downgraded to a top-two position in the ICC Test Championship and the ICC One-Day Internationals Championship, which meant that losing to the number one nation, whoever that was, became part of an official ECB objective.

The strategy had virtually nothing on access for fans to the England team at grounds or through television, but it did outline the ECB's spending plans[13] for the five years between 2005 and 2009. These plans showed that the ECB spends its money in three principal areas. In 2005, 50% of that spending would be on support for county cricket, 20% on Team England and 17% on what the plan called 'participation'[14].

Cricket Australia also published its four-year strategy in 2005. It stated that 'Television for cricket fans is vital. Cricket Australia wants as many Australians as possible to see cricket on television' and set a 13% audience target. The strategy also said that 'One of Australian cricket's main aims over the coming years is to build the at-match experience for fans, and create an event-style atmosphere for children, families, young people, adults and cricket's traditional fans.' It set an audience goal for Australia games of four million over the four years (physically impossible in England).

The overriding goal, though, was that Australia be the:

> *Number one ranked senior male and female team in all game formats.*

Cricket Australia also carries out a periodic census to determine how many people play the game. The target set in the strategy was 555,000. The ECB carries out no such census, and has no such target.

## Finances

In 2005, the business model of England cricket remained unaltered since 1976 except for the dozen central contracts that bound the top players to the ECB rather than to their counties. The England team made revenues of £95 million[15], of which £49 million came from the sale of broadcasting rights. The 18 counties together made £24 million from their own cricket, of which £6 million apiece came from members, gate receipts and sponsorship & advertising and £5 million from their share of the broadcasting pie.

In 2005, then, the one England team made 80% of professional cricket revenues and all 18 county teams put together made 20%. These revenues reflected the preferences of cricket fans, who spent about 90% (295 million) of their viewing hours[16] on England and only 10% (30 million) on the counties. This was despite the introduction of Twenty20 in 2003, which has made little difference so far to the finances of the county game because the few Twenty20 games have mostly replaced other one-day cricket.

Costs, on the other hand, were unrelated to the interests of cricket fans. England's costs were £53 million, and the England team's performance off the field in 2005 was as good as it was on the field. It generated profits of £42 million. The counties' costs were also £53 million, of which £23 million—almost their entire cricket revenues—

went on players. The counties lost £29 million on their cricket in 2005.

Of England's £42 million profit, £23 million[17] was spent on supporting county cricket by the ECB. The MCC kept about £5 million under its staging arrangement, £8 million went to an ECB charity for safe-keeping and £5 million was spent by the ECB on grassroots[18].

The counties made up their £29 million cricket loss through the £23 million from the ECB (over 40% of their costs) and by a catering surplus of about £6 million. As a group, they roughly broke even when these two additional sources of cash are included.

The £23 million ECB support for county cricket was 40% more than the £16.2 million of ECB spending on the England team and grassroots cricket combined. Furthermore, little appears to have been spent on grassroots by the counties in 2005.

## County finance and strategy

All 18 first-class counties sustained heavy losses on their own cricket in 2005, regardless of their position in the class structure of England cricket. One official commented to me that, without England money, 'They're all bust.'

The typical minor major county—Somerset, say—made about £1 million in cricket revenues in 2005. It paid players £1.2 million and incurred another £1.4 million in ground and administration expenses, leading to a cricket loss of about £1.6 million. The payment of £1.4 million from the ECB and catering & events profits allowed it to register a small profit or loss in the £100,000 range.

For these clubs, barely bigger financially than a *Costcutter* mini-supermarket, £50,000 gained here or lost there made a big difference. Were the ECB payment to be cut by as little as £250,000 a year, then almost all of these clubs would be sunk within a year or two.

Graffiti on a sign at Lord's in 1999. Many fans believe that the MCC runs the game. In fact, the MCC and the 18 first-class counties run it, mostly through the ECB.

(Photo by Graham Chadwick/Getty Images)

MCC members look down on the winning Australian team after the 1999 World Cup final. Australia has completely dominated the international game since then.

(Photo by Graham Chadwick/Getty Images)

David Graveney and Nasser Hussain face the press after the England
team was booed at the Oval Test against New Zealand in 1999.

(Photo by Graham Chadwick/Getty Images)

Ian MacLaurin (foreground) and Tim Lamb (background) drove through
the Team England reforms in the late nineties, leading to England's
improved performance between 2003 and 2005.

(Photo by Getty Images)

Ian Chappell and Richie Benaud in 2007. England fans have listened to Benaud, but England administrators have not listened to Chappell.
(Photo by Simon Fergusson/Getty Images)

England selector Rod Marsh in 2004. His career has also included 96 Tests for Australia, two years with Kerry Packer and more than a decade as head coach at both national academies. Plus the small matter of the 45 beers.
(Photo by Stu Forster/ Getty Images)

Australian selector Allan Border in 2000. Since retiring, Border has held a number of management positions in Australian cricket.

(Photo by Darren England/ Getty Images)

Writer and TV & newspaper pundit Mike Atherton in 2007. England's longest-serving captain is yet to take up a management position in England cricket.

(Photo by Leon Neal/AFP/ Getty Images)

The
unrelenting
pursuit of
excellence is
rare in England
cricket. Kevin
Pietersen
shows the way
with his left-
handed sweep
for six against
Sri Lanka in
2006.
(Photo by Stu
Forster/Getty
Images)

Some ECB officials in 2006. Giles Clarke (front right) helped negotiate
the 2004 Sky deal. David Morgan (front centre) was ECB Chairman at
the time and David Collier (back left) defended the deal to a House of
Commons Select Committee inquiry in 2005. As ECB Chairman in 2008
and 2009, Clarke is responsible for producing the next deal.
(Photo by Christopher Lee/Getty Images)

John Buchanan and Adam Gilchrist hold the ICC World Cup trophy in April 2007 after the latter's fabulous innings. 'All men can see these tactics whereby I conquer, but what none can see is the strategy out of which victory is evolved.' (Photo by Hamish Blair/Getty Images)

Andrew Flintoff leaves the field during the ICC Twenty20 World Cup in September 2007. The press reported earlier in the month that Flintoff had received a steroid injection to get through the tournament.
(Photo by Tom Shaw/Getty Images)

Chinaman-bowler Brad Hogg during the 2007 Boxing Day Test between Australia and India at the MCG. For the second time in eight years, Australia won 15 Test matches in a row.
(Photo by Mark Dadswell / Getty Images)

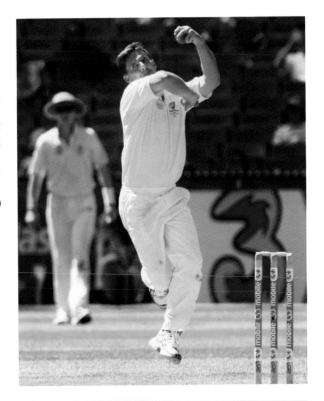

New model England cricketer Alastair Cook leaves the field after helping England avoid defeat at the Third Test against Sri Lanka at Galle in 2007. England lost the series 0-1, making three losses out of four in 2007 to go with failure at the two ICC tournaments.
(Photo by Deshakalyan Chowdhury / AFP / Getty Images)

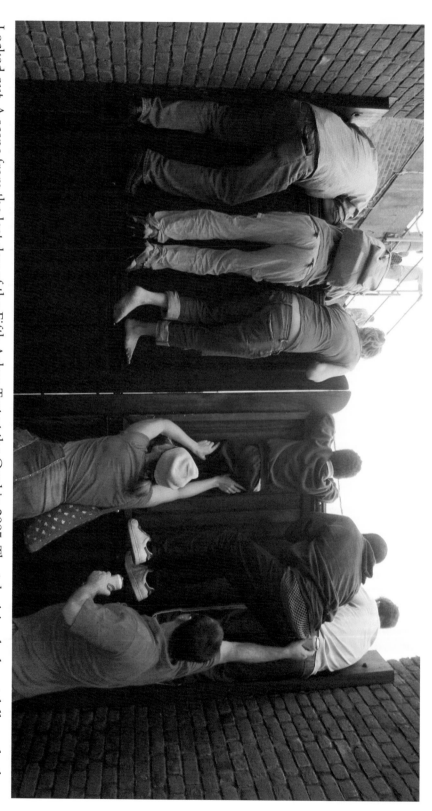

Locked out. A scene from the last day of the Fifth Ashes Test at the Oval in 2005. The television lock-out followed a few hours later and England team performance then collapsed. (Photo by Scott Barbour / Getty Images)

The typical major major county—Surrey, say—was in exactly the same position as far as its own cricket was concerned. The difference for them was that the mighty, mighty England came in 2005 with the slightly less mighty Australia in tow. As a result, the club had more members, bigger sponsors, more advertising and a more substantial catering & events business. The downside was an echoing ground that ate maintenance cash.

The typical major major generated two or three times more revenue than the average minor major, still barely more than a smallish supermarket, and made a profit in the £300,000 range. Like the average minor major, it also depended completely for its existence on the ECB payment of £1.4 million, but its finances were marginally less parlous month to month because of the inflow of cash from staging England games.

As in the nineties, the sensible strategy for each of the 13 minor majors was to expand its very small ground of 5,000 seats into a small ground of 15,000 seats and lobby for a One-Day International. The sensible strategy for all 18 major counties was to expand non-cricket revenue with a sports centre, housing, a hotel and the like. Increasingly, cricket was becoming a secondary commercial activity at many of England's 18 professional grounds.

The counties still needed, at all costs, to keep the torrent of England cash flowing in their direction and to increase it year by year. Otherwise they would topple, altogether now, like two sets of ninepins.

These 18 county cricket clubs, together with the MCC, effectively controlled the ECB. As a successful business, BSkyB is likely to have been well aware of who it was actually dealing with when it negotiated the television rights for 2006–2009. BSkyB agreed to make an offer to a small subset of England cricket fans. The offer began:

*All members of first class counties, minor counties, and the MCC will be eligible for special offers. New subscribers can get Sky Sports free for 12 months when ...*

## The message

Before the investigation each party submitted evidence to the committee, which then held hearings where representatives were questioned by Members of Parliament. Afterwards, the committee published a report and the Department for Culture, Media and Sport followed up with a statement of its own.

In its evidence and at the hearings, the ECB message came through loud and clear. The England team and grassroots cricket required considerable funding, and that money could only come from the sale of broadcasting rights. If the ECB was forced back to free-to-air television then it would lose £20 million a year and the result would be cuts to the England team and to grassroots funding. Therefore, the argument ran, the ECB had to resolve a clash of priorities between England and grassroots cricket, on one side, and audience demand for access, on the other. Reluctantly, in the public interest, it had chosen the former.

In essence, MPs were being asked whether they wanted to deprive Big Freddie, who had just won the Ashes, and Little Freddie and Little Franny in the under-10s. Put like that, there was only one answer.

In reality, the battle for ECB funds was between England, grassroots and the counties, on one side, and TV access on the other. The ECB neglected to mention that county cricket was by far the biggest of these three beneficiaries of ECB funding, and the ECB's evidence and testimony failed to alert MPs to the £23 million provided to county cricket in 2005 from profits made by the national side. In fact, in its evidence and testimony, the ECB hardly mentioned the counties at all.

Furthermore, the ECB failed to describe any way that it could save the £20 million difference between the two bids without cutting England and grassroots funding. Actually, it could have saved the £20 million by, for instance, cutting its support for county cricket by half and cancelling the charity payment.

This option may not in practice have been available to ECB executives because of the effective control of the organisation by the MCC & Counties and the various provisions in its Articles of Association that protect their interests. But, if that was the case, the ECB failed to inform the Select Committee that this or any similar alternative option was constitutionally impossible.

## The six claims

During the inquiry, the ECB made six principal claims in support of its message. Only one of these claims can be shown to be correct according to publicly-available information. The remaining five are, to say the least, questionable.

The first claim was that the cost of accepting the combined BSkyB and Channel 4 bid for the 2006–2009 television rights would have been £20 million a year. The difference was £82 million over the four years, so this claim was correct.

The ECB then claimed that broadcasting revenue constituted 80% of its revenues. This claim was also mentioned by the Secretary of State for Culture, Media & Sport, Tessa Jowell, in a letter to *The Daily Telegraph* in September 2005, and the ECB appended this letter to its evidence to the committee. Where Jowell got that number from is not clear.

The figures suggest that domestic broadcasting revenue[19] was 80% of the ECB's spending and not 80% of its revenues. Domestic broadcasting revenue for 2004 was actually 63% of the ECB's revenues. And, because broadcasting revenue goes into an ECB pot which is used to fund county cricket, England and grassroots cricket, the relevant comparison was between broadcasting revenue and the game's overall revenue, not with just ECB revenue. The relevant figure is about 42%.

The ECB's third claim was that 'cricket in England and Wales' invested 18.5% of its total income on grassroots in 2005[20]. The accounts of the ECB and MCC & Counties detail less than £10 million of spending in this area. This is a little over 8% of the £119 million generated by England professional cricket in 2005, and is so far short of the 18.5% claim that any unidentified spending is unlikely to bridge the gap.

The ECB claimed, fourthly, that extra money from television had in recent years allowed it to invest in central contracts, the national academy and in grassroots cricket. This claim was correct so far as central contracts was concerned, but failed to mention that Sport England had paid almost all of the construction costs of the National Academy[21] out of lottery funds. It also disregarded the fact that by far the biggest chunk (£11 million per year) of the increase in television rights, ticket revenues and sponsorship & advertising between 1995 and 2005 had gone on increasing ECB payments to counties from their already high levels.

Another claim stated that when cricket was on List A of sports to be available on free-to-air television, the revenue from television was £33.5 million[22] over four years versus the £220 million during 2006–2009. This claim did not remotely compare like with like. Instead, it compared part of an 11-year-old deal with a whole contemporary deal without adjusting either for inflation (33%) or for England's expanded schedule (37%).

Lastly, David Collier was asked by one MP how it was that other countries, especially Australia, managed to maintain cricket on free-to-air television. Collier responded that Channel Nine[23] paid 'substantively more in rights fees as a terrestrial broadcaster than we have enjoyed in this country.' In fact, as of 2005, Channel Nine's deal with Cricket Australia for all Australia's home games was worth $25 million a year, equivalent to about £11 million. Channel 4 paid nearly £20 million per year from 2003 to 2005 for six of the seven Tests and none of the One-Day Internationals, nearly twice as much as Cricket Australia received from Channel Nine for all its Tests and all of its One-Day Internationals.

# Eighth in the world

Reading through the evidence and the transcript of the testimony, the overriding impression I get is that the ECB was acutely vulnerable to detailed questions about its constitution and finances. Had Collier been asked these questions during his testimony, then he would have had no choice but to admit that ECB support of county cricket in 2005 was 15% more than the £20 million difference between the exclusive and the sharing bids, and 40% greater than its spending on the England team and grassroots cricket combined.

Any MP could then have suggested that the ECB implement a programme of cuts centred on county cricket to save the £20 million, leading to the conclusion that the ECB did not actually need Sky's money. Had an MP done a back-of-the-envelope calculation of county and England viewing hours and looked at the ECB Articles of Association, he or she could then have asked some further searching questions about what led the ECB to agree the deal in the first place. Had ECB executives then bleated that their constitution prevented them from cutting the funding to counties (if it does), MPs could have suggested that the constitution be changed in the public interest and then required the presence before them of the people who do actually run this game.

For Collier, caught between informed representatives of the population of the United Kingdom on one hand, and the members of the ECB on the other, these lines of questioning would have left him nowhere to go. If pursued to the end, they would probably have brought 19 representatives of the MCC & Counties to Westminster and exposed the business model of England cricket to full scrutiny by those ultimately responsible for the public interest.

However, no MP asked the key questions and the ECB got through relatively unscathed. It was also helped by a large slice of luck: the Sports Minister, Richard Caborn, bought the message whole. On the consequences of £80 million less over the four years, he said, 'Do we deny them that? If you do then that is fine. That is a decision which will mean we will go back to being eighth in the world and we do not want to do that.' As with Tessa Jowell, one can only wonder where Caborn's analysis came from.

The committee published its report in April 2006. While supporting the free-to-air principle, the report stated that there should be no return to the days of an impoverished ECB. It concluded that 'If the ECB truly believes that ... the future of cricket is best served by selling its rights to the highest bidder ... then it is inconceivable that in years to come its conclusion could be any different.'

## TV logic

The logic behind this ominous statement is derived from developments over the last 25 years in British television. The UK is currently completing a long-term transition from a single universal analogue system with no charging mechanism (good old BBC1, BBC2, ITV and Channel 4) to three digital platforms, all delivering multi-channel television and all equipped with the means to charge the viewer a subscription. Two of these systems provide universal coverage.

The first system is BSkyB and its satellite. The second is Digital Terrestrial Television (DTT) and its set-top box, which processes a digital signal broadcast by the old terrestrial mast network. Cable, the only non-universal system, is the third. As of September 2007, eight million households subscribed to BSkyB, nine million had DTT, and three million subscribed to cable. Only four million households continued with the old analogue five-channel system, and they will be compulsorily converted by 2013 under a process called 'Digital Switchover'.

Pressure from *Keep Cricket Free* in 2005 prompted Tessa Jowell to mention a review of the listing system 'around 2008–09', but she also stated that the context of the listing review will be Digital Switchover. So, this review may not happen in time for the next set of cricket television rights. Actually, it may not happen at all. And, even if it does, there is every reason to expect that the UK government will again permit the TV rights to be sold to the highest bidder. After all, according to the ECB, the England team and grassroots cricket need the money.

This fatuous argument worked in 2005. The net effect of the Parliamentary investigation into the sale of television rights by the ECB was exactly the same as the typical ECB or TCCB review. It was exactly equal to the number of Tests won by England in the subsequent Ashes series, plus the number of cricket stadiums in England & Wales with over 30,000 seats, multiplied by the number of international-standard wrist spinners in England, multiplied again by the number of Tests Australia did not win in 2006 and 2007.

Zero.

## Priority order

The ECB, in suggesting to the Select Committee that the loss of £20 million per year from retaining Test matches on free-to-air television would cause the end of central contracts, the loss of the national academy and reduced funding for grassroots, provided yet further confirmation, as if any were needed, of the game's priority order in 2005.

That order ran, and still runs:

1) Sustaining county cricket
2) Achieving England success
3) Funding grassroots
4) Providing England access for fans

To make sure, I asked an official what would have happened had the ECB been forced to return Test matches to free-to-air television. He said:

> I can absolutely guarantee that the first-class counties would have remained. The soft end of the game would have gone, including development and central contracting.

Shortly after this investigation, in March 2006, Cricket Australia Chief Executive James Sutherland told a newspaper about his strategy. 'Our core business is about the game of cricket,' he said, 'but there are two arms to that. One is ensuring that Australian representative teams are the best in the world. The other side is also about growing the game in a participation sense and making it more accessible to Australians.'

The order in Australia runs:

1)   Achieving Australia success
2=) Providing Australia access for fans
2=) Funding grassroots

## Descent from 2005

Ever since its famous, one-off Ashes victory, England has endured a continuous fixtures crunch. In the 27 months from October 2005 to December 2007, the team played 28 Tests, 59 one-day games, 10 Twenty20 games (counted as half a day) and 30 tour days, equal to 28% of the calendar days. In that period, England had a six-week Christmas break in 2005 and three other breaks of less than a month each.

The ICC stipulates a minimum schedule for full members of 18 series every six years, each of two Tests and three one-day internationals. These commitments, and the various ICC tournaments, give a total of under 50 playing days per year. Since 2005, though, England has been playing other full members at nearly twice this rate. In 2005, over half of England team profits went to county cricket and another £5 million to the MCC. There is no reason to believe that anything changed on that score in 2006 and 2007.

One player at the sharp end of this meat mangler, Darren Gough, told the *News Of The World* in May 2004:

> *The international schedule is relentless and burnout is a problem. But the tours just get tougher and extra Tests and one-dayers are*

*squeezed in as we are sacrificed in the quest for more money to keep the counties afloat.*

As a result of the fixtures crunch, England went full circle and the bad old days of the nineties returned. It won eight of the 28 Tests and lost 11, with only two series victories out of eight, and continued to flop at the shorter forms of the game. Three of the pace quartet and Giles were injured at one point or another before 2007, and all four of the quartet in the summer of 2007.

Post-Ashes, England used 27 players in Tests. Only eight batsmen were selected, but 11 pace bowlers, four spinners and three wicket-keepers were picked. Vaughan, Flintoff, Strauss and Trescothick all captained the team and Test debuts continued at the long-term rate of five per year. Just one player played all the Tests: Pietersen. By the end of 2007, even he appeared to be struggling with the relentless grind.

For the 2005/06 series against Pakistan and India, Simon Jones was injured and the pace quartet broke up, probably for good. Giles also suffered a hip injury, leaving England with just three experienced bowlers. Although they took 36 wickets in the three games against Pakistan, these cost 33 apiece versus Shoaib Akhtar's 17 at 25. England lost 0–2.

Against India, England lost Trescothick to some combination of burnout, emotional breakdown and a virus, the press reporting that he had been away an average of 250 days for each of the previous six years. In Vaughan's absence with a knee injury, Flintoff was made captain, and two more players produced by the new development system, Alastair Cook and Monty Panesar, were given debuts in the First Test. Harmison failed to perform, but Hoggard did, and England sneaked a 1–1 draw with a makeshift team achieving a determined victory in the Third Test.

The subject of burn-out again hit the headlines. Duncan Fletcher said in February 2006, 'Burnout doesn't happen overnight. Once it's happened it's too late. By the end of the 2007 World Cup we are going to have some very tired players, then we go into home series against West Indies and India.' Australia's Brett Lee said in April 2006 he was 'out of gas and bowling on fumes', while Ricky Ponting castigated the international programme as 'hectic and unacceptable'. In the same month, Trescothick said, 'We play so much. We spend 300 nights of the year out of our own house, either travelling the world or in hotels preparing for games in England, so I think there are times when you do need to have a rest.'

At home in 2006, the pace bowlers took turns missing series. Jones missed both, Harmison the first against Sri Lanka and Flintoff the second against Pakistan. Only Hoggard played throughout but he faded towards the end, taking 10 wickets at an uncharacteristic 47 in the four-Test series against Pakistan. Panesar came through with 27 wickets in the seven games, and England drew 1–1 with Sri Lanka and beat a Pakistan side missing both its opening bowlers 3–0.

Panesar added lustre to an increasingly forlorn England team, celebrating his wickets like a puppet whose strings were being jerked by an invisible hand 250 feet above. He was not initially risked in one-day cricket and it was fortunate that he was not playing at Headingley in July when Sri Lanka launched the most remarkable display of hitting ever seen in an international match in England. Sri Lanka scored 324–2 in 37 overs to overhaul England's 321, thereby taking the series … 5–0.

In 2006, the first year of the BSkyB television deal, Sky had eight million subscribers out of the 25 million households in the UK. Of these, five million took the sports option, meaning that 80% of all households did not subscribe to Sky Sports. Press reports indicated that the average live television audience for the summer's Tests was 250,000, which represented a reduction of 80% from the 1999–2005 average of 1.3 million achieved by Channel 4.

This means that Sky Sports subscribers are equally as likely as the whole population to watch Test cricket. Any argument that Sky reaches disproportionate numbers of youth, women, the retired, cricket fans as a whole, or whatever, must answer the fundamental point: 80% of the population is cut off, and the average number of cricket viewers has fallen by the same percentage.

## Grounds and money

In 2006, the ECB paid £30.7 million out to county cricket, 7% up on 2005 despite a 2% reduction in ECB revenues and the promise in its 2005 strategy that support for county cricket would decline as a percentage of its spending. But, even though the BSkyB deal had secured the future of county cricket for a further four years, the counties continued to squabble about grounds and money.

In February, three minor majors who had made a loss in 2005 requested a further ECB handout to reflect the increased revenues generated by the MCC and the four major majors that had hosted an Ashes game in 2005. Jack Simmons, the Lancashire Chairman, responded through the media that the major majors had kept county cricket going for 30 years. After a ding-dong, David Morgan commissioned a review to report back sometime in 2007.

In April, the ECB decided to award an Ashes Test for 2009 to Cardiff, making it the eighth Test ground in England & Wales. The use in 2009 of this new 15,000-seat ground at the expense of Old Trafford (21,000 seats) will further reduce the total capacity for the 2009 Ashes from the hopelessly inadequate level provided in 2005.

Other counties expressed dismay, although not about the loss of capacity for fans. The Hampshire Chairman, Rod Bransgrove, said, 'We stepped aside to make way for Durham, and I expected them to get the Test. We felt it was right they got one … But Lord's giveth and Lord's taketh away … I am angry and deeply disappointed. Quite clearly the "W" in the ECB is silent, but powerful.'

Bransgrove then joined Michael Parkinson and Bob Willis in suggesting the Kerry Packer solution for England cricket. 'The way to do it,' he said, 'is to buy the whole shooting match. The ECB turns over about £60 million. Just buy the game.'

The MCC kept quiet, but three major majors spoke out. Lancashire's Chief Executive Jim Cumbes called the decision a 'kick in the teeth' for his county. Yorkshire Chief Executive Stewart Regan said, 'The whole system needs to be clarified because the bottom line is that too many grounds are bidding for too few international fixtures.' Surrey Chief Executive Paul Sheldon said, 'the ECB have decided on expanding Test-match grounds to 11 or 12 and there are only seven Tests [per season] to go around. That means some of these grounds could go out of business.' In August, Regan said that the number of counties should be reduced from 18 to 12. When asked how, he said, 'I haven't worked that one out yet.'

In November, the ECB conferred international status on Hampshire's Rose Bowl. This means that eight small grounds and one medium-sized one (Lord's, the Oval, Trent Bridge, Old Trafford, Headingley Carnegie, Sophia Gardens, Chester-le-Street, The Rose Bowl and Edgbaston) will be battling it out to host a Test each year.

Nottinghamshire also produced plans to increase capacity by 2,000 to a gigantic 17,500, and in 2007 the Oval announced a 2,000-seat expansion to a monumental 25,000. Among the minor majors, Somerset proposed a £60 million expansion at Taunton and Derbyshire launched a plan to build 6,000 additional seats. Its Chief Executive, Tom Sears, said, 'We want to give Derbyshire a stadium that is capable of staging One-Day Internationals and Twenty20 finals. If we could even get one international match every three years, that would give us a lot more financial security.'

## 2012 stadium

In November and December 2005, my editor Robert Franklin and I proposed that the ECB use the 80,000-seat 2012 Olympic Stadium to enhance access and make money. We did not begin to suspect that access to England games for fans is fourth priority for the ECB and hence irrelevant. Nor did we know that the MCC & Counties effectively control the ECB and come first in the priority order. We did not appreciate that our proposal, if carried out, would have upset the delicate balance of power and interest between the MCC, the major major counties, the minor major counties and the ECB itself, and that in this context the extra cash that it would have generated was meaningless.

This proposal therefore had about the same chance of being adopted as the ideas put forward by the Cricket Reform Group and the proposal that Test cricket be kept on free-to-air television. The problem for the ECB, though, was how to reject something that served its customers and made money. That is not an easy thing to do, especially in writing.

In September 2006, we received a letter from John Perera, the ECB's Commercial Director, in response to our letter to Giles Clarke. Perera provided five reasons[24] for inaction. None of them stacked up and together they were even less convincing than the utterances of David Collier in Parliament nine months before, which took some doing.

In 2007, I mentioned our proposal to an official. He immediately said that county grounds were 'a problem' for the idea. When I suggested that the six main grounds be reduced to three and their capacity hugely expanded he said that was 'obvious'. When asked why not get on with it, he replied, 'Too political … fighting the counties on this issue and that … not possible.'

The MCC launched a new debenture scheme for Lord's at about the same time. An eight-year debenture (actual tickets extra, as at the Oval) was priced at an average of £10,000, equivalent to at least £150 a day at a big game. The brochure was headlined 'Seat In The Upper House' and contained the sentence: 'May we respectfully suggest a call to your accountants?' The small print mentioned that Lord's did not technically have any England games after 2009.

The MCC then opened negotiations with the ECB for staging rights post-2009. Having earlier put out a press release promising an expansion of the ground, the MCC's strategy is clear and perfectly sensible: build more seats and make more money for the ECB in exchange for keeping two Tests.

But, with nine anointed grounds and Bristol all tussling for 47 England days, the MCC may be hard-pressed to retain its privileged allocation of 12 days. Sometime in 2008, England's cricket fans may be treated to the extraordinary spectacle of the ECB removing a Test from the country's only medium-sized ground.

Even MCC membership provides no protection against the consequences of being fourth in the priority order. It seems that no fan, anywhere, is safe.

## 2006/07 Ashes

Midway through the hectic post-2005 schedule came the 2006/07 Ashes series and the 2007 World Cup tournament. For the Ashes, England's strongest XI was Trescothick, Strauss, Vaughan, Cook, Pietersen, Flintoff, Chris Read, Simon Jones, Hoggard, Harmison and Panesar. This side, essentially the 2005 Ashes team strengthened by Cook, Read and Panesar, was fully capable of competing with Australia. And, with Bell, Paul Collingwood, Geraint Jones, Giles, Anderson and Tremlett making up a squad of 17, England had on paper the strongest tour party for decades.

However, Simon Jones and Vaughan were injured. Flintoff was injured but played anyway, Trescothick left the tour before the series started, Harmison completely failed to perform, and Panesar and Read were not picked until the third game. This left a side between five and seven players short of peak strength. And, by not picking Mark Ramprakash, who scored 2,278 runs in 2006 at an average of 104, and preferring Mahmood, Anderson and Plunkett to established county bowlers, the selectors showed exactly what they thought of county cricket.

Set against England was an Australian side that had benefited from such a long rest (four months) during the English summer that John Buchanan felt it necessary to arrange a boot camp in September 2006 for his players. Buchanan also conjured up a replacement for the support bowling that had been battered in 2005. Stuart Clark, a state cricketer aged 31 and an on-and-off nationally-contracted player, ably filled the gap left by Gillespie and Kasprowicz.

Huge crowds turned out to watch the Australia machine pulverise England. On the first day at the Fourth Test, with the Ashes already won, 89,155 people saw the local hero Shane Warne start his last Test at his home ground. At least 15,000 England supporters were in the crowd during each of the three days of this game, as many as will be accommodated at the 2009 Ashes Test at Cardiff's new ground. But on Radio 4's *Test Match Special* there were several jibes about the concrete bowls in Brisbane and Melbourne and few references to the sheer number of spectators that these grounds can accommodate.

After the MCG game, John Buchanan tossed an exploding sledge back at England's exploding batsman, Kevin Pietersen, saying through the media, 'It surprises me that he always seems distanced from the rest of the group. He certainly talks of himself as a team player, but I don't personally see any evidence of that.' This exquisite piece of psychological manipulation reminded England that their best player is not a Pommy either by birth or by inclination and gently suggested that Pietersen regretted having headed north to a number two cricket country rather than south to the number one cricket country.

Over 40,000 people turned up at the SCG on the last day of the series to see Hayden and Langer take Australia home and rub out the memories of 12 September 2005. Afterwards, Warne and McGrath's children cavorted on the outfield, looking every bit like the kids in the 2012 London Olympics video. Once again, four Australian bowlers played the entire series, capturing between 20 and 26 wickets each at a combined average of 25. England did play only five bowlers, but none of them averaged under 37.

Harmison promptly announced his retirement from the one-day game, probably to get a holiday before the next Test in May. Bob Willis commented that Harmison's bowling was partly caused by the ineffectiveness of the county system and that Anderson, Plunkett and Mahmood were all learning the game in England colours rather than in county cricket. Mark Nicholas wrote: 'The locals here are staggered by the second-rate culture and systems of English cricket. We have young Test cricketers who cannot even field properly. Most of them don't know what hard work is, because county cricket rewards them and their colleagues for being ordinary. And the counties run the game.'

But most commentators preferred instead to focus on local, short-term factors, such as inadequate warm-up time, the ICC Champions' Trophy just before the tour, and the coach for not selecting Panesar and Read.

In January 2007, after a day-night game in Adelaide, a newspaper reported that England's management was concerned that Strauss and Collingwood were close to exhaustion. Strauss had played all 15 Tests and 25 one-day games in the previous 11 months (equal to 30% of calendar days), and Collingwood had played in all but two one-day games in the same period. The Aussies, on the other hand, rotated their squad before the World Cup, leaving England a short moment in the sun when they won the Commonwealth Bank one-day series.

Two months later, Australia waltzed through the World Cup. England made the Super Eights but beat only one of the six top-eight sides that they played in the tournament. Duncan Fletcher resigned as England coach and Peter Moores, former Sussex coach and Director of the Academy, was appointed as his replacement. In interviews following his resignation, Fletcher said that there was far too much county cricket and that the county game lacked intensity.

## Schofield

After eight years, Fletcher bequeathed a strong squad and a good elite youth conveyor belt to his successor. Forced by injuries and a lack of adequate county replacements to rely on youth in his last 18 months in charge, he reportedly did not consult county coaches or build relationships with them as much as he could have.

In the end, Fletcher came up against the hard facts about England cricket. Because its second tier does not provide cricket to national Second XI standard, Team England has not been enough to sustain success in an international calendar of 80–90 days per year, especially against an Australian side that has long since moved to another plane altogether. The result has been an even more cyclical performance in Test cricket and the effective sacrifice of the one-day form of the game.

In January 2007, the ECB announced a review into the Ashes defeat. Ken Schofield, a former European Professional Golfers' Association Executive Director, was appointed Chairman. The ECB press release stated that 'The composition of the Review Team is fully independent of the ECB Board and the Team England Management structure'. Press reports said that six experts would help, one of whom would be Mike Atherton. However, he withdrew, saying he didn't want to feel compromised when talking about the game in the media.

After every disaster, there is a moment when the governed see that their governors are not competent and ask themselves whether others would do better. Ordinary governors fear this moment because it is the dwelling place of revolution and the entrance to a bottomless pit into which their privileges and power can permanently be cast. The astute governor knows that the moment will eventually pass because the governed want more than anything to return to daily life. Standing on the podium, he offers reassurance and promises to solve the problems that led to disaster. He steps off the podium and the independent review begins. Experts are hired, witnesses heard and weighty considerations given. The months pass by and the disaster recedes into history. Suddenly, on a good news day, the results of the review are announced. This person is promoted, that person is shunted sideways and a stakeholder implementation taskforce is created. The governed feel a minute twitch on the rudder of the ship of state and without looking up they carry contentedly on.

The experts eventually appointed were Brian Rose, Angus Fraser, Nasser Hussain, Hugh Morris, Nick Knight and Mickey Stewart. Of these, two were employed within England professional cricket: Rose was Director of Cricket at Somerset County Cricket Club and Morris was Deputy Chief Executive of the ECB. Two more, Knight and Hussain, worked for BSkyB, the ECB's broadcast partner. Fraser was a cricket writer on *The Independent* and was also on the ECB Cricket Committee. Stewart was a former manager / coach of the England team and former director of coaching at the ECB. Schofield himself had never held an ECB or county appointment or worked for a partner organisation.

These seven individuals were not the only people 'fully independent of the ECB Board'. For example, Richie Benaud, Ian Chappell, Greg Chappell, Rod Marsh, Clive Lloyd, Tony Greig, Mark Taylor, Viv Richards, Mike Brearley, Allan Border, Steve Waugh, Bob Woolmer, Imran Khan and Tom Moody were, among many others, also fully independent. None worked for the ECB or a partner organisation and almost all had extensive experience of England professional cricket. Several had captained sides that had thrashed England and a proportion had cricket management experience too.

By and large, former England captains come across in the media as an independent lot suitable for the task at hand. Collectively, they form a kind of Privy Council to be consulted on matters of constitutional importance. But, in addition to Atherton, Greig and Brearley, the review team also did not feature Ian Botham, Bob Willis, Graham Gooch, Mike Gatting, David Gower or Alec Stewart. Just the one former captain—Hussain—was included.

Any six of these 20 famous names would have been likely to provide a comprehensive answer to the two key questions:

*What does England have to do to maximise its chances of a)
beating Australia 5–0 in 2009 and in every Ashes series thereafter
and b) winning the ICC World Cup in 2011 and every tournament
thereafter?*

But the ECB did not set its experts this simple one-sentence task.
Instead, it instructed them to answer a list of twelve pleonastic
questions. The list is unreadable and baffling and not worth
printing. Most importantly, it precluded almost all discussion of the
commercial issues that lead to the tight schedule, burn-out and
injury and the structural issues that weaken England. One official
told me that the review 'was not up to much' and another said that
it was a big PR exercise.

A summary of the Schofield report, but not the report itself as had
been promised, was released during the Second Test against the
West Indies in May. The one substantial recommendation—that a
county one-day tournament be scrapped—was referred on to a new
Domestic Structure Review Group. Those few cricket fans paying
attention witnessed a priceless governance spectacle: the handing
of the baton in Perpetual Review Relay.

## Warning signs

Australia coach John Buchanan also stepped down in spring 2007,
after eight years. In May, he told the BBC what he had learned from
his spell as coach at Middlesex in the late nineties:

*I made a few mistakes ... but it opened my eyes to the English
system and made me see why England find it difficult to field
competitive sides consistently. The talent and the numbers are
there, but the county system is a real anchor on the players. There's
no doubt that they play too much cricket, and that promotes
mediocrity.*

In summer 2007, new England coach Peter Moores immediately
moved to reconnect England to county cricket, picking a county

bowler, Ryan Sidebottom, for the Test series against West Indies and permitting England players once again to play county fixtures. One official said to me, though, 'We've always got to have players playing at the highest possible level. If we want to compete, we have to have an elite system. But everything else is elite except for county cricket.'

Despite the absence of Flintoff and Simon Jones, England easily disposed of a dreadful West Indies team featuring no world-class players at all for the first time in over 30 years. Angus Fraser commented on radio that the First Test was 'a low-key affair ... this is ripping people off ... it is the poorest bowling I can remember.'

Against India, England failed to field any of its pace quartet. The second-string attack, flattered by spring weather that continued into July as well as by the West Indies, ran into a superior team and lost the series 0–1. The England county cricket season consisted, yet again, of 85-90 playing days.

During the summer, Professional Cricketers' Association Chief Executive Richard Bevan demanded an annual three-month break for bowlers, an end to back-to-back Tests and sufficient rest in between games. Pointing out that England cricketers spent more than 250 nights away in 2006, Bevan reminded *Test Match Special* listeners in May that 'cricketers are the product' and suggested that the 2008 Champions' Trophy may fall victim to player fatigue.

In July, *BBC Radio Five Live* carried an interview with Pietersen. Complaining of serious fatigue, he said:

> *The England team is a team that never, ever stops ... A good four to six weeks is about right for a proper break ... I'm not a robot. I'm going away now for a few days, which isn't a real break, but hopefully it will help in some way before the Test series against India.*

As was the case with the player grievances that led to World Series Cricket, the signs of conflict to come are quite clear.

# Full circle in 2007

From the end of April to the end of August, again, the Australian side played no cricket while England played seven Tests and 10 One-Day Internationals. The inaugural Twenty20 competition in South Africa, staged at the end of our summer, was for Australia a welcome pre-season warm-up, whereas for England it was a nuisance that prevented the squad getting a proper rest between the 2007 and 2007/08 seasons.

England picked an 'A' team for this tournament that combined the best county Twenty20 players with the biggest-hitting frontline batsmen. The selectors took a weak bowling outfit, leaving Panesar at home and picking only Flintoff out of the pace quartet. He was again injured and things got so bad that Ricky Ponting suggested through the media that he be given six months off, adding one more to the number of Aussies who have felt obliged to tell England how to manage its game.

England won only against Zimbabwe and failed to make the semi-finals, setting in the process a new record—four years—for the time this country has taken to lose its lead in a game that it invented. This record is unlikely ever to be beaten. But, by comparison with the Ashes nine months before, there were few complaints in the media and there was therefore no need for the ECB to launch an independent review of this latest humiliation.

The 2007 Rugby World Cup overlapped with this tournament. Having achieved a score-line in a first-round game to match Stuart Broad's 0–36 in one over against Yuvraj Singh in the Twenty20 competition, England came from nowhere to complete a full cycle of success, collapse and success between 2003 and 2007. The tournament was screened on ITV, a free-to-air advertising-funded channel, and the nation tuned in en masse. One cricket official told me, 'There is now no doubt in my mind that rugby union has eclipsed cricket as the nation's number two sport and, in part, this is down to cricket's sheer incompetence and parochialism.'

After a commendable 3-2 one-day victory against Sri Lanka in October, England's bowling crisis continued in the three-test series against the same opposition in December. With Flintoff out until 2008, Hoggard injured for one game, Jones still in long-term lay-off and Harmison perceived as unreliable, England bought their wickets at an alarming 48 runs apiece and Sri Lanka exceeded 440 in three out of their four innings. The batsmen fared badly too, selling their wickets at 26 each, with Pietersen failing in a series for the first time. England was lucky to get away with a 0-1 defeat.

Perhaps attempting to develop a long-term replacement for the injured Flintoff, England gave three games to Ravi Bopara, a 22-year-old all-rounder who had come through the new development system. This move again highlighted the lack of support provided to the England team by county cricket, which does not have in its 400-strong ranks an England-qualified player ready to occupy even part of the hole left by Flintoff. Forced to learn on the job, Bopara had a horrible time, averaging eight with the bat and 81 with the ball. England still needs a second all-rounder and Bopara still needs more training, but both now have to face the same question: where from?

During the Sri Lanka series, the ECB finally began to face the question of bowler injuries and player burn-out in public. There are only three approaches to this problem. Blunder on and accept the pain, as at present, or reduce the England fixture list, or introduce player rotation. Blundering on is getting harder by the day as the schedule gets pinned in the press for damaging England's performance. A cut of 15 days per year, to about 70, would cost about £20 million in lost revenues. With Sky already having been tapped, ECB executives would have to turn to the counties for savings and the government for support. They would be likely to receive the same pair of monosyllables from each.

So, player rotation it is. In December, the signs of the cricket public being prepared for this policy were unmistakeable. However, without drastic measures to increase the standard in the second tier and produce a strong England Second XI, national team performance is likely to drop yet further if this policy is adopted.

Down at the Melbourne Cricket Ground, in the 2007 Boxing Day Test, Australia's new bowling attack of Brett Lee, Stuart Clark, Mitchell Johnson and Brad Hogg took 20 Indian wickets for fewer than 360 runs, helping Australia complete its 15th Test victory in succession. Its form in 2006 and 2007 was 5-0.

England's two-year form was between 1-1 and 1-0, roughly where it was before the great revival began in the Oval Test against South Africa in 2003 but still, mercifully, a couple of notches above the level before the advent of Duncan Fletcher and central contracts. This performance means Australia and England are further apart than at any time since the end of World Series Cricket in 1979. It also means that England's form was closer to Bangladesh's than to that of its historic rival.

The Pommy cricket Establishment, always uncomfortable with excellence and the irritating burden of adulation, expectation and hope, has successfully muddled its way back to mediocrity.

Just before Christmas, the MCC sent out its annual invitation to fans to enter the public ticket ballot for games at Lord's in 2008. For the South Africa Test in July, the adult price for all seats bar those in the lower tier of the Compton and Edrich stands hit a new record of £75. The child price, though, was reduced to £24. This peculiar figure allows the MCC, should anybody complain, to say that an adult and a child can go to 'The Home of Cricket' for less than £100.

In all, there was no joy for England fans during Christmas 2007, but plenty for the Aussies. Despite the levying of vast tithes from its supporters, the England team will spend 2008 sagging under the weight of the 90 days of international cricket required to make up the financial losses incurred by the 18 major counties.

## Clarke, turkeys and Christmas

Towards the end of the summer, the Chairmanship of the ECB came up for re-appointment after David Morgan landed the ICC

Presidency. Giles Clarke and Mike Soper, from major major county Surrey, contested the election. On 11 August, Clarke went on *Test Match Special* and was asked about the BSkyB deal that he had helped negotiate in 2004. After claiming that the ECB spent 21%[25] of its revenues on grassroots cricket and that BSkyB's money helped, Clarke told a sweet little story about boys and girls learning the game at an event near his village in the West Country. Again, the official message about the Sky deal came through loud and clear.

I tuned in, eagerly anticipating insights into why £30.7 million had been provided by the ECB to county cricket in 2006 and why about 1/18th of this merry fortune had gone to Clarke's own club, Somerset. Despite listening carefully and shouting questions at Jonathan Agnew on the radio, I learned nothing on either score.

Seven years before, after the failures against Australia and New Zealand and at the 1999 World Cup, Clarke had been quoted by the sports journalist Mihir Bose to the effect that the longer county cricket survived in its current state, the more difficult it would be to halt the decline of English cricket.

'As a businessman,' said Clarke, 'I hate subsidies, because subsidies make for inefficiency. But county cricket would not survive but for the subsidy from Test cricket. That's the basic problem. If county cricket were a business product, then it would have gone bankrupt years ago.' The culprit, according to Clarke, was 'the structure of cricket. It's fundamentally flawed. County cricket is no longer a viable economic activity. It does not create a Test-winning team. It's a bit like the British motor industry.'

Clarke concluded with a revolutionary proposal. 'I would abolish county cricket,' he said, 'but the problem is, the counties control cricket in this country. And turkeys don't vote for Christmas.'

In September 2007, the turkeys voted instead for Clarke to be the Chairman of the England & Wales Cricket Board. If he still thinks that county cricket should be abolished, the politics could get even more complicated. If he no longer thinks county cricket should be abolished, then what has led him to change his mind?

That is as may be. Giles Clarke, like all his predecessors, does not actually run this game. Heavily constrained by the ECB Articles of Association, he merely represents those who do. But during his term as Chairman in 2008 and 2009, the ECB will conclude the next television deal, which starts in 2010. From the perspective of the MCC & Counties, it seems, Clarke's heretical words have more than been erased by his noble work on the current deal in 2004.

As 2008 begins, access and success are in bad shape at the same time. Once again, the unreformed business model of England cricket is hamstringing the game despite the ever greater largesse provided by television.

# CHAPTER 7

# FUTURES

*The English game has access to better resourcing than the Australian game, the whole TV / commercial side is much stronger, so I think there is every reason why England should prosper. Everything is there for cricket to take off.*

John Buchanan, 2007


## REVIEW

In the 35 years since Australia held England to a 2–2 draw at the Oval and Rod Marsh first led the now ritual incantation of *Under The Southern Cross*, the West Indies set the pace on the field until the early nineties and Australia has done since then.

Managerially, Australia has led the pack since the mid-eighties. England professional cricket has been introspective, self-absorbed and reluctant to face the modern world. Owned and run by the MCC & Counties, it has lagged badly behind.


## Failure to keep up

The England team has played 319 Test matches since the end of World Series Cricket, won 92 of them, lost 114 and drawn 113. It has not won any of the nine World Cup tournaments. This is a lamentable record in the context of our vast playing and fan base, the rapid growth in the game's finances, the status of cricket as our national summer sport, the UK's relative economic wealth and the advantages conferred by participation in international cricket since 1877.

The principal reason for this failure is that England has emphasised domestic cricket virtually throughout. The ultimate control of the TCCB and then the ECB by the MCC & Counties has compromised the national side and delayed the adoption of the innovations produced mostly by Australia.

Table 4 lists the 20 major differences between England and Australia at some point between 1972 and 2007 in descending order of importance. Each of these is classified in the right-hand column as relating either to domestic cricket or to national team access, success or finance. The year of its introduction is shown in bold in the column of the more advanced country and in plain text in the column of the copying country.

Of these 20 differences, four originated in England and 16 in Australia. England produced Twenty20 cricket, ran a fully-professional second tier and made its second-tier tournament two-divisional before the Aussies did. All three relate to domestic cricket and one of them does not apply to Australia. England has introduced exactly one innovation relating to international cricket: in 2004, it placed all England's home games on subscription television from 2006 onwards. By law, this is not permitted in Australia unless free-to-air television firms are not interested.

England has adopted 13 of the 16 Australian innovations an average of 21 years after they were introduced Down Under. Excluding four-day domestic cricket, which distorts the average upwards, the average adoption time is 17 years. Three important features of Australian cricket are yet to be adopted here. A right-sized second-tier system, an 80,000-seat stadium (and big grounds in general), and a national Under-19 competition are all pending. On average, England is 74 years behind in these areas.

Successive generations of England pace bowlers have not reached their full potential because of injury. Ian Botham and Graham Dilley in the eighties and Angus Fraser, Andy Caddick, Darren Gough and Dominic Cork in the nineties were, in the absence of central contracts, over-used by country and county to an alarming degree. Steve Harmison, Matthew Hoggard, Andrew Flintoff and Simon Jones enjoyed a brief period of success as a quartet between 2003 and 2005, but the hectic international schedule and the need to generate money for the counties have, precisely as predicted by Gough, exacted a heavy toll. The best batsman in each generation— David Gower in the eighties, Graham Thorpe in the nineties, and now Kevin Pietersen—has complained of burn-out and fatigue.

Our elite youth conveyor belt has been weak in relation to Australia's all along, but improvements in the last few years have closed the gap so that, today, it is missing only the Under-19 component. The second tier has been too big by a factor of three, leading to the dispersal of talent and a widening gap with international cricket. Precious Test experience has been wasted on players that the second tier has failed to expose as inadequate and denied to players not identified early enough as stars.

There have been some changes in England cricket, as Table 4 shows. But it took a decade of dreadful England performances, press ridicule bordering on contempt, declining audiences, a polemic from Ian Botham, and five years between 1997 and 2002 to drive the Team England reforms through. Until then, England success had largely been permitted to come and go of its own accord, leading to cyclical performance.

The next three years was a golden era during which fans could and did follow a winning team. But the MCC & Counties curtailed the evolutionary process in 2003 and have since consolidated their position. The net effect of the MacLaurin reforms was to bolt a professional England team management structure to unreconstructed Victorian foundations.

For the last twenty years, then, England has slowly been copying the Australian system with a time lag of between 15 and 20 years. The last three of the 16 Aussie innovations, together with free-to-air television, are the four major remaining differences between the two

## TABLE 4: DEVELOPMENTS 1972–2007[1]

| Difference | Aus | Eng | Difference | Category |
|---|---|---|---|---|
| Team on subscription TV only | - | **2006** | 1 year + | Access (5) |
| Five-or-six-team second tier | 1892 | - | 115 years + | Success |
| National player contracts | 1977 | 2000 | 23 years | Success |
| Four-day second-tier cricket | 1892 (1) | 1993 | 101 years | Success |
| 80,000-seat stadium | 1937 (2) | - | 70 years + | Access |
| Professional coach | 1986 | 1987 | 1 year | Success |
| Captaincy as job | 1986 | 2000 | 14 years | Success |
| National Academy | 1988 | 2001 | 13 years | Success |
| Sunday play in Tests | 1977 | 1991 (4) | 14 years | Access |
| National U19 competition | 1969 | - | 38 years + | Success |
| Admission of women by MCC | 1984 | 1997 | 13 years | Access |
| Floodlit evening cricket | 1977 | 1997 | 20 years | Domestic |
| T20 domestic tournament | 2005 | **2003** | 2 years | Domestic |
| Adverts between overs | 1977 | 1999 | 22 years | Finance |
| First-class player contracts | 1996 | **1963 (3)** | 33 years | Domestic |
| 2-tour format | 1977 | 2000 | 23 years | Access |
| White ball & coloured clothing | 1977 | 1992 | 15 years | Access |
| Fielding circle | 1978 | 1993 | 15 years | Access |
| Two divisions in second tier | n/a | **2000** | n/a | Domestic |
| National team song | 1978 | 2003 | 25 years | Access |

countries. In the last few years, external lobbyists have proposed three of them: a big ground, a right-sized second tier and a restoration of free-to-air television. None of these made any progress at all.

The England team today is mostly divorced from its second tier. When injuries strike, the best substitutes are the young elite and not older, trained professionals. This young elite learns the international game while playing for England rather than in the second tier, and has not yet been dulled by the two treadmills. The end result is a weaker England team.

Under the Australian system, substitutes are called up in their prime from a competitive second tier. By contrast, English domestic cricket has not helped the England team. County cricket has, for decades, been a millstone around its neck.

## England fans and our money

Since 1976, the revenues of the England team have grown by a factor of 15 in real terms, equal to 10% a year. Television has led this rise, with fees increasing by 18% per year above inflation. England ticket revenues have increased by 8% a year, and England sponsorship has grown from nothing in 1976 to over £10 million. County revenues, though, have risen by only 6% a year, and have steadily been reduced to irrelevance by England's financial success.

Since the Second World War, television coverage of England's home Tests has made the national side freely accessible to everybody. County cricket, which is largely a vestige of the pre-television era, has been the loser. Why would the average fan physically go to a county match when he or she can watch England at home on the TV simply by flicking a switch and collect beer from a refrigerator a few feet away?

At the end of 2004, the ECB cut off this free access to generate the money necessary to preserve the status quo, and 80% of the audience for England games was instantly disenfranchised. Today, the few million viewing hours annually spent on county Twenty20 cricket are dwarfed by the nearly 200 million England hours lost after 2005.

Grounds, too, are a disaster. The politics surrounding the allocation of England games has led to a proliferating set of small venues.

Resources are wasted keeping ten England and eight other county grounds going, and England games are dispersed instead of concentrated. As a direct result, national seat capacity for fans is lower and ticket prices are higher than they would be if venues were organised to maximise capacity.

It seems that the main purpose of the England team today is to generate profits to sustain a domestic system that has failed as a commercial entertainment proposition and which fails to support the England team cost-effectively. Because a successful England team delivers more profits for the counties, it has therefore made sense for the MCC & Counties to reinvest a few million pounds a year in an elite development system to produce enough success to keep the profits coming.

The bulk of England's profits, however, have been spent to sustain county failure rather than to reinforce the success of the national team and fans' access to it. With the exception of a few short weeks in 2005, this has prevented the virtuous circle of success, access and money from kicking in.

The purpose of a national sports team is to win and to please the entire country, man, woman and child. But the business strategy of the ECB is effectively to deny access to the England cricket team to most fans in order to raise the price paid by richer ones. They now cough up excessive sums for ground and television access that the ECB then gives to county clubs to pay overseas players to play in front of pitiful crowds at county grounds.

Apart from its patent economic absurdity, this strategy is a perversion of the ethic of a national sports team.

## The fundamental problem

The fundamental problem in England cricket is the constitution (Articles of Association) of the England & Wales Cricket Board. Not only does this constitution fail to set England success and access as objectives for the ECB, it doesn't even mention them. Instead, it is a finely-crafted compromise between the five interest groups among the 40 ECB members. Furthermore, the 19 private clubs that make up the MCC & Counties effectively control the ECB through appointments to its Management Board.

Under the constitution, the MCC & Counties are not accountable to anybody except their own members for their business activities. These members, accountable only to themselves, possess the power to control this game without commensurate responsibility.

This constitution and the lack of accountability mean that the ECB is the protector and guardian of county cricket, a Victorian folly that should have been knocked down in the seventies. Over the years since, hundreds of millions of pounds in today's money that might have been used to improve the England team, improve access for fans and support grassroots cricket have been wasted. Never in the history of sport have so many been paid so much to perform so often in front of so few as are today by the 18 counties that for obscure historical reasons have the right to play first-class cricket.

The MCC & Counties use their ECB as a forum to squabble about grounds, players, money and control and as a blame magnet when things go wrong. The language and management techniques of the ECB resemble those of government-run business. Reviews and committees produce political compromises. Official statements are sometimes questionable or incorrect. Executives are given responsibility without power, customers are taken for a ride and muddling through is the *modus operandi*.

## Unfit

In 1977, Kerry Packer was accused of bringing commerce into the hallowed vestries of cricket. But he saw that providing better cricket for more people generated more money for his television company and for the players. Australian cricket is unquestionably the better for the competition, innovation and enhanced access that resulted.

Commerce also entered the England cathedral during World Series Cricket. But the new money from television and advertising & sponsorship merely entrenched the existing Victorian structure. The net effect has been to paste a veneer of faux commercialism on to a core of feudalism and produce an enterprise that is, fundamentally, an old-style unregulated monopoly run in the interests of its members.

Despite these members, the recreational game rolls on as it always has, played by a vast hinterland of cricketers young and old, black, white and brown, male and female, fat and thin. But the England side represents neither this hinterland nor the population of England & Wales because, without universal access and participation in the team's successes and failures, there can be no such representation. Instead, like a Victorian touring side put together by a landed Lord, this team represents only its owners.

There is today a crisis of legitimacy in professional cricket in England & Wales. On overseas tours until 1977, England used to be called *MCC*. Today, a more truthful title for this team than *England* would be *MCC & Counties*. The MCC & Counties, and their ECB, are self-serving, privately-owned organisations that are not fit to run a team called *England*.

## THE OFFICIAL FUTURE 2007–2012

More than ever, cricket is today an integrated global game. Innovations spread and developments make themselves felt more quickly than in the seventies. The future of professional cricket in England depends to some extent on international as well as local factors.

### International challenges

The future of the game globally is of course uncertain. However, three issues are particularly relevant to England.

The first is a budding economic giant, India. To some extent, success in international sport is correlated with the size of a country's economy. At the Olympics, for instance, the three biggest medal winners are the world's three biggest economies. In descending order, they are: the European Union, the United States and China. The two deviations from this correlation in the Olympics—India (down) and Australia (up)—result from cultural, historical and managerial factors.

Economic size, culture and history all favour India in the game of cricket to the extent that it now leads the game commercially and is always strong on the field. Should this country ever gets its cricket management in order and fill the gap between its national side and recreational cricket with a domestic structure based on the logic that suggests five or six professional domestic teams, then it could potentially dominate the game to an even greater degree than Australia has since 1999.

The same goes to a lesser extent for the two other large-population, cricket-mad countries in Asia, Pakistan and Bangladesh. Should England continue on its present profligate course, it is not hard to envisage a situation in 20 years where the three big Asians dominate the game commercially and they and that highly-organised minnow, Australia, rule the field.

In this scenario, England would be definitively second-division, alone in an Asian world with no Uncle Sam on hand to maintain pretences. How many fans would get up early to watch England getting whacked in Dhaka as they have been in Australia and at the World Cup?

The second issue is the exploitation of cricketers. In large-population countries, a national cricket team and its stadiums can be run for a lot less than is generated from television rights, ticket receipts and sponsorship & advertising. Consequently, the principal teams today seem to be giant cash tills from which their governing bodies are unable to prise their paws. The more this goes on, the quicker leading players will get rich and knackered and hence less willing and less able to remain on the international treadmill.

Who gets these profits? In England, the MCC & Counties take most of them. In Australia, they are divided between the national players and the six states, which then fund state and grassroots cricket. In India, the top players are rich but it is not clear where all the money goes.

In sport, though, the players are the product and the governing bodies and the television companies are mere clerks that mine, organise and exploit talent. The system for doing this, perfected in Australia in the last 20 years, is easy to operate once politics, muddle and compromise are shunted aside. There is not a lot to prevent players banding together and demanding greater control of the incumbent clerks, or even hiring their own.

It is perfectly possible that a group of international players could retire early with a couple of million in the bank each and set up their own circuit. Because they would keep a much higher proportion of the income generated, they could cut their playing time by half and still make more than if they stayed on the treadmill.

The third challenge is Twenty20 (T20). Originally invented to reduce the losses of English county cricket, this form of the game has obvious potential to increase the audience appeal of second-tier cricket around the world, not least in India. There, and in the West Indies, the failure of the governing body to create a domestic competition has left openings that entrepreneurs are now trying to exploit.

National governing bodies without domestic T20 competitions are likely to create them quickly, and there may also be an international second-tier competition under the auspices of the ICC. Some countries, especially England, may be tempted to expand domestic T20 competitions dramatically in order to reduce financial losses.

At international level, T20 is destabilising the settled Test-and-ODI equilibrium that evolved in the decade after World Series Cricket. The average international tour programme of three Tests and five One-Day Internationals is likely to evolve, perhaps to two Tests, three One-Day Internationals and five T20s.

So far, the format looks likely to be financially successful, and if it reduces the volume of Tests and One-Day Internationals then it may also reduce injury and burn-out, especially if different players are used for each of the three formats. With a fair wind, the overall effect of T20 will be to refresh the two existing forms of the game, just as one-day cricket refreshed Tests back in the eighties.

Finally, a combination of the three challenges of India, exploitation and Twenty20 could produce a single, mighty challenge to the entire global game.

## Future England success

Because the success of the England team is necessary to generate cash for the MCC & Counties, the immediate future looks reasonably good if one puts aside the second-tier problem. For Test cricket, it has a strong first-choice pace combination as well as Monty Panesar, and a squad of batsmen all averaging over 40. On paper, this side is good enough to win all its home series and to compete strongly against India, Pakistan and Australia away. The problem, as always, is bowler injuries and bowling back-up.

Between January 2008 and June 2009 Australia will play about 15 Tests. In theory, this is enough to develop two bowlers to supplement Stuart Clark, Brett Lee and Stuart MacGill. In this case, Australia will be strongly competitive in the 2009 Ashes. But if England can field its strongest side then we could be in for another classic series. If it cannot field that side then it will come second.

England's one-day and Twenty20 teams are likely to continue to suffer from player drop-outs in response to the intensive schedule, the small number of contracted players, the poor second-tier system, and from the country's preference for Test cricket.

## Future England access

Significantly improved access to the England team would require a dramatic change in ECB priorities. But the abolition of the First Class Forum in 2005 and the granting of independence to the ECB executive mean that the MCC & Counties are likely to employ safe Chairmen and Chief Executives so that county cricket remains first on the priority list. Access is therefore likely to remain a distant fourth.

Two things are certain for the 2009 Ashes. The series will be played in small, packed grounds dotted around England and Wales and will be screened on Sky to an average live audience about a quarter of the average 2.1 million that watched the 2005 series. The face-value of public tickets in London may reach £100 and who-knows-what on the secondary market. There may be continuous complaints in the media and perhaps a renewed campaign by *Keep Cricket Free*.

Ground disputes are likely to continue as minor major counties strive to obtain England games to make money and to cement their role in the professional game. The crunch is whether the MCC can retain two Tests at Lord's in the face of political pressure from the owners of the other eight Test grounds. In this environment, any proposal for a bigger non-county stadium will continue to have little chance of success. England's grounds are instead likely to expand by a couple of thousand here, a couple of thousand there, into the indefinite future, as increasing ticket prices justify small capacity enhancements at grounds with between one and seven big days a year.

The next set of England television rights covers the years from 2010 and is due on sale in 2008. In the absence of a government review of the listing regime, the ECB is likely to enjoy the same free hand as it did for the 2006–2009 rights. If so, the set of bidders could include the BBC, any advertising-only channel that goes out on both Digital

Terrestrial Television (the set-top box) and BSkyB's satellite, and BSkyB itself.

BSkyB should be able to outbid the advertising-only channels because it collects revenue from both advertising and subscriptions. The BBC is unlikely to be able to outbid BSkyB given the many demands on the licence fee, and a new channel using the same model as BSkyB, such as Setanta, will start with zero subscriptions versus Sky Sports' likely six million at that date.

Television rights, then, will probably go to BSkyB again. Moreover, its position is so strong that it could drop its bid from the current £52 million per year and still trump any rival, prompting one official to tell me that the situation is looking 'a little precarious'. However, the ECB and BSkyB both seem to want each other, and the election of Giles Clarke as Chairman of the ECB in October 2007 may lead rapidly to a new deal that secures the future of county cricket beyond 2009.

If BSkyB does win again, then the number of fans will surely fall and England cricket will find out in the 2020s just how powerful the Inspiration Effect was between 1938 and 2005. With small stadiums, limited TV coverage and the Lord's Effect all working in tandem, this game could end up as an expensive indulgence for the upper middle classes in London and the shires, like the opera.

That may have been the idea all along.

## Future England finance

The England team has enjoyed a long boom in television, ticket and sponsorship & advertising revenues, resulting in 10% annual revenue growth after inflation. A continuation of this growth rate would require television rights for 2010 onwards to go for around £85 million per year, up from £52 million today. In the absence of a credible rival to BSkyB, this seems highly unlikely and, unless there is a boom in another area, the game may be nearing the end of the growth road.

The most likely boom area is the domestic Twenty20 (T20) competition. Each T20 game generates revenues of about £100,000, roughly equivalent to eight days of the County Championship, so the temptation to substitute T20 for large parts of the current fixture list must be strong.

For instance, a 50% reduction in the first-class programme to 32 days (two divisions of nine playing each other once) would allow an increase in T20 days from 10 to 34 (18 counties playing each other home and away). All the T20 games would be played in the two months beginning in mid-June, and first-class cricket would be played at each end of the season.

Home T20 games for each county would rise from five to 17. Average crowds would fall, perhaps by as much as half, but would still be far greater than at County Championship matches. The effect would be to improve each county's revenues and profits (costs would hardly change) by perhaps £350,000[2], about a quarter of the annual support currently provided from England profits.

Any critic who complained that the reduction in the first-class programme damaged the counties' support of the England Test team could be told that Australian states only play 10 first-class matches and their Test team is pretty good. This reasoning would contradict previous lines of argument, but that's business.

Should a financial crisis occur, there is also substantial room for cuts according to the priority order that places county cricket at the top. £5 million can be lopped off grassroots spending and payments to the ECB charity can be cut from £8 million down to zero. A Team England pay cut of 30% would save £1 million and county pay cuts of 30% would save £6 million. These amount to cuts of £20 million without threatening the existence of any counties and, together with the £6 million from more T20 cricket, provide an effective buffer of £26 million or thereabouts.

## More of the same

This is a large buffer. County cricket as presently constituted, therefore, is vulnerable only if BSkyB drops its bid dramatically. But the official mentioned above thinks that BSkyB will 'act responsibly'. As for T20, even though it is merely the latest and possibly last adrenaline shot into the groaning corpse of England domestic cricket, there is a quite a lot of adrenaline left in the syringe.

It looks, then, as if the financial crisis predicted by Ian MacLaurin will not now occur. Under present management, county cricket is completely safe and the ancient business model of England cricket will persist for another decade at least.

Unless England learns from its history, it is doomed to repeat it. One commercially-successful team will continue to carry 18 failures. Up will follow down will follow up, the players and the fans will be milked for cash, bowlers will fall like skittles and the Aussies will march on.

From the foot of the Himalayas, three teams representing over 1.6 billion people are only just setting out.

## AN ALTERNATIVE FUTURE

Imagine that our game is one day run in the public interest. What would that look like? I went to see a cricket official to ask him what he would do. He was reticent but, after some prodding, this experienced and decent man came out with the following, in no particular order:

1) Subordinate everything to the national team.
2) Do more to make the county game subservient.
3) Restore free-to-air television.

On the subject of free-to-air television, he said, 'This is hugely important. We are in a very unhealthy situation.'

# Public-interest objectives

In any conceivable set of public-interest objectives, the England team and access to it come at the top because England enjoyed 90% market share when all fans could watch it live on the television. Grassroots cricket features in the list because nearly one million adults and several hundred thousand under-16s play the game. On the other hand, county cricket is subservient because it had 10% market share. This gives:

1)   Ensure the success of the England side
2=) Ensure access for the public to the England side
2=) Support grassroots cricket

This priority order is the one operated in Australia. Second-tier cricket does not feature because it cannot at any scale pay more than half of its costs. Its only purpose, therefore, is to assist with objective one. Also, the *Inspiration Effect* can more efficiently be generated by exposing large numbers of youngsters to the recreational game (2=), to the England team (2=), and by creating national cricket heroes (1), than by persuading relatively small numbers of them to attend second-tier games, even if they are Twenty20.

This order is not perfect, however. A conflict between funding grassroots cricket and ensuring access on free-to-air television, as cited by the ECB in 2005, could theoretically arise even in the absence of the huge dividend paid to county cricket.

However, this conflict has not happened in Australia. England has a population two-and-a-half times bigger and correspondingly greater television and sponsorship & advertising revenues but the same number of national teams. It should easily be able to generate a sufficient surplus from its team to fund the second pair of objectives adequately and avoid conflict between them. In 2005, with Test cricket still on free-to-air television, that surplus was £42 million.

# A strategy

At the moment, success is in moderate shape and access is awful, so the strategic emphasis must therefore be on access. The first and most important task is to restore England cricket to free-to-air television. The second is to buy the television rights for England's away games from the host country and put them on free-to-air television too. The third is to build up the main England venues to allow many more fans direct exposure to their team.

Restoring free-to-air television for Tests could mean a reduction in cricket revenue of about £20 million per year, using the difference between the bids for the 2006–2009 rights as a guide. Given the failure of the ECB negotiators to coax BSkyB into paying as much per day for 2006–2009 as it had for 2003–2005, this sum is likely to be an over-estimate. However, it acts as a ceiling on the cost of a restoration of free-to-air television. For overseas England games, the rights are likely to cost around £5 million a year but would be sold on for perhaps £3 million. To accomplish these two goals, the game therefore has to find a maximum of £22 million.

The three sources for this are the funding of the England team, the funding for grassroots cricket, or the £29 million loss incurred in the domestic game. The first two are out because they are top in the priority order. On the other hand, the domestic game is far bigger than it needs to be to support England and is not a public-interest priority.

The Cricket Reform Group proposed three leagues of six teams, made up of 18 associations based on the current first-class counties with the minor counties folded in. This proposal was explicitly designed to support success only and, by maintaining 18 first-class grounds and 18 professional sides, it would not have saved anywhere near the £20 million required to get England back on to free-to-air television.

A cut in the number of second-tier teams from 18 to five would reduce domestic cricket losses by £23 million[3], and further cuts in player salaries and in the number of games would save another £1 million. These steps would reduce losses in the second-tier system to about £5 million. By comparison, the six states in Australia lost $20 million (about £8 million) in 2006 on their cricket operations.

This step would help with England success, as identified by the Cricket Reform Group. The higher standard of cricket would close the gap between the domestic and international game and provide a better-prepared reservoir of players for England. It would also provide the final component of the elite youth conveyor belt.

The 47 days in the England home calendar, and the 80–90 in the annual calendar, are too much under the existing system. However, a stronger elite youth conveyor belt and stronger second tier should in time provide the squad of 25 players required to rest tired players. The overall unavailability rate should also improve from today's alarming level, even counting players on their break, because of reduced injuries, burn-out and fatigue.

This cut in the number of domestic teams would reduce the number of England venues to five. England games would then be concentrated into fewer grounds and those grounds expanded to improve access to the game still further.

## Four-level pyramid

These changes would help achieve the success and access objectives but would also require a re-jig of the England pyramid. At present, this consists of one England team, the 18 counties and about 500 elite clubs. The size ratio between each layer is high at 18 (counties per national team) and 27 (elite clubs per county team). Hence the large standard gap between layers.

The five[4] second-tier teams must cover the entire area of England & Wales and should therefore be regional. The most obvious regions are London & Southeast, Wales & Southwest, Midlands, Northwest and Northeast. The four grounds outside London would be Cardiff, Edgbaston, Old Trafford and Riverside (Durham). All other first-class grounds would be cut to save money and to allow the expansion of the remaining grounds, at no cost to most fans in terms of travel time. Those who currently go to games in London would still do so. Trent Bridge customers would go to Edgbaston and Headingley fans to Old Trafford.

Although the teams would be regional, their identities could be a mixture of regional and city. A title like 'Birmingham and Midlands Cricket Association', or 'Birmingham' for short, would be both definitive and marketable. The teams would maintain an even standard through player transfers, to a greater extent than the counties do today.

The five would play each other both home and away (eight games) in each of the three forms of the game. Finals for each of the three tournaments, and two full-strength four-day games against touring sides, would make between 55 and 60 days for each team. This is the quantity of cricket that successive ECB reviews have stipulated and would allow for the necessary recovery, practice and review between games demanded by countless players and commentators.

The teams would play a better standard of cricket that should, in time, prove more attractive to the paying customer. All games would be played in Test grounds with at least 20,000 seats situated in major cities, and it is reasonable to expect the average audience for these games to double from today's level, although crowds would still be far too small to turn these teams into commercial propositions.

All 100 professional players in the second tier would be learning how to be England cricketers, practising to become one, or passing on experience to younger players, and there would be no journeyman cricketers eking out a life as a professional sportsman. To enable control over the number of overseas players, all professional cricketers would have to be contracted to the governing body. Each of the five sides could employ one outstanding former overseas Test cricketer as a player or player / coach and one young overseas cricketer under reciprocal arrangements with other national boards.

The next level would be the existing 38 counties, playing on the same amateur basis that minor counties do today. If the 38 were divided into five regions, then each county could play the others in its region in one three-day game and one one-day game, with finals, for about 30 days per county. If all games started on a Sunday, players would have to take about three weeks off work to play the entire schedule.

The county structure would provide cricket about the same standard as Australian first grade, and would constitute the bridge between club and professional cricket that is presently lacking and which the ECB has spent years trying and failing to erect. It would cost about £2 million (£50,000 per county) and provide historical continuity with the present structure.

In all, this new pyramid would have four levels versus the present three. There would be one England team, five regions in the second tier, 38 counties in the third tier and 500 elite clubs in the fourth. The size ratio between each successive level is five (i.e. five regions to one England), seven (38 counties to five regions) and 13. This renovated pyramid, with one more level and smaller gaps, would be considerably smoother than the present structure.

Under this architecture, elite youth development would be carried out by clubs and by county youth teams up to the age of 17 or so. Regional Under- 15, 17 and 19 teams would support the corresponding England teams and five academies would prepare the best young cricketers for the professional game.

Finally, touring teams would play strong domestic teams rather than county Second XIs. An England Second XI would play local Associate ICC members such as Scotland, Ireland and the

Netherlands and help these countries improve. England would, at last, become a good cricket citizen.

## Grounds

The 47 England days could be divided between the five cities roughly on the basis of the population served by each one. London gets 18 days (the same as now), Manchester and Birmingham 12 apiece, Durham two days and Cardiff three. The heavy allocation to Manchester and Birmingham would allow these grounds to be increased to 40,000[5] seats each. Durham and Cardiff would be out-grounds with 20,000 seats.

London is tricky because, like all cities, it needs just one stadium but already has the world-famous but medium-sized and exclusive Lord's Cricket Ground. The capacity- and revenue- maximising strategy for London[6] would be to scrap both Lord's and the Oval and build a new National Stadium. A compromise strategy that also increases revenue and capacity sharply, but which maintains historical continuity, is to expand Lord's to 60,000 and lose the Oval.

England has a superb bargaining position with the MCC because, without England games, as one official put it, 'Lord's is a nice bit of ground in St John's Wood'. The basis of a deal with the MCC could be the increased volume of England games for its members. In exchange, the MCC would be asked to consign the *Lord's Effect* to the dustbin of history. This would entail an expansion of the membership, a two-sex children's section, the admission of at least 5,000 women and short-term ethnic minority quotas. These measures amount to social engineering but are justified by decades of drift in the other direction by an organisation that has called itself 'a private club with a public role'. If cricket is to be run in the public interest, then the public interest has to hold sway at the country's biggest ground.

If the members of the MCC or the local authority were unwilling to permit this expansion or tolerate the conditions that went with it, or the single London Underground line were unable to cope with the crowds, then Lord's should be replaced by a National Stadium.

Retaining the Oval only makes sense if, in the absence of Lord's, it becomes that National Stadium. However, the 2012 stadium, depending on availability and design, would be the better option for reasons of finance and location. This facility would make £1.2 million profit a day for the seventh and subsequent England days and is located at what will be one of the best connected places in Europe.

This leaves either an expanded Lord's or a new National Stadium. As Arsenal has done in North London, the history and memories of the Oval, including the Ashes, must be bottled up and transferred either to Lord's or to a new, bigger ground.

Under the strategy that retained and expanded Lord's, total seating capacity[7] would more than double to over two million and £11 million more profit would be generated. This would allow the England team to be marketed at last to its entire audience, including children, ethnic minorities and women, and capacity in England & Wales would rise from 19 to 41 seats per thousand population. Remarkably, this is still only 44% of the 93 per thousand in Australia today.

This strategy has one apparent downside. The 30% of cricket fans located in the East Midlands, on the South Coast or in Yorkshire would be an average of 45 minutes further away from the nearest England ground than they are today. The other 70% of fans would be unaffected. However, this 30% would trade increased distance for restored free-to-air television access and a higher chance of getting tickets. They would still be better off than they are today.

There are, therefore, no losers apart from a small minority of fans who would prefer to watch one of the 13 demoted counties instead of their national team. For each of these losers, at least 40 other fans gain.

# Summary of public-interest measures

These seven measures amount to a long-overdue rationalisation of the England professional game in the interests of the fans. Table 5 summarises how each measure generates increased national team success, access and finance.

The measures transform the England team into an operation that serves the public interest. The net financial effect on the game is to increase its profits by about £10 million. This money can be used to increase funding for the grassroots game from its current level (whatever that is), or it can be used to fund the transition between the current structure and this new one.

The opportunity exists to improve the success of the England team, make it more accessible to fans, and make more money for grassroots. It is the mirror image of the insanity of maintaining county cricket in its present state and is easily the biggest business and customer opportunity in British professional sport today. It is probably the biggest such opportunity that there has ever been in this country.

### TABLE 5: RESTRUCTURING OF ENGLAND CRICKET

| Measure | Success | Access | Finance |
|---------|---------|--------|---------|
| Five regions | Bridge county-country gap | None | +£24m |
| Five grounds | Increase Inspiration Effect | × two | +£11m |
| England home free TV | Increase Inspiration Effect | × five | –£20m |
| 25 contracted players | Reduce injury rate | None | –£1m |
| Youth teams | Improve elite development | None | £0 |
| England away free TV | Increased Inspiration Effect | × five | –£2m |
| Amateur counties | Bridge club-professional gap | None | –£2m |

## Action in the public interest

Rather inconveniently, and probably not by accident, the ECB executive is prevented from implementing this agenda by various clauses in the ECB Articles of Association that protect the interests of the minor major counties. Any person who wishes to carry the agenda forward must therefore circumvent the ECB or take control of it. Control requires a vote by 30 of the 40 members to insert the new priority order into the ECB Articles of Association and remove the protective clauses.

These measures are not as detrimental to the interests of the MCC & Counties, and the minor counties, as they may appear. Five major counties form the basis of the regional associations and four of those, along with the MCC, get more England days at their ground. The 20 minor counties become a part of the cricket pyramid rather than stranded dangling outliers, and the Minor Counties Cricket Association gains because of the increased status of its members. This makes 27 ECB members.

However, the other 13 major counties are downgraded to the amateur third tier of England cricket and their grounds are no longer visited by England. Although the return of free-to-air television and an offer of free membership of the nearest of the five associations would be compelling, they would be unlikely to secure the acquiescence of a sufficient number of the 60,000 members of these 13 counties.

Assuming that all ECB members vote according to their interests, the score is 27–13, which is not quite enough to take control of the ECB. The 13 counties constitute, therefore, a blocking minority that must be removed from the equation if this agenda is to proceed. Once removed, these counties keep their grounds, and what they then do with them is their business.

# Government mitigation measures

There are three ways that the effects of this blocking minority can be mitigated and four ways that it can be removed altogether. All of these require intervention by an outside party acting either in the public interest or out of self-interest but in a manner that also delivers public benefits.

The mitigation measures are: listing; rights-splitting; an investigation by the Office of Fair Trading (OFT). All three of these require government action in the public interest. The removal methods are: government regulation; nationalisation; a friendly takeover; a hostile takeover. The first pair involves government and the second pair an external business. All four would compensate the 60,000 members of the 13 downgraded counties for the loss of property.

Government measures would be appropriate because the England cricket team, like all national teams, is by definition a monopoly business that faces no competition. In 2005, this monopoly made an operating profit of about £42 million on revenues of £95 million. County cricket, on the other hand, lost £29 million on cricket revenues of £24 million. The vast ECB payments (£23 million in 2005) to its member counties to make up this deficit are only possible because the England team is a monopoly.

There is a further distinction in the definition of a monopoly governed by the destination of its profits. In essence, the England team is either a malign monopoly that pays a dividend to its shareholders or it is a benign monopoly run in the public interest that recycles its profits to further that interest.

A malign monopoly tends to abuse its customers with high prices and restrictive terms of access in order to maximise profits and hence shareholder dividends. Benign monopolies tend not to do this because they act in the public interest. Populations employ governments to serve their interests, one of which is to control malign monopolies, so governments in well-run countries tend to take a hard line against this type of monopoly.

Cricket executives could argue that the England team is a benign monopoly whose profits are recycled into cricket, rather than handed out to shareholders, and that the whole game is therefore a public-interest business. Despite this argument, action by government could be undertaken on an argument that 18 of the 19 controlling members of the ECB are effectively receiving a shareholder dividend in the form of support for county cricket, a separate product for a separate market, making the England team a malign monopoly.

The first of the three mitigation measures, the television listing system, is supposed to ensure access via free-to-air television for important sports events. But England cricket has already been through this process and out the other side, thanks to the successful argument that the public interest required the extra cash from subscription television to fund the England team and grassroots cricket.

The UK government could also interfere directly in the sale of television rights to ensure that multiple broadcasters secured them. The football Premier League was forced by the European Commission (EC) in the last few years to divide its television rights into pieces and ensure that more than one broadcaster won a piece in the latest auction in 2006.

This resulted in a new entrant, Setanta Sports, winning two chunks and BSkyB the other four. But, not surprisingly, the enforcement of competition among television firms by the EC resulted in higher revenue for the Premier League. It negotiated fees 65% greater than those secured in the previous BSkyB deal three years before.

This rights-splitting approach appears to be a failure because monopoly control over access to the one national side, or to a set of football teams that negotiate collectively, is unaffected and may even be reinforced by a government-mandated split of TV rights. Nonetheless, there is a possibility that either the UK government or the EC could attempt to force the ECB to break up its television rights in a similar fashion. New entrants would be attracted, there would probably be a further increase in prices, England profits and hence the counties' dividend would rise, but the number of subscribing fans would fall.

A successful approach to the problem of national sports team monopoly must involve more direct control of prices and the terms by which fans access their team. This leads to a third mitigation approach, which has never been tried in UK sport.

In UK and European law, the abuse of a dominant position in a market is prohibited by Chapter II of the Competition Act 1998 and by Article 82 of the European Community Treaty. An organisation has to be both dominant and to abuse its position for these rules to apply. The European Court has defined a dominant market position as:

> *A position of economic strength enjoyed by an undertaking which enables it to prevent effective competition being maintained on the relevant market by affording it the power to behave to an appreciable extent independently of its competitors, customers and ultimately of its consumers.*

Abuse can take one of several forms. The two most relevant here are:

> *Directly or indirectly imposing unfair purchase or selling prices or other unfair trading conditions.*

> *Limiting production, markets or technical developments to the prejudice of consumers.*

It appears that the ECB has a position of economic strength as far as the England team is concerned. It could further be contended that the ECB is afforded the power to behave independently of its customers in the market for access to the England cricket team and that it has both indirectly imposed unfair purchase or selling prices and limited production to the prejudice of consumers.

An analysis could be mounted by the Office of Fair Trading (OFT). If evidence of dominance and abuse were found, the OFT would then refer the matter to the Competition Commission for a full investigation.

The outcome of such an investigation could be positive for fans of the England cricket team.

## Removing the blocking minority

These mitigation measures are no more than fingers in the dyke. The MCC & Counties would retain overall control of the game and could attempt to stay one step ahead of the government. The job at hand is to remove the blocking minority and operate the game in the public interest.

The first option is the establishment of an independent economic regulator for UK sport. The water, electricity, power generation, gas, rail and communications industries all exhibit monopoly economics, and each is regulated by an independent regulator authorised by Act of Parliament.

The absence of a sports regulator has been particularly glaring in the case of English football. It has been the European Commission, and not the UK government, that has forced the Premier League to divide its television rights into packages and sell them to a number of different broadcasters. In cricket, too, the lack of a sports regulator became critical during the Parliamentary inquiry into the ECB's deal with BSkyB, when Members of Parliament appeared to have had little if any assistance with the constitution and economics of the game and the deal was allowed to pass even though it was flagrantly against the public interest.

A sports regulator would be likely to establish that England cricket is charging the fans of the national team excessive prices to subsidise a loss-making county circuit that does not cost-effectively support the England team. If a gas company produced three times as much gas as consumers required and flared the excess, or a water company processed three times as much water as its customers needed and poured the surplus into the North Sea, the relevant regulator would be unlikely to permit the utility to charge its customers the cost of running this redundant capacity.

The usual course for a regulator in these circumstances would be to set England team revenues at a level that paid its costs on the assumption that those costs were spent efficiently. The regulator would be likely therefore to cut the fees paid to county cricket. This situation, similar to that envisaged by Ian MacLaurin when he speculated about a fall in the value of television rights from 2006 onwards, would generate a wave of mergers in which the major major counties would buy out the others. The distribution of grounds may not be as geographically equitable as in the agenda described above, but the number would fall.

The second way to remove the blocking minority is for the government to nationalise the game and inject it into a trust that operated it in the public interest. This trust would effectively be a new ECB with a constitution that set England success and access and supporting the grassroots as the game's three objectives. The trustees would be a mixture of ex-captains, fans from the world of commerce and the usual members of The Great and The Good.

This nationalisation would require the government to compensate the 60,000 members of the 13 downgraded clubs for expropriating their property. A payment of £1,000 to each member, for instance, produces a bill of £60 million. The government could then levy interest at 6% from the trust to produce £4 million a year and render the nationalisation self-financing. The trust, £10 million better off after implementing the agenda, would still have £6 million more per year than the game does now to feed into grassroots cricket and to build up a reserve.

The third possibility is a friendly takeover by an external party. An entrepreneur could do a deal with the MCC and the five counties and then offer £60 million to the members of the other 13 clubs if they agreed to fall in with the agenda and vote his way at the ECB. A payment of £500,000 to each of the 20 minor counties, plus the prospect of a fuller and more equitable role for them within the association structure, should be sufficient to secure their acquiescence. The total cost would be £70 million.

Depending on how he structures the relationship with the MCC and the new associations, this entrepreneur could keep some of the extra £10 million a year to generate a return on his £70 million and to compensate him for his time and effort. Like Kerry Packer, this individual could retain an interest in the game through the ownership of a ground or by awarding himself the television rights. He could also appoint himself Chairman of the Board of Trustees in order to safeguard the new structure against unenlightened seekers of a restoration of the *status ante quem*.

The fourth and last scenario is a takeover of the game by an entrepreneur without the cooperation of the MCC & Counties. This would require the entrepreneur to grab one of the game's key assets and use it to drive the official game into the ground.

In cricket, as in all professional sports, the big assets are the players, the grounds and the television rights. Kerry Packer wanted the television rights, co-opted the leading players as willing hostages and cobbled together a set of grounds. Once the ACB and the ICC accepted that their least-bad option was to grant Packer his beloved television rights, they caved in.

Packer found that the easiest asset to obtain is the players. That remains the case today because players, unlike grounds and television rights, can walk. An offer to the top 25 players in England

& Wales of double their present salaries, guaranteed for three years, may secure enough of them to constitute a player grab and would cost about £30 million. They could be put to work coaching and playing exhibition games while negotiations took place. They certainly need a break.

Like the ACB in 1977/78 and 1978/79, the ECB would be forced to field a third XI. The team would be thrashed, audiences would collapse and there would be some tight games with Bangladesh a few years earlier than is currently likely. The ECB and the counties have few financial reserves, like the ACB and the state associations back then, because they have spent their money keeping the county circuit afloat all these years. Official cricket would probably last a matter of months before collapsing and, in these circumstances, an offer of £60 million for 13 counties would seem like a gift. The entrepreneur would then be able to use his players productively and recoup some of his upfront player purchase costs.

A hostile takeover could therefore be mounted for about £90 million plus the cost of the obligatory court cases. For most of the 97% of serious fans who are not members of the 13 counties, and probably some of them too, the public relations battle would be the off-field equivalent of the last day of the 2005 Ashes series.

Two worlds would thud together in an epic collision and there could only be one winner. The whole country.

## Tradition

This programme of measures entails the loss of three historic Test grounds at Headingley, Trent Bridge and the Oval and the reduction in status of 13 teams that have played first-class cricket in some cases since 1864. Looking at the situation rationally, these sacrifices are overwhelmingly justified by the restoration of free-to-air television to a cricket public that has clearly indicated that it wants to watch England and not the counties, by the increases in capacity at surviving grounds and by the construction of a pyramid and in particular a second tier that maximises our chances against the Aussies and others in the years ahead.

But anybody, whether it is a government regulator, the government itself or an entrepreneur, who tries to drive forward this agenda would be bound to run into the argument that county cricket and these three Test venues are 'traditional'. The animosity against Packer of a generation ago would be magnified 100-fold, the media would quickly fill up with the ululations of famous ex-players from the downgraded counties, and dusty old *Wisdens* detailing great games at the Oval and Headingley would be liberated from the shelves of many an harrumphing editorialist.

Two cricketers have addressed themselves to this problem. One, Mickey Stewart, said in 1966:

> *Cricket is based on tradition, and I personally am a lover of tradition, but if the game suffers because of tradition then tradition must go.*

Justin Langer, when imagining a merger of Middlesex and Surrey, wrote:

> *Tradition matters and, while the thought of Middlesex and Surrey merging may be met with scepticism and a sentimental heart in the short-term, there is no reason why new traditions cannot be formed. Like planting a seed, the merging of counties could grow into a beautiful flower. Not only would it produce more attractive county games but it would be the catalyst to rejuvenating English cricket overall.*

Tradition is not by itself a sufficient reason for continuing with the status quo in any field of life. Those invoking tradition like the status quo because it reminds them of times gone by in their own lives and support the status quo simply because it exists. By appealing to tradition, they generate the appearance of an argument without any of the essential components of argument, such as reason and evidence, and manufacture a meretricious wrapping of principle for what is actually a combination of circular reasoning and plain self-interest.

Michael Parkinson, for all his eloquence, did not have it quite right. Self-interest cannot masquerade as tradition because tradition, once the circular reasoning has been stripped away, is self-interest. It is this self-interest that has got England cricket into its present situation.

## Best outcome

The proposal that 13 counties be bought out and the game restructured around the remaining five and the MCC is simple. But it is also risky.

The regulatory scenario is an indirect way of achieving the required outcome. There is a risk that cost cuts would be driven by the current ECB order of priority rather than by the public interest. It would be unwise to underestimate the further damage that the MCC & Counties could do to the public interest if cost cuts were enforced by a regulator but they were still free to organise the England team.

The nationalisation scenario depends on the competence of the Department of Culture, Media and Sport. But it was this department whose ministers parroted various claims made by the ECB about the game's finances and which had a hand in the Wembley and 2012 Olympics stadiums. Also, 18 county clubs feuding over the allocation of England games and England profits is quite enough without government inserting its priorities too. One can imagine the game becoming the plaything of a new set of conflicting and vested interests.

The entrepreneur scenario depends on an alignment of interest between the entrepreneur and the public. But, once he has his hands on the game, an entrepreneur may be tempted to implement the whole agenda except for the part relating to free-to-air television, especially if he has had to spend a fortune locking up the England players and waiting for the official game to fold.

The fans would be better off than now—how could we not be?—because of the measures to enhance the success of the England team and to expand grounds. But the agenda would be incomplete and England would be as unlikely as it is now ever to return to free-to-air television.

The best outcome for this game is a combination of the money, drive and ingenuity of an entrepreneur and the concern of government for the public interest. The entrepreneur's job is to get rid of the feudalism in England cricket and effect the transition to modern, customer-centred capitalism. The government's job is to ensure that the entrepreneur does not simply replace a feudal monopoly with a capitalist one.

I advocate a friendly takeover of the 13 counties co-ordinated by an external investor with the co-operation of the MCC, the other five counties and the 20 minor counties. This group would take control of the ECB, alter its Articles of Association to emphasise success, access and grassroots and hire new management to drive through the seven measures. To prevent the new owners from perpetuating existing monopoly practices, a statutory sports regulator is also required to protect the public interest.

Under this hybrid scenario, the cricket public wins big, the investor makes a little money and the public interest is safeguarded for the future. England cricket would at last be liberated from the shackles of its historical structure and our team would at last break out of the centripetal grip of mediocrity.

## Back to The Home of Cricket

Sitting at the Melbourne Cricket Ground in December 2002, watching Mark Butcher bowl and hearing the reactions of my Australian neighbours to the sound of the Barmy Army singing, I realised that my neighbours knew that the Aussies are not better than us at cricket. They perceived that they are merely better organised. They saw that if we do organise ourselves as they have done and as the Barmy Army has done then they are going to come second. They sensed that within 10 or 20 years the superior resources available in England & Wales of population, facilities and hard cash could change the balance between England and Australia so that it would be them, and not us, who would have to scrabble for the occasional victory in The Ashes, the best sporting competition on Earth.

So do many Australian cricketers and commentators. Again and again, these Australians have told us what to do. Rod Marsh came over here to lend a hand for four years, and it is hard these days to hear a sentence about England cricket from Ian Chappell that does not include the term 'over-complicated'. On our team, the heroic Bob Willis continues his 26-year marathon stint to this day and was partnered by Mike Atherton in the first years after his retirement.

This model would move our cricket architecture from the nineteenth to the twenty-first century. It is consistent with the three public-interest objectives and is derived from first principles. Not coincidentally, as well, it adapts the successful Australian example for our geography and population size.

But no committee or executive hired to carry out the wishes of the MCC & Counties has the remotest chance of carrying the transition through. Organising England cricket to win and to serve its fans requires an act of supreme will by an external party to give forcible birth to a new MCC and a new set of regional associations. This act cannot be carried out by anybody who is muddled and all at sea, or who is traditional, sophisticated and political.

He, or she—you—must keep your head when all about you are losing theirs and blaming it on you. There will be lies and triumph and disaster. You must make one heap of all your winnings and risk it on one turn of pitch-and-toss, and hold on when there is nothing in you except Will.

A similar revolution of greater scale and impact took place a long time ago in a big, desert country a long way from here. Yet despite the example and the lessons we remain clinging to the flotsam of the past, like deluded children.

That's why they call us: Pommies.

# NOTES

## Chapter 1

### 1.    Grovel

Tony Greig said, 'But when they are down they grovel. And I intend to make them grovel, with the help of Closey and a few others.' When Greig was out in the first innings there was a full-scale pitch invasion. During the West Indies second innings, he went down on his hands and knees and grovelled.

### 2.    Caribbean section

Clive Lloyd later said that the Oval was a home game for the West Indians.

### 3.    Holding

In his biography *Whispering Death* Michael Holding writes:

> *'There is nothing that thrills a fast bowler more than seeing the stumps flying from behind a batsman and at the Oval I hit them nine times. Not only to my own delight but to the unrestrained delight of every West Indian on the ground as well, I clean bowled Tony Greig in both innings.'*

### 4.    Agnew and Lawrence

David Lawrence played five Tests for England, taking 18 wickets at high pace, but his career was wrecked by an injury sustained against New Zealand in 1992. According to the Gloucestershire captain in the early 2000s, Mark Alleyne, 'Dave Lawrence wanted to bowl quick because he saw Michael Holding at the Oval.'

Jonathan Agnew played three Tests for England, taking four wickets including those of Greenidge and Richards. He retired at 30 and went into the media. He mentioned on *Test Match Special* in 2007 that he saw Holding during the 1976 game.

## 5.    Fixture list

The following is a summary of the 2002/03 fixtures in Australia:

| Tournament | Participants | Games |
|---|---|---|
| Tests | Australia v England | 5 |
| VB series | Australia, England & Sri Lanka | 15 |
| England tour | England v Various | 9 |
| Sri Lanka tour | SL v Various | 4 |
| Pura Cup | Six states first-class | 31 |
| ING Cup | Six states one-day | 31 |
| South Africa 'A' | SA 'A' v Various | 7 |

The VB series involved Australia, England and Sri Lanka playing each other four times, with a final of up to three games for the top two sides. Both England and Sri Lanka also played various other tour matches.

Australia 'A' played all three visiting international sides during 2002/03, for a total of three four-day and eight one-day games, giving the selectors the opportunity to keep an eye on their next-best players.

The Pura Cup (four-day) and ING (one-day) inter-state tournaments both involved each state playing the other five both home and away, giving 10 matches in each competition for each state. The four-day and one-day matches between each pair of states were played consecutively to avoid unnecessary travel. Each tournament then had a final between the two top teams.

The season structure had been more or less the same for 25 years.

## 6.    George Orwell

These are the concluding sentences of *Homage to Catalonia* (1938)

# Chapter 2

### 1. Arena

A standard Track & Field layout consists of a 400-metre athletics track with the throwing events and high jump situated inside the track and the remaining jump events outside it.

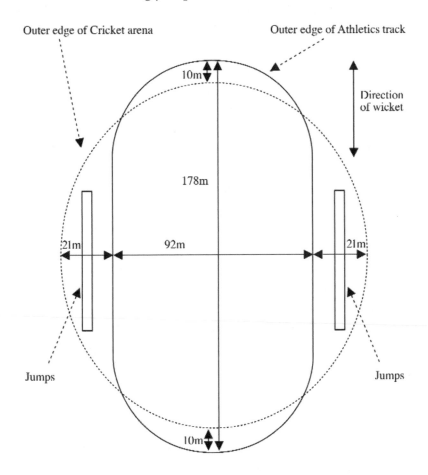

The Track & Field layout is 178 metres long and 134 metres wide. The cricket oval shown is 158 metres long and 134 metres wide. This provides side boundaries of 63 metres (4 metres leeway each side) and straight of 82 metres (7 metres leeway each end).

The Track & Field layout is the same width as for cricket but 20 metres longer. The stand at one end is built down to a height of five metres for Track & Field and filled down and inwards for cricket. The pavilion is built at the other end.

## 2.     Tony Banks

Tony Banks made a difference whenever he popped into the public consciousness. Apart from forcing the MCC finally to admit women to its membership, he memorably described the Tory politician William Hague as a foetus and fought against the culling of Canadian seals.

## 3.     Complexities

The complexities relate to a) playing rectangle sports in oval stadiums and vice-versa b) hybrid stadiums that allow both oval and rectangle sports c) converting an oval stadium to rectangular and d) the UK government's legacy plan for the 2012 stadium.

### a)     Mixing

An oval sport cannot be played in a rectangular stadium because the arena is too narrow by half. A rectangular sport can be played in an oval stadium, but the spectators in the front row are at least 40 metres from the action all around the circumference. Some oval stadiums, notably the 1972 Munich Olympic Stadium, have been used for football notwithstanding this disadvantage. Bayern Munich used this ground, but decamped in 2005 to a new, rectangular facility.

### b)     Hybrid

There are two hybrid forms that accommodate sports of both shapes. Each form is essentially an oval stadium modified to bring some spectators at rectangular events a little closer.

The first, *Stade de France*, is equipped with lower side stands that slide in for rectangular sports and back out for oval. The second, the new Wembley stadium, uses moveable platforms to raise and lower the arena. The lower arena is rectangular, and Wembley was built on the assumption that this setting would dominate. The upper arena is oval. To convert Wembley into an athletics stadium, the operator builds a platform six metres above the football pitch and takes out the first 29 rows of seating in the lower stands, which are built at a low angle to the horizontal to enable greatly expanded width. The seating capacity goes down from 90,000 to 68,000 and, hey presto, there is an athletics stadium.

These two hybrid forms work for rectangular sports, after a fashion. Those in the lower side stands are reasonably close to the action. But 70% of the spectators are in the end stands, which are curved like an athletics track, or in the upper tier of the side stands. These spectators are heavily disadvantaged when watching rectangular sports: people in the first row of the upper tier of the side stands are at least 57 metres from the edge of the playing field at *Stade de France* and 55 metres at Wembley.

Wembley is primarily an athletics and cricket stadium. How that came about is a long story of politics, muddle and compromise. During the design and financing process, various parties wanted to improve the UK's chances of winning a bid for a major athletics event such as the Olympics by building Wembley as a hybrid stadium. In doing so, they damaged its function as a football stadium. But when the UK did actually bid for an athletics event, the 2012 Olympics, it was decided not to use Wembley after all. Instead, another oval stadium would be constructed in East London. The UK won the 2012 Olympics and is now building that other stadium.

And that's not all. See point d).

c)     *Conversion*
There is one further twist: the Manchester solution. This technique permanently converts an oval stadium into a rectangular one by lowering the arena and filling the stands downwards and inwards. The 2002 Commonwealth Games stadium was turned into Manchester City's new ground, with a smaller athletics stadium built anew next door. For the 2012 stadium, though, both Ken

Livingstone and Seb Coe made it known early in the piece that they wanted the original oval stadium to be retained rather than rebuilt next to a football ground. That effectively ruled out the Manchester City option for the 2012 stadium.

*d)      Legacy*

For the new 2012 stadium, the UK government legacy plan from the outset was to cut down the upper stands, reduce the stadium to 25,000 seats and dedicate it to athletics. Franklin and I were curious about why the government wanted to cut the stadium back after the Games. By means of *Yes, Minister*-style winks and nods, we extracted the answer from a government official. Haunted by the spectre of the Millennium Dome, the government evidently decided that it preferred the carcass of a white elephant to a whole white elephant.

London needs two national sports stadiums: a rectangular ground for football and rugby and an oval for cricket and the occasional major Track & Field event. It currently has four, with a fifth under development: one big rectangular stadium for rugby (Twickenham), one big oval stadium for football (Wembley) and two smallish ovals (Lord's and the Oval) for cricket. These four stadiums are all badly underused by the relevant national team. London is now adding a large oval stadium for just four weeks of Track & Field in 2012.

Yet another public scandal is slowly brewing. The UK government should have marched into Lord's in 2006, made the ECB an offer it could not refuse, and used the press to bounce the ECB into accepting. Whether it made the offer, or not, I do not know.

**4.      Arsenal stadium**

Algebraically, set F as the fixed cost per year and V as the variable cost per event. The cost of each physical seat per year is £F + Vx, where x is the number of events. The cost of providing a seat at each event is therefore £(F/x) + V. As x rises, the cost per seat falls and the lower prices attract more spectators. As x falls, the cost of each seat rises and spectators are priced out.

The Arsenal stadium cost about £400 million to construct, equal to £390 per seat per year at an interest rate of 6%. Depreciation over 50 years adds another £130 and maintenance, insurance, rates and management costs another £115. Arsenal makes about £82 per seat in sponsorship and advertisements, making a net fixed cost for each seat of £553.

The costs shown in the table are generated from the expression $(553/x + 7)$, plus VAT at 17.5%, plus ticket sales cost of 3%.

According to Arsenal's financial report for 2006/07, match-day revenues increased to £90.6 million from £44.1 million the year before. An average of 60,000 people went to each of 27 games, giving per-seat revenue (excluding VAT and ancillaries such as programmes and catering) of around £50. Arsenal's operating profits rose to £51.2 million from £13.7 million, giving manager Arsène Wenger greatly increased buying power in the transfer market and setting in motion the virtuous circle.

Note that mine is an economic analysis and not an accounting analysis and that I have calculated economic profit rather than accounting profit. Because Arsenal built the stadium with a mixture of debt and equity, rather than entirely from debt, the stadium's reported profit will differ from its economic profit.

## 5.    Seating capacity

The tables on the following page provide additional information on grounds and capacities in England & Wales and Australia. They are based on the typical recent season in each of the two countries.

The population column shows the population for whom the ground is the nearest facility used by the national team. The seats / 1,000 column shows how many seats are provided per 1,000 of the population for whom the ground is the nearest.

In order to serve its population as well as other Australian cities, Sydney needs to start using its Olympic Stadium.

| City | Capacity | Days | Seats | Population | Seats / 1,000 |
|------|----------|------|-------|------------|---------------|
| Nottingham | 15,000 | 6 | 90,000 | 2.4 m | 37 |
| London | (1) | 18 | 489,600 | 18.0m | 27 |
| Birmingham | 21,000 | 6 | 126,000 | 7.2m | 17 |
| Manchester | 19,000 | 6 | 114,000 | 6.7m | 17 |
| Leeds | 14,000 | 6 | 84,000 | 5.6m | 15 |
| Southampton | 20,000 | 2 | 40,000 | 2.9m | 14 |
| Durham | 17,000 | 1 | 17,000 | 3.0m | 6 |
| Bristol | 15,000 | 1 | 15,000 | 3.8m | 4 |
| Cardiff | 5,000 | 1 | 5,000 | 2.0m | 2 |
| TOTAL | | 47 | 980,600 | 51.7m | 21 |

(1) Lord's holds 29,300 and the Oval 23,000.

| City | Capacity | Days | Total seats | Population | Seats / 1,000 |
|------|----------|------|-------------|------------|---------------|
| Adelaide | 32,000 | 8 | 248,000 | 1.5m | 161 |
| Melbourne | 100,000 | 8 | 800,000 | 5.0m | 159 |
| Perth | 24,000 | 7 | 168,000 | 2.0m | 84 |
| Brisbane | 40,000 | 7 | 280,000 | 4.0m | 70 |
| Hobart | 16,000 | 2 | 32,000 | 4.8m | 66 |
| Sydney | 43,000 | 9 | 387,000 | 6.8m | 57 |
| TOTAL | | 41 | 1,923,000 | 20.6m | 93 |

## 6.    £1.2 million

This figure and the six-day break-even estimate are calculated from the following assumptions. The UK government tears down the upper stands but builds the stadium so that they can be restored at a cost of £100 million. The annual cost of converting from athletics to cricket and back is £2 million. 75% of the capacity is sold at average ticket price of £40 including VAT. 10% of days are lost to weather and early finishes.

Six days of England cricket sells 324,000 seats and generates a small profit of £100,000. 17 days sells 918,000 seats and generates a profit of £13 million. Therefore, the stadium breaks even in six days and generates £1.2 million in profit for each subsequent day.

If the UK government elects to retain the upper stands then the stadium becomes even more profitable for cricket. Robert Franklin and I attempted to persuade it but ran into the Millennium Dome syndrome described above.

## 7.    750,000

This estimate for the number of serious fans within range of London, and the estimate of 1.5 million casual fans, are derived from an estimate of two million serious cricket fans and four million casuals in England & Wales. These numbers are derived as follows.

According to Sport England's General Household Survey in 2002, 2.5% of the over-16 population of England played the game in the previous 12 months. This converts to about one million people. The age profile is heavily skewed to youth: 10% of 16–19s and 4% of 20–29s played, compared with under 2% of 45–59s.

Applying a percentage of 50% gives half a million people who played cricket and were serious fans in that year. Multiply that by three because most fans who have played cricket no longer do so because of age. That gives 1.5 million. A quarter of the television viewers of the first day of the 2005 Ashes Test at Lord's were female, rising to 39% for the last day at the Oval. Adding in women, very few of whom play or have played, and the under-16s, gives a figure of about two million serious fans.

A Sport England survey in 2006 and 2007 showed that 4.3% of the 39 million 16+ population of England plays cricket at least once per year. Adding in Wales, this gives 1.8 million over-16s playing. This appears to be an over-estimate, but I checked with the statistician and she said that the estimate was sound. An oft-quoted Sport England survey done in 2005 produced a figure of 0.9% of over-16s playing the game, but the survey was carried out over 12 months and asked about sports played in the last month only – a dreadful methodological error given the seasonality of cricket. This is therefore an under-estimate.

Television and Radio figures for England Test matches are vast. Channel 4's average TV audience from 1999 to 2005 was 1.3 million and its reach (defined as the number of individuals who watched at all) averaged 13 million each year. About four million people tune in to a home Test on BBC *Test Match Special*, the same as the continuous average (see below) audience for the last two Tests in the 2005 Ashes.

This leads to rough estimates of two million serious fans and four million casual fans in England & Wales. I subsequently checked them with two cricket officials. One said 'about right' and another 'a bit under'.

## 8.     Continuous average
This is the average number who were watching TV coverage at any one time.

## 9.     Excluding themselves
In the London metropolitan area about 9% of the population is composed of people with a South Asian or Caribbean background. It is reasonable to assume that they are equally likely to follow cricket as whites.

Let's say 11,000 seats at Lord's go to MCC members and friends who, because the club has a 20-year waiting list, do not reflect London-area demographics. This leaves 18,300 seats available to the general public. If you randomly select 18,300 people from a very large group with an ethnic distribution of 91% white and 9% not, your chances of picking fewer than 1,000 non-whites is about one divided by 10 to the power of 72, not far off the number of atoms in the universe, exponentially speaking.

So, if there are fewer than 1,000 non-whites at Lord's when it is full, we can safely say that either non-whites themselves, or the MCC, or both, are deselecting non-white people. Every time I go to Lord's, the number of non-whites is well under this figure. The MCC is highly unlikely to be doing this, so non-whites as a group must be deselecting themselves.

**10.    Form line**
Each line contains one data point per quarter, calculated at the end of March, June, September and December. To calculate each data point, I took all the Test results for the country in the two years up to the end of the quarter in question and calculated average points per game on the football league basis of three points for a win, one for a draw and zero for a loss. The vertical axis therefore runs from zero to three. I then converted this 0–3 rating into 'performance in a five-Test series'. An average of 2.6 points per game is equivalent to a 4–0 win in a five-Test series, with one draw. 1.6 points per game is equivalent to a 2–1 victory, with two draws. 0.8 points per game is equivalent to a 0–1 loss, with four draws. And so on.

The form lines therefore illustrate the form of each country over time. They are less good than the ICC rankings in that there is no weighting for the strength of the opposition. They are better in that they cover two years rather than five or six. The ICC rankings are designed to rank all 10 Test teams in a hierarchy, whereas this method is designed to show the recent form of one team over time.

**11.    Each year**
For ease of computation, Test caps awarded in the northern winter are allocated to the following calendar year. So, for instance, caps awarded in the 1979/80 and 1980 seasons are counted as having been awarded in 1980.

# Chapter 3

### 1.    County Championship

15 of the 17 first-class counties in 1976 took part in the 1899 County Championship. Northamptonshire joined in 1905 and Glamorgan in 1921. No counties that took part in the 1899 tournament have left first-class cricket since.

### 2.    £2 million

This is the first of six figures for the years 1976, 1985, 1989, 1995, 2001 and 2005. The following table divides cricket revenues in 1976 between England, the counties and the MCC.

|  | £m |
|---|---|
| **England** | |
| Broadcasting | 0.09 |
| Ticket receipts | 0.56 |
| Sponsorship & advertising | 0.00 |
| **Total** | **0.65** |
| | |
| **Counties** | |
| Broadcasting | 0.01 |
| Memberships & tickets | 0.63 |
| Sponsorship & advertising | 0.27 |
| **Total** | **0.91** |
| | |
| **MCC** | |
| Total | 0.27 |
| | |
| TOTAL | 1.83 |

The England ticket receipts figure comes from *Wisden*. The broadcasting figure of £100,000 is based on the deal with the BBC worth £270,000 for the 1975 and 1976 seasons, including the 1975 World Cup. 10% of the value of domestic broadcasting rights is allocated to the counties and 90% to England. The counties' memberships & tickets and the MCC membership figures are my estimates. The sponsorship & advertising figures are from press reports.

These figures exclude revenues from catering, corporate boxes, debentures and other uses of cricket grounds.

### 3.      Strategy

The 'bounce / slog the cunt' quote is taken from *Cricket War: the inside story of Kerry Packer's World Series Cricket* by Gideon Haigh. This magnificent book is essential reading for anybody who wants to understand Australian cricket. To my knowledge it has never been published in the UK. The six Legal Deposit libraries probably have most of, if not all, the copies in this country.

### 4.      Cans of beer

The *Weekend Australian Magazine* for 20–21 December 2003 carried a marvellous article about the various attempts to set the drinking record between Sydney and London. The article is available on *The Fanatics* web-site. Alternatively, entering 'Marsh Tindall Boon Australian beer' into a search engine should produce results with the article at or near the top. England's best performer is Mike Tindall, reputed to have disposed of around 50 tins on the way back from the 2003 Rugby World Cup.

### 5.      Aussie Rules

Aussie Rules was invented in 1858 with the express purpose of keeping cricketers fit. The original rules from 1859 state that 'The game shall be played within the space of not more than 200 yards wide'. This makes the game stadium-compatible with cricket, which demands a space of not less than 140 yards wide.

All five of Australia's main cricket grounds have been extensively used for Aussie Rules, which explains their vast boundaries as well as their vast stands (the second law of stadiums). Adelaide's Football Park today holds over 50,000 spectators and is equipped with light towers to permit evening events. This stadium, with 60% more capacity than England's biggest cricket ground, has not been used for a major cricket match since 1979.

## 6.    £8 million

The following table divides cricket revenues in 1985 between England, the counties and the MCC.

|  | £m |
|---|---|
| **England** |  |
| Broadcasting | 0.4 |
| Ticket receipts | 2.5 |
| Sponsorship & advertising | 0.9 |
| **Total** | **3.8** |
| **Counties** |  |
| Broadcasting | 0.03 |
| Memberships & tickets | 2.2 |
| Sponsorship & advertising | 1.6 |
| **Total** | **3.9** |
| **MCC** |  |
| **Total** | **0.7** |
| **TOTAL** | **8.3** |

The England ticket receipts figure comes from *Wisden*. The broadcasting figure is based on the deal with the BBC worth £1 million for three years plus an estimate for overseas sales. 10% of the value of domestic broadcasting rights is allocated to the counties and 90% to England. The counties' memberships & tickets and the MCC membership figures are my estimates. The sponsorship & advertising figures are from press reports.

These figures exclude revenues from catering, corporate boxes, debentures and other uses of cricket grounds. Inflation averaged 10.1% per year between 1976 and 1985.

## 7.     Englishman

The poem is *If* – by Rudyard Kipling. Kipling was born in India.

# Chapter 4

### 1.    Steve Waugh
In his autobiography, Waugh identifies the person responsible for telling Packer whom to protect with PBL contracts. It was Tony Greig.

### 2.    Vomited
Dean Jones' innings in Madras is featured in the ABC TV programme *Rookies, Rebels & Renaissance* (available on DVD) and in the book of the same name by cricket writer Mike Coward. The images of Jones chucking up all over the square are unforgettable.

### 3.    Elite youth conveyor belt
Determining who is elite does not appear to be difficult. Dennis Lillee, who has coached at the Australian Cricket Academy, has said he can tell a good fast bowler in three balls. Former England coach Keith Fletcher has written that he can watch a player of 16 or 17 for about 15 minutes and make a judgement.

Organising representative Under- 15, 17 and 19 sides does not appear to be difficult either, politics apart. The real trick with elite youth seems to be to get them to play cricket in the first place and then persuade them to choose it over other sports. Hence the importance of the *Inspiration Effect*.

### 4.    142 England days
These days came in seven series, as shown in the table opposite.

### 5.    Dilley and Botham
In the 15 months, Graham Dilley played 12 of the 16 Tests and 16 of the 33 one-day games as well as a couple of other tour games in Australia. For Kent and Worcestershire (where he moved after the 1986 season), he played 20 first-class games and another 24 one-day games in the two home seasons.

In the 21 months, Ian Botham played 15 of the 21 Tests and 20 of the 37 One-Day Internationals, as well as some tour games in Australia. For Somerset and Worcestershire (Botham left Somerset in 1986 after Viv

| Total days | Season | Opponent | Tests | ODIs |
|:---:|:---:|:---:|:---:|:---:|
| 29 | 1985/86 | West Indies | 5 | 4 |
| 17 | 1986 | India | 3 | 2 |
| 17 | 1986 | New Zealand | 3 | 2 |
| 39 | 1986/87 | Australia | 5 | 14 |
| 4 | 1986/87 | (Sharjah) | | 4 |
| 28 | 1987 | Pakistan | 5 | 3 |
| 8 | 1987/88 | (World Cup) | | 8 |
| **142** | | | **21** | **37** |

Richards and Joel Garner were sacked), he played 23 first-class games and another 28 one-day matches. Botham had four breaks. Other than the second—the TCCB ban—the first was 10 days between the end of the West Indies trip and his first game for Somerset in the 1986 season. Like Dilley, Botham had a month off before going to Australia and 10 weeks between the Australia trip and the 1987 season – he did not go to Sharjah. Botham missed the Third Test versus Australia at Adelaide in December 1986 with a rib muscle injury.

As a commentator, Fred Trueman had little time for any argument that players should be protected against over-use and fatigue. Year in, year out from 1952 to 1965, Trueman would play most of Yorkshire's 32 three-day games along with all five England Tests, making 90 days in the average season.

The thing was, Trueman only played 18 professional one-day games in his career, and one wonders how often he dived in the field. He also went on only four overseas tours, so his typical year included six months away from the game.

The tours were in 1953/54 to the West Indies, 1958/59 to Australia and New Zealand, 1959/60 to the West Indies and 1962/63 to Australia and New Zealand. Trueman's two West Indies tours both started in January and were therefore preceded by four-month breaks. His two Australia tours were four-month affairs with one first-class match per week, not all of which he played. There were also long boat rides each way with plenty of time for rest, recuperation and deck quoits.

## 6. David Boon

Boon is currently a member of the Cricket Australia selection board, along with Merv Hughes. One assumes that attempts to beat his record will be both encouraged and discouraged.

## 7. Few first-class games

Like Bob Willis, Mike Atherton was an England player first and a county player second. When he made his Test debut, Atherton had played about 25 first-class games for Cambridge University and another 25 for Lancashire.

## 8. £16 million

The following table divides cricket revenues in 1989 between England, the counties and the MCC.

|  | £m |
|---|---|
| **England** | |
| Broadcasting | 1.3 |
| Ticket receipts | 5.1 |
| Sponsorship & advertising | 1.1 |
| **Total** | **7.5** |
| | |
| **Counties** | |
| Broadcasting | 0.1 |
| Memberships & tickets | 4.4 |
| Sponsorship & advertising | 2.5 |
| **Total** | **7.0** |
| | |
| **MCC** | |
| **Total** | **1.2** |
| | |
| **TOTAL** | **15.7** |

The England ticket receipts figure comes from *Wisden*. The broadcasting figure is based on the deal with the BBC worth £1.25 million each year for three years plus an estimate for overseas sales. 10% of the value of domestic broadcasting rights is allocated to the counties and 90% to England. The counties memberships & ticket receipts and the MCC membership figures are my estimates. The sponsorship & advertising figures are from press reports.

These figures exclude revenues from catering, corporate boxes, debentures and other uses of cricket grounds. Inflation averaged 5.1% per year between 1985 and 1989.

### 9. Martin McCague
Martin McCague was one of three England players to have been to the Australian Cricket Academy. The others were Craig White and Jason Gallian.

### 10. Three successors
Four players have held the job of Australian national cricket captain since 1985. The other three are Mark Taylor, Steve Waugh and Ricky Ponting. Bob Simpson has also had only three successors. Geoff Marsh and John Buchanan took the team through to 2007, and Tim Nielsen took over after the 2007 World Cup.

# Chapter 5

### 1.     Medical research

This research was published in 2003 in the *Journal of Science and Medicine in Sport*. Cricket Australia also prepares an annual injury report. The 2005 report stated that the follow-on and back-to-back Tests are also factors in bowler injuries and reported a 2.1% injury risk per bowler per innings based on several seasons' worth of data.

Simple arithmetic suggests that the probability of an injury to a fast bowler (who is more vulnerable than a spinner) quickly mounts up as he bowls in more innings.

A similar survey was carried out by Dave Newman on behalf of the ECB in the early 2000s. I asked for access to this survey, but this request got nowhere.

### 2.     £41 million

The table on page 293 divides cricket revenues in 1995 between England, the counties and the MCC.

The England ticket receipts figure comes from *Wisden*. The broadcasting figure is based on the deal with the BBC and Sky worth £58.5 million for 1995–1998 plus an estimate for overseas sales. 10% of the value of domestic broadcasting rights is allocated to the counties and 90% to England. The counties memberships & ticket receipts and the MCC membership figures are my estimates. The sponsorship & advertising figures are from press reports.

These figures exclude revenues from catering, corporate boxes, debentures and other uses of cricket grounds. Inflation averaged 4.4% per year between 1989 and 1995.

### 3.     England and Wales Cricket Board

The Articles of Association dated December 1996 stated that any proposals for domestic and international cricket, selection of venues, and the registration of players, had to be approved by the First Class

|  | £m |
|---|---|
| **England** |  |
| Broadcasting | 11.3 |
| Ticket receipts | 10.1 |
| Sponsorship & advertising | 5.8 |
| **Total** | **27.2** |
| **Counties** |  |
| Broadcasting | 1.2 |
| Memberships & tickets | 6.6 |
| Sponsorship & advertising | 4.2 |
| **Total** | **12.0** |
| **MCC** |  |
| **Total** | **1.8** |
| **TOTAL** | **41.0** |

Forum. ECB budgets also had to be approved, and the FCF nominated eight of the 14-person ECB Management Board. It also nominated the ECB Chairman and the chairmen of the four principal committees – Cricket, Finance, Marketing and England.

Management Board members were explicitly allowed by the articles to vote on decisions and contracts in which they were interested. Finally, in order to prevent a putsch by the major major counties, a three-quarters majority was required to change the articles.

### 4. Ian MacLaurin

MacLaurin had been Managing Director and then Chairman of Tesco and was appointed a non-executive director of Vodafone in 1997. He played cricket for Hertfordshire.

## 5.    Regulations

In 1996, Parliament passed a new Broadcasting Act that closed a loophole in the 1990 Act regarding listed events. This loophole lay in the definition of what 'free-to-air' meant. The 1990 Act incorrectly assumed that services that were not free-to-air must necessarily be pay-per-view. In fact, they could also be paid for by subscription.

The 1996 Act tidied this loophole up, defining services as either free-to-air or not free-to-air and getting rid of the muddle between subscription and pay-per-view.

## 6.    £71 million

The following table divides cricket revenues earned from cricket in 2001 by England, the counties and the MCC.

|  | £m |
|---|---|
| **England** |  |
| Broadcasting | 25.4 |
| Ticket receipts | 13.2 |
| Sponsorship & advertising | 9.2 |
| **Total** | **47.8** |
| **Counties** |  |
| Broadcasting | 2.6 |
| Memberships & tickets | 10.5 |
| Sponsorship & advertising | 7.2 |
| **Total** | **20.3** |
| **MCC** |  |
| **Total** | **2.5** |
| **TOTAL** | **70.6** |

The England ticket receipts figure comes from *Wisden*. The broadcasting figure is based on the deal with Channel 4 and BSkyB worth £104 million for 1999–2002 plus an estimate for overseas sales. 10% of the value of domestic broadcasting rights is allocated to the counties and 90% to England. The counties memberships & ticket receipts and the MCC membership figures are my estimates based on press reports. The sponsorship & advertising figures are from press reports.

These figures exclude revenues from catering, corporate boxes, debentures and other uses of cricket grounds.

# Chapter 6

**1.    Canard**
One official with an intimate knowledge of this argument told me
that it was 'a good line to fend off the questioner.'

**2.    David Willis**
All David Willis' statements quoted here were made in conversation
with me in 2007.

**3.    Giles Clarke**
Giles Clarke is a former investment banker and serial entrepreneur
who founded Majestic Wines and co-founded Pet City and Safestore.
His first year as Chairman of Somerset County Club was 2003.

**4.    Official**
All statements by people described as an official were made to me in
2007 on condition that he or she not be identified.

**5.    Market research**
Of the sample of 4,100 people studied, about two thirds were not
interested in cricket at all, and one third were. 12% of the population
were potentially interested in this new form of the game. The most
favourably-disposed new market groups were women, people aged
between 15 and 44, and families.

Interestingly, according to one official, Anglo-Asians expressed such
a strong sense of exclusion from the mainstream game that the ECB
decided to leave this group for another day. Until then, one
imagines, many will continue to support what the ECB calls their
'country of origin'.

The research was funded not from ECB resources but out of the
Channel 4 marketing budget.

**6.    Six departures**
Henry Blofeld wrote in *The Independent* about Des Wilson, Tim
Lamb, John Read and Mark Sibley:

*Ian Fleming wrote in one of the Bond books, 'Once is happenstance, twice is coincidence and three times is open warfare.' He might have added that four times is meltdown.*

Richie Benaud has written: 'There may occasionally be a case of a minor official getting the chop but it is rare indeed for the more established ones to feel the touch of cold steel on the neck. It has always intrigued me that this should be so.'

It is also intriguing why the opposite was the case in this instance.

## 7.    Paying

The following table shows the value per day for the 2006–2009 television rights of two actual and one potential bids. This value is calculated on the basis that a Test is four days, a One-Day International one day and a Twenty20 game half a day. The 'per day' column on the right includes the effect of a 10% allocation to county cricket, but the 'value' column next to it shows the full face value of the bids without this deduction.

Bid 1 is the actual exclusive bid received from BSkyB. Bid 2 is the sharing bid actually received from Channel 4 and BSkyB. Bid 3 is the

| Bidder | Description | Tests | ODIs | T20s | Value | Per day |
|--------|-------------|-------|------|------|-------|---------|
| 1. BSkyB | Actual exclusive | 28 | 40 | 8 | £208 million | £1,200,000 |
| | | | | | | |
| 2a. Channel 4 | Actual sharing | 18 | 0 | 0 | £54 million | £680,000 |
| 2b. BSkyB | Actual sharing | 10 | 40 | 8 | £72 million | £770,000 |
| 2. Total | Actual sharing | 28 | 40 | 8 | £126 million | £730,000 |
| | | | | | | |
| 3a. Channel 4 | Possible sharing | 18 | 0 | 0 | £54 million | £680,000 |
| 3b. BSkyB | Possible sharing | 10 | 40 | 8 | £154 million | £1,650,000 |
| 3. Total | Possible sharing | 28 | 40 | 8 | £208 million | £1,200,000 |

sharing bid that would have happened had the ECB negotiating team managed to drive BSkyB's fee per day back up to the £1.65 million in effect during the 2003–2005 deal (see the second table). The Channel 4 component of this putative bid is the same as in Bid 2.

The value per day of the BSkyB part of the sharing bid, marked *2b*, is less than half the fee it paid per day during 2003–2005 (see the second table).

It is interesting to note that the value of Bids 1 and 3 are the same – £208 million. Why did the ECB team not manage to drive BSkyB's per-day fee back up to what it already was and close the gap between Bids 1 and 2?

This second table shows the value per day of the 2003–2005 deal.

| Licensee | Description | Tests | ODIs | T20s | Value | Per day |
|----------|-------------|-------|------|------|-------|---------|
| Channel 4 | Actual sharing | 18 | 0 | 0 | £59 million | £740,000 |
| BSkyB | Actual sharing | 3 | 28 | 0 | £75 million | £1,650,000 |
| Total | Actual sharing | 21 | 28 | 0 | £134 million | £1,070,000 |

## 8.     Kolpaks

The existing rules allowed two overseas players to play for a county in any given game, and a total of four in a season. In May 2003, the European Court of Justice handed down a judgement that became known as the Kolpak ruling. Non-EU citizens of a country with an Association Agreement with the EU could, if they had a work permit, play professional sport in any EU country. Then, in August 2003, changes to the UK Working Holiday Visa rules meant that anybody from Commonwealth countries aged between 18 and 30 could obtain a UK work permit.

The combination of the two meant that players from countries in both categories could play county cricket without being regarded as an overseas player. South Africa and Caribbean countries are members of the Commonwealth and are also covered by EU Association Agreements.

This opened the floodgates. In February 2005, the UK government announced that those on Working Holiday visas would not be allowed to play professional sport, meaning that players from Association countries would need to get a work permit – a harder proposition. But in 2005, 51 came in under the EU banner anyway as foreign cricketers traced their European Union antecedents and took up remunerative winter employment in England.

## 9.     113 days

After three games in the September 2004 Champions Trophy in England, Australia went to India for a four-Test series in five weeks in October and November, winning 2–1. Then they returned home for five more Tests against New Zealand and Pakistan, winning all five. 10 One-Day Internationals against New Zealand, West Indies and Pakistan followed, Australia winning these 7–2. After two weeks off, Australia went to New Zealand in mid-February for three more Tests (2–0) and five One-Day Internationals (5–0).

The net result for 2004/05 was 9–1 in 12 Tests and 14–3 in 18 One-Day Internationals.

## 10.     Articles

The ECB now has 40 members. They are the Chairmen of the 18 major counties (for some reason, Glamorgan has become Wales), the 20 county boards in the areas known as the minor counties, the MCC and the Minor Counties Cricket Association.

County boards are the vehicle by which funding for grassroots cricket from Sport England, the ECB and various other sources is disbursed. Although the county boards in the minor counties are members of the ECB, the county boards in the major counties are not. If they were, then these 18 boards and the 20 others would constitute a 38–20 majority on the ECB and could put in an executive that handed England's profits to the boards, or reinvested them in

England, rather than give most of them to the 18 county clubs.

## 11.    Effectively controlled

The 40 members appoint an ECB Management Board of 12 directors. Of these 12, three including the Chairman and the deputy Chairman are proposed by the 19 Chairmen of the MCC & Counties and then approved by all 40 members. Three more are appointed by a vote of the major counties. This makes six. Two more are appointed to represent the recreational game by a body named the Recreational Assembly, and one is nominated by the MCC.

That makes nine, of which six are effectively controlled by the major counties by either nomination or appointment and one by the MCC, making seven. The Chairman appoints a 10th, 'independent' director (currently Bill Morris, the former TUC General Secretary), and the remaining two are the Chief Executive and the Finance Director. The Chief Executive is appointed by the Board, which is likely to mean the first 10 directors. The articles are not clear on how the Finance Director is appointed, but it is likely that this position too is appointed by the first 10 directors.

These first 10 directors are effectively in charge. Seven of these are appointed or nominated by the MCC & Counties and one by the Chairman. Therefore, this setup is effectively controlled by the MCC & Counties.

## 12.    Protective clauses

The Management Board controls the professional game subject to the proviso that the Board 'not cause ECB's affairs to be conducted in a manner which is unfairly prejudicial to the interests of the Members of the ECB or of some part of the Members of the ECB'.

This clause, a standard company law mechanism to protect minority shareholders, prevents an alliance of the five major majors, the MCC, the MCCA and the 20 (minor) county boards ganging up on the 13 minor majors and taking their annual ECB payout for themselves. Another clause states that the Board cannot stop any first-class county club from participating in first-class competitions. This also protects the minor majors.

Finally, the 2005 Articles of Association stipulate that they can only be altered with the support of 30 members. This means that the 13 minor major counties can prevent a change to the articles that harms their collective interests.

## 13. Spending plans
The figures provided for ECB spending in the first year (2005) and the last year (2009) were:

| Item | 2005 | 2009 |
|------|------|------|
| County cricket | £31 million (50%) | £33 million (43%) |
| England | £12 million (20%) | £17 million (23%) |
| 'Participation' | £11 million (17%) | £16 million (21%) |
| Governance | £8 million (13%) | £9 million (9%) |
| Total | £62 million | £75 million |

## 14. Participation
The strategy document did not define what it meant by this term. It could mean 'grassroots' (discussed below), or it could mean a whole lot more.

## 15. £95 million
The table on page 302 divides cricket revenues in 2005 between England and the 18 major counties.

The England ticket receipts figure comes from *Wisden*. The broadcasting figure is based on the deal with Channel 4 and BSkyB for 2003–2005 plus an estimate for overseas sales. 10% of the value of domestic broadcasting rights is allocated to the counties and 90% to England. The counties' membership & ticket receipts are derived from annual reports for 14 counties for 2005 and one for 2004. I was

|                            | £m   |
|----------------------------|------|
| **England**                |      |
| Broadcasting               | 49.2 |
| Ticket receipts            | 31.0 |
| Sponsorship & advertising  | 15.2 |
| **Total**                  | **95.3** |
|                            |      |
| **Counties**               |      |
| Broadcasting               | 4.6  |
| Memberships & tickets      | 11.5 |
| Sponsorship & advertising  | 7.8  |
| **Total**                  | **23.9** |

unable to obtain reports for Durham, Hampshire and Worcestershire, so I assumed that non-England cricket revenues and costs for these counties were equal to the average for the other minor major counties except Middlesex. The sponsorship & advertising figures are from press reports. I also used the ECB 2005 accounts.

These figures are not directly comparable with those provided earlier for 1976, 1985, 1989, 1995 and 2001. For 2005, the extra detail in the annual reports has allowed me to calculate a more exact division between England and the counties. I have allocated 80% of MCC member subscriptions to England, along with the extra sponsorship & advertising and corporate box income earned by the clubs which hosted Ashes games, over and above those earned by the counties which did not.

I am confident that the figures of £95 million for England and £24 million for the 18 counties are reasonably accurate. The following table divides cricket costs in 2005 between England and the 18 major counties.

|  | £m |
|---|---|
| **England** | |
| Team | 10.9 |
| Grounds | 7.2 |
| Admin & matches | 22.9 |
| ECB Cost of Sales | 12.0 |
| **Total** | **53.0** |
| | |
| **Counties** | |
| Teams | 22.8 |
| Match expenses | 10.9 |
| Admin | 12.1 |
| Grounds | 7.0 |
| **Total** | **52.9** |

These calculations include current costs only and ignore depreciation.

The England team costs figure is taken from the ECB 2005 annual report. The England grounds figure is calculated from the MCC report and from my estimate of the excess costs generated at the major grounds over and above those generated at the minor grounds. All ECB administration costs, most of those at the major major counties and much of the MCC's are allocated to England. Finally, I have allocated a mysterious item (£12 million) in the ECB report called 'Cost of Sales' to England. I suspect, but do not know for sure, that this item represents costs incurred by the ECB and the MCC & Counties in staging England games.

The counties' team costs are calculated from the 15 county reports. The match expenses is calculated from those reports and £4.5 million spent directly by the ECB on county cricket added in. The administration cost is calculated from the county reports with England-related costs backed out, as mentioned above. The same goes for ground costs.

I am confident that the costs estimate of £106 million for England professional cricket is accurate. I am less confident about the division of costs between England and the counties because not all the necessary detail is available in the various reports and I am uncertain about the definition of the ECB Cost of Sales item. Where doubts existed, I allocated cost to England rather than to the counties. A reasonable range for England costs is £48–£55 million. A reasonable range for counties' costs is £51–58 million.

These revenue and cost figures produce an England profits estimate of £42 million and a counties loss estimate of £29 million. The game overall made £13.4 million, which is close to the sum (£13.7 million) of ECB payments to its charity and in support of grassroots cricket.

## 16.    Viewing hours

County cricket in 2005 generated an audience of 1.43 million, of which 470,000 was for the County Championship and 550,000 for Twenty20. This generated a total of about eight million viewing hours. This number was unrestricted by either price or ground capacity.

Some county cricket was televised, but viewing figures are unavailable. A county final might be watched by 500,000, generating 3.5 million hours, and an ordinary one-day game by 75,000 (according to an official), giving 500,000 viewing hours. An estimate of 20 million television viewing hours is probably a mild over-estimate.

Overall, county cricket garnered less than 30 million viewing hours in 2005.

England cricket was watched by 800,000 people in 2005, generating five million viewing hours. This number was heavily restricted by price and ground capacity.

An average of 2.1 million people (at any one time) watched Channel 4 in 2005, but this was distorted upwards by the Ashes series. The average for 1999 to 2005 was 1.3 million. 31 Test match days (assuming four days lost to early finishes and the weather) of six hours each gives 242 million viewing hours. 10 One-Day Internationals and one Twenty20 were on Sky. Viewing figures are unavailable, but an estimate of 400,000 is reasonable for each of 70 hours. This gives 28 million. Highlights figures are also unavailable, but an average of 500,000 people for 42 days of cricket produces another 20 million hours or so.

This makes, roughly, 295 million England viewing hours and 30 million for the 18 counties. It is highly likely that England generated at least 90% of the viewing hours for professional cricket in 2005.

This calculation includes ground attendance and television, but excludes voice broadcast over radio and internet. Including this would drive the England proportion towards 95%.

**17.    £23 million**
In 2005, the ECB paid £24.3 million in fees to the major counties and directly supported county cricket to the tune of £4.5 million (as mentioned above). This totals £28.8 million. Of this, £4.6 million was the counties' 10% share of the £46.3 million earned from domestic broadcasting and £1.9 million was the value of county tournament sponsorships. I assume that these two items are included in the ECB fee payment. Backing out this county-earned money gives £22.3 million. Finally, adding in the surplus kept by the counties from England games (£1.1 million) gives £23.4 million.

This figure represents the ECB support provided to the counties in 2005 out of profits generated by the England team. If the assumption that the ECB fee payment includes county-earned money is wrong, then the ECB support to the counties in 2005 was even higher. The figure of £23.4 million therefore represents a minimum estimate.

The ECB strategy document mentioned a little earlier stated that the ECB provided £31 million to the counties in 2005. I can locate only the £28.8 million mentioned above in the ECB accounts, and I use this lower figure as a starting point before backing out county-earned money.

At various points in the book I mention fees paid by the ECB to the counties. These fees probably included television and sponsorship money generated by county cricket, and are therefore no more than somewhat comparable with this £23.4 million figure, which is much more exact.

That said, only a small proportion of ECB fees to the counties over time is likely to have been derived from county cricket, so the fees mentioned throughout the book give a reasonable picture of how TCCB and ECB support of county cricket has increased over time.

## 18. Grassroots

Grassroots cricket has been defined for me by two officials as consisting of everything unrelated to the professional game. It includes kids, clubs and schools, but excludes county and national Academies and county second XI cricket, whose purpose is to produce professional cricketers.

The officials were at pains to point out that the use of this term is so fuzzy as to include almost anything except county and England cricket. If so, then the costs of finding and producing professional cricketers from among the general population, which are substantial, could then be labelled 'grassroots'.

If this were true, they said, then the spending reported under the label 'grassroots' would be higher than it would be under the narrower definition.

## 19. Domestic broadcasting revenue

In 2004, according to its annual report, ECB revenue was £75.1 million. Domestic broadcasting revenue in that year—£47.4 m—represented 63% of its revenues. The average figure for the three years of the 2003–2005 Channel 4 / BSkyB contract was also 63%. However, the most relevant percentage for the ECB to have presented to the Select Committee for 2004 is domestic broadcasting revenues divided by overall game revenues. Game revenues in 2005 were £119 million, of which domestic broadcasting revenues constituted around £50 million, or 42%. In 2004, the year cited by the ECB, overall game revenues were similar to those in 2005 because television fees, ticket receipts and sponsorships & advertising fees were much the same.

The relevant figure, then, is about 42%. Not 80%, and not 63% either.

## 20.    18.5% of its total income on grassroots in 2005

The ECB's accounts for 2005 state that £5.3 million was spent on 'recreational and grassroots' in that year, but 2005 spending on 'grassroots' reported in the 2006 accounts mysteriously rose to £8.7 million. The county reports for 2005 show spending of about £5 million on academies, but these are not grassroots according to the 'kids, schools and clubs' definition. The MCC report for 2005 shows grants of £780,000 to the game, including £390,000 to the six University Centres of Cricketing Excellence.

I have seen documents which propose ECB spending of £6 million on grassroots for 2005, and an official told me that the ECB grassroots budget in 2004 (not 2005) was £7 million.

Identifiable grassroots spending comes, then, to under £10 million. However, the 18.5% 'cricket in England and Wales' figure presented by the ECB suggests that the ECB and the MCC & Counties together spent over £22 million on grassroots in 2005, using the £119 million game revenue figure calculated above.

There appears to be a gap of at least £10 million between the claim and publicly-available information. The ECB's use of two charities, the Cricket Foundation and the England & Wales Cricket Trust, to disburse money further confuses the picture.

The ECB evidence reads: 'Cricket currently invests 18.5% of our total income into the grass roots game'. Notwithstanding this, it may be that the ECB used only its income as denominator, rather than that of the whole game, as suggested by the statement. The £8.7 million spent by the ECB on grassroots in 2005, according to the 2006 accounts, is 11% of the ECB's 2005 revenue of £78.8 million. So, if that was how the percentage was calculated, then it would still have been incorrect.

I asked three officials what they thought of the 18.5% figure. All three were scathing. There are fertile grounds here for a more thorough investigation.

This ECB claim should be buttressed by a precise account of spending by the ECB and the MCC & Counties on kids, clubs and schools cricket that specifies the ultimate source of the funds and includes only those generated by professional cricket. Any accounting that lumps in Sport England money, or defines grassroots vaguely or so widely as to include items outside the definition above, or that counts the ECB's 2005 charity donation of £8 million, will not do.

## 21.    National Academy

According to a report in *The Times* on 26 September 2002, the Lottery Sports Fund, administered by Sport England, paid £4 million of the costs of constructing the National Academy. The total budget was about £4.5 million. The report also stated that the lottery would cover the £2 million running costs for at least four years, and that the ECB paid about £350,000 per year for the use of the site in Loughborough.

## 22.    £33.5 million

This figure must be referring to the 1995–1998 period, when coverage was shared by the BBC and BSkyB, because the deal before that (1992–1994) was worth only £15 million over three years. For 1995–1998, the BBC paid £33.5 million over four years for the Test matches and BSkyB paid £25 million for the one-day games, giving an overall value of £58.5 million.

With this comparison between £33.5 million and £220 million, David Collier got it wrong in three different ways. First, he compared only the Test match part of the 1995–1998 deal with the whole of the 2006–2009 deal. Second, he failed to mention that the whole-deal £58.5 million figure needed a 33% upgrade to allow for 11 years of inflation. Third, he failed to mention that it needed another 37% upgrade to allow for the increased England home schedule from 2000 onwards.

The relevant comparison was between the whole deal for 1995–1998, adjusted once for inflation and then again for England's expanded schedule, and the exclusive BSkyB deal for 2006–2009.

This, incidentally, would have produced a comparable figure of £106 million for 1995–1998. This is not so far from the combined Channel 4 and BSkyB bid to share the 2006–2009 rights.

## 23.    Channel Nine
The new Channel Nine deal worth $45 million (£18 million) per year started in April 2006, about the same time as BSkyB started its new contract here. This new deal could not therefore be used as a comparison to the ECB deal with BSkyB and Channel 4 for 2003–2005. The exchange rate in 2005 hovered around $2.40 to the pound.

## 24.    Five reasons
John Perera's five reasons are in italics below. Each is then contrasted with an analysis based on publicly-available information and one piece of inside information.

1.  *Firstly there are a number of long term Staging Agreements in place with our counties that would be affected by a new stadium capable of staging international cricket. These are legally binding documents.*

In fact, only the Oval (2022) and Headingley (2016 or 2020 – reports vary) had staging agreements past 2012. There was plenty of room to re-jig grounds to accommodate an 80,000-seater. I asked two officials whether there are secret long-term agreements with certain grounds. They both said definitely not.

2.  *Secondly the venue that the plan is based on — the MCG — has a completely different business model to your proposal. The MCG operates on a minimum of 26 weeks per year of AFL, which has a clearly defined season, and, does not clash with the summer season. Last weekend they staged three AFL matches with average crowds of around 45,000 which generated substantial revenue.*

This is true but irrelevant because the economic case that we presented in the proposal for the use of the 2012 stadium did not include Aussie Rules football as this game is not played professionally in the UK. The use of the stadium for cricket alone is economically viable because most of the stadium's capital costs are borne by the UK government. The MCG was in fact used to illustrate the technical feasibility of a dual-use facility rather than as the basis for the economic case.

3.  *Having UK Athletics as a partner would not present anywhere near the same level of revenue opportunity as the sport in this country struggles commercially.*

This is true but irrelevant. The revenue opportunity presented by cricket appears easily sufficient to justify cricket's use of the stadium. Athletics does lose money but that doesn't destroy the economics for cricket and is in any case UK Athletics' problem.

4.  *To have an athletics track would mean either a drop in track or a track that creates a greater distance between the spectators and any cricket action.*

The second point is incorrect – the proposal stated that the athletics track goes under the outfield, as at the MCG. The first is also incorrect. Drop-in pitches can be used, or the square protected by matting or turf, or athletics events scheduled after cricket in the summer to give the square plenty of time to recover from any damage by the following summer.

5. *Athletics would also pose an issue as it is a summer activity.*

The small number of athletics events each year means that both cricket and athletics could be scheduled in the same summer.

All five of the points made in this letter by Perera were either irrelevant or incorrect.

**25.    21%**
The ECB spending plans outlined in the 2005 strategy show that its planned 2009 spending on participation is 21% of its overall spending in that year. But Clarke was speaking in August 2007. More importantly, the definition of 'participation' and 'grassroots' are not clear, spending is not the same as revenue, and ECB revenue is only part of that of that earned by professional cricket.

A precise accounting of spending and funding sources is required to justify this questionable claim.

# Chapter 7

**1.    Table 4**

(1)    Australia's Sheffield Shield competition was inaugurated in 1892/93. Games were timeless until 1926/27 and then five-day for three seasons. In 1930/31, the Shield went four-day.

(2)    Over 87,000 people attended the third day of the Third Test between Australia and England on 4 January 1937. I use this date as the opening day for the MCG.

(3)    I have used 1963 for England, the year the distinction between amateur and professional was abolished.

(4)    Sunday play was tried in England in the early eighties but discontinued.

(5)    In the Category column, Access includes any development relating to fans of the national team.

**2.    £350,000**

This calculation runs as follows. An audience of 7,500 (the actual 2006 average) generates revenues of about £100,000 and game profits (i.e. revenues minus costs on the day) of about £70,000 after staging costs. Five home games (in 2008) generate game profits of about £350,000.

If there are 17 games, say the average audience drops to 5,000, revenues to £65,000 and game profits to £45,000. This gives overall profits of £765,000. Four Championship games are lost, causing a drop of £50,000 in game profits. The overall gain is £365,000.

This is quite clearly a back-envelope calculation. The point is to show what substituting T20 games for half of the four-day County Championship games could do for the average county's finances. The effect is likely to be a profit gain in the £250,000–£400,000 range.

£350,000 for the average county and £6 million for the 18 counties combined seem reasonable estimates.

### 3.    £23 million

Domestic cricket lost £29 million in 2005. Removing the £4.6 million earned in television rights gives a loss of £34 million. Scaling domestic cricket back by 13/18$^{ths}$ gives a cricket saving of 13/18$^{ths}$ of £34 million, which is £24 million. Putting back television rights fees of £3 million reduces the saving to £23 million.

This assumes that the value of television rights for domestic cricket drop by 40%. Even with five domestic teams, there would still be plenty of cricket to fill up the airwaves.

The £5 million loss in county cricket mentioned in the text is equal to the £29 million lost in 2005 less the cricket saving of £23 million mentioned above, less another £1 million from further savings in the number of games and reduced salaries.

Catering & events profits are assumed not to change. In fact, with three much bigger grounds and facilities to match, they would probably rise.

### 4.    Five

A case could be made for a sixth region to cover the East Midlands, East Anglia and the counties north of London. This would reduce the preponderant size of the London & Southeast region. However, it would cost £1.5 million of fans' money that would be better spent on helping secure more valuable goodies such as free-to-air television, bigger England grounds and grassroots cricket. This sum, for instance, would allow 75,000 under-16s per year to go to an England game for £20 instead of £40. It would also pay for any number of indoor nets, coaches, groundsmen, rollers, et cetera.

A sixth region would provide little if any benefit to the England team because the job of attracting and training elite youth is to be carried out by free-to-air television, attendance at England's expanded grounds, the various academies and participation in youth sides run by the 38 counties. It would also require a sixth ground, which would inevitably be awarded England games, in breach of the second law of stadiums, that would then reduce overall national capacity and push up ticket prices.

The same reasoning holds for Leeds / Yorkshire and the South Coast. The question is not the number of regions, which really should be five, but their boundaries and the location within each of the one big ground.

### 5.    40,000 seats

The doubling of England days to 12 at each of Old Trafford and Edgbaston allows the second law of stadiums to work in favour of fans instead of against them. Investment of over £50 million in each ground to boost capacity to 40,000 seats produces extra England team profits of between £2 million and £3 million per year, assuming that the grounds are 75% full, 10% of days are lost to the weather and the average ex-VAT price is £35 (including box seats). This profits figure includes maintenance costs and interest on construction loans.

### 6.    Strategy for London

Allocating the Oval's games to Lord's and boosting it to 60,000 produces extra profits of about £9 million, assuming that it is 85% full, 10% of days are lost to the weather and the average ex-VAT price is £40 (including box seats). Allocating all Lord's and Oval games to the 2012 Olympic Stadium increases profits by £11 million, assuming a price of £35.

The construction costs of doubling the capacity of Lord's and bringing the 2012 Olympic Stadium into use are roughly similar, and the Olympic stadium would have to be converted between athletics and cricket and back once a year. This gives the stadium only a small financial advantage over an expanded Lord's, although it would have another 20,000 seats.

The Olympic Stadium, and the whole concept of a new National Stadium, comes into play if Lord's cannot be doubled in size for some reason. If so, then the choice is between a) putting five days at Lord's and 13 at the Olympic Stadium (extra £3 million profits) and

b) putting all 18 on at the Olympic Stadium (extra £11 million profits, as noted above).

The £8 million difference between a) and b) is earned through the sale of 800,000 more seats, which means a lot of happy punters. This money pays for a lot of free-to-air television, pavilion refurbishments, et cetera. What can I say?

## 7.    Total seating capacity

The following table shows seating capacity if England games are concentrated at five expanded grounds.

The population column shows the population for whom the ground is the nearest facility used by the national team. The seats / 1,000 column shows how many seats are provided per 1,000 population.

| City | Capacity | Days | Total seats | Population | Seats /1,000 |
|------|----------|------|-------------|------------|--------------|
| London | 60,000 | 18 | 1,080,000 | 20.1m | 54 |
| Manchester | 40,000 | 12 | 480,000 | 10.9m | 44 |
| Birmingham | 40,000 | 12 | 480,000 | 10.1m | 47 |
| Cardiff | 20,000 | 3 | 60,000 | 6.8m | 9 |
| Durham | 20,000 | 2 | 40,000 | 3.8m | 11 |
| TOTAL | | 47 | 2,140,000 | 51.7m | 41 |

Even after the redevelopment of Lord's, Old Trafford and Edgbaston, the seats-per-thousand figure for all five England & Wales regions would still be lower than that of the worst-served region in Australia, New South Wales, which has the Sydney Olympic Stadium in reserve.

Maybe we should also invent an oval game that re-uses cricket grounds in the winter and exploits the second law of stadiums. On that score, we are now 149 years behind the Aussies.

# OFFICIALS

## England Captains

The following 11 players have captained the England Test team for 10 or more of the 319 games between June 1979 and January 2008:

| | | |
|---|---|---|
| Mike Brearley | 12 games | 1977–1980 & 1981 |
| Ian Botham | 12 games | 1980–1981 |
| Bob Willis | 18 games | 1982–1984 |
| David Gower | 32 games | 1984–1986 & 1989 |
| Mike Gatting | 23 games | 1986–1988 |
| Graham Gooch | 34 games | 1988–1993 |
| Mike Atherton | 54 games | 1993–1998 |
| Alec Stewart | 15 games | 1998–1999 |
| Nasser Hussain | 45 games | 1999–2003 |
| Andrew Flintoff | 11 games | 2005–2007 |
| Michael Vaughan | 42 games | 2003–2007 |

Keith Fletcher (7 games), Andrew Strauss (5), Allan Lamb (3), Marcus Trescothick (2), John Emburey (2), Chris Cowdrey (1) and Mark Butcher (1) have also captained the team.

## England Coaches

The following have coached the England Test team since 1987:

| | |
|---|---|
| Mickey Stewart | 1987–1992 |
| Keith Fletcher | 1993–1995 |
| Raymond Illingworth | 1995–1996 |
| David Lloyd | 1996–1999 |
| Duncan Fletcher | 1999–2007 |
| Peter Moores | 2007– |

## England Chairmen of Selectors

The following have been the Chairman of Selectors since 1982:

| | |
|---|---|
| Peter May | 1982–1988 |
| Ted Dexter | 1989–1993 |
| Raymond Illingworth | 1994–1996 |
| David Graveney | 1997– |

## TCCB and ECB Secretaries or Chief Executives

The following have been the Secretary / Chief Executive of the TCCB or the ECB since 1973:

| | |
|---|---|
| Donald Carr | 1973–1986 |
| Alan Smith | 1987–1996 |
| Tim Lamb | 1997–2004 |
| David Collier | 2005– |

## TCCB and ECB Chairmen

The following have been the TCCB or ECB Chairman since 1978:

| | |
|---|---|
| George Mann | 1978–1983 |
| Charles Palmer | 1983–1985 |
| Raman Subba Row | 1985–1990 |
| Frank Chamberlain | 1990–1994 |
| Dennis Silk | 1994–1996 |
| Ian MacLaurin | 1996–2002 |
| David Morgan | 2003–2007 |
| Giles Clarke | 2007– |

# BIBLIOGRAPHHY

## Books

*Wisden Cricketers' Almanack* 1961–2007
*Wisden Australia* 2001/02–2005/06

I recommend the books marked with a star.

| | | |
|---|---|---|
| Mike Atherton | *Opening Up* * | Hodder & Stoughton |
| Hilary Beckles | *A Spirit Of Dominance* | Canoe Press |
| Richie Benaud | *My Spin On Cricket* | Hodder & Stoughton |
| Richie Benaud | *The Appeal Of Cricket* | Hodder & Stoughton |
| Derek Birley | *A Social History of English Cricket* | Aurum |
| Allan Border | *Beyond Ten Thousand* | Souvenir Press |
| Ian Botham | *The Botham Report* | CollinsWillow |
| Ian Botham | *My Autobiography* | CollinsWillow |
| Ian Chappell | *Hitting Out* * | Orion |
| Mike Coward | *Rookies, Rebels and Renaissance* * | ABC Books |
| Graham Dilley | *Swings and Roundabouts* | Pelham |
| Keith Fletcher | *Ashes to Ashes* | Headline |
| Gideon Haigh | *Cricket War* * | Text |
| Graham Halbish | *Run Out* | Lothian Books |
| Chris Harte & Bernard Whimpress | *History of Australian Cricket* | Andre Deutsch |
| Michael Holding | *Whispering Death* | Andre Deutsch |
| Nasser Hussain | *Playing with Fire* | Penguin |
| Ray Illingworth | *One Man Committee* | Headline |
| Justin Langer | *From Outback to Outfield* | Headline |
| David Lloyd | *The Autobiography* | CollinsWillow |
| Ian MacLaurin | *Tiger by the Tail* | Macmillan |
| Alastair McLellan | *Nothing Sacred, The New Cricket Culture* | Two Heads |
| John Major | *More Than A Game* | HarperPress |
| Mike Marqusee | *Anyone but England* * | Aurum |
| Bob Simpson | *The Reasons Why* | HarperCollins |
| Steve Waugh | *Out Of My Comfort Zone* * | Penguin |
| Bob Willis | *The Cricket Revolution* | Sidgwick & Jackson |
| Graeme Wright | *Betrayal* | H.F. and G. Witherby |

# Newspapers & magazines

*Wisden Cricket Monthly, The Cricketer, The Wisden Cricketer.*

*Guardian, Daily Telegraph, Times, Independent, Sun, Daily Mail, Daily Mirror, Financial Times, Daily Express, News of the World, Mail on Sunday, Observer, Independent on Sunday, Sunday Telegraph, Sunday Times, Sunday Business, Express on Sunday, Sunday Mirror.*

*Western Morning News, Birmingham Post, Nottingham Evening Post, Argus (Brighton), Lancashire Evening Post, Evening Standard (London), Evening Chronicle (Newcastle), Taunton Times, Yorkshire Post, Daily Post (Liverpool), Manchester Evening News, Derby Evening Telegraph, Coventry Evening Telegraph, Western Mail, Liverpool Echo, Bristol Evening Post.*

*Sun Herald, Australian, West Australian, Sydney Morning Herald, Age, Hobart Mercury, Sunday Tribune, Adelaide Advertiser, Sunday Herald Sun, Sunday Age, BRW, Sydney Daily Telegraph.*

*Singapore Straits Times.*

*Marketing, Accountancy, Economist, Sports Marketing, Spectator, Real Business, Marketing Week.*

# Web-sites

Cricinfo, Sports Business, PCA, ECB, Cricket Australia, Glamorgan CCC, The Gabba, MCC, BBC, Wikipedia, Nottinghamshire CCC, Arsenal FC, Surrey CCC, Sport England, 2012 London Olympics, Office of Communications.

# Reports & Accounts

| | |
|---|---|
| England & Wales Cricket Board | 1997–2006 |
| Cricket Australia | 2003/04–2005/06 |
| Essex CCC, Glamorgan CCC, | 2005 |

Gloucestershire CCC, Kent CCC,
Leicestershire CCC, Lancashire CCC,
Middlesex CCC, Northamptonshire CCC,
Nottinghamshire CCC, Somerset CCC,
Surrey CCC, Sussex CCC, Warwickshire CCC,
Yorkshire CCC

| | |
|---|---|
| Derbyshire CCC | 2004 |
| Rose Bowl plc, Hampshire Cricket Ltd | 2005 |
| Kennington Oval Ltd | 2005 |
| Marylebone Cricket Club | 2005 |
| Arsenal Football Club | 2005/06 & 2006/07 |
| Rugby Football Union | 2006 |
| Western Australia Cricket Association | 2005/06 |
| Queensland Cricket Association | 2005/06 |
| International Cricket Council | 2005/06 |

## ECB Documents

| | |
|---|---|
| Articles of Association & amendments | 1997–2005 |
| Directors Appointments | 1997–2007 |
| Certificate of Incorporation | 1996 |
| *Building Partnerships* | 2005 |
| *National Strategy for Cricket* | 2001 |
| *Raising The Standard* | 1997 |
| *Strategic Plan For Cricket – Community Cricket* | |
| *Issues Report* | 2004 |
| *Playing Cricket Making A Difference* | 2007 |

## UK Government & Parliamentary publications

House of Commons Select Committee on Culture, Media and Sport *Broadcasting Rights for Cricket First Report of Session 2005–06* (Parliamentary Copyright)

Department of Culture Media and Sport *Government Response to the Culture, Media and Sport Select Committee Report on Broadcasting Rights for Cricket Session 2005–06* (Crown Copyright)

Broadcasting Acts 1990 and 1996 (Crown Copyright)
Office of Fair Trading *Abuse of a Dominant Position, Understanding Competition Law*
Office of Fair Trading *Market Definition, Understanding Competition Law*
Office of Fair Trading *Services of General Economic Interest Exclusion, Understanding Competition Law*

| | | |
|---|---|---|
| Sport England | *General Household Survey Participation in Sport* | 2002 |
| Sport England | *Sport by Sport fact-sheet* | 2006 |
| Sport England | *Taking Part Survey* | 2007 |
| Sport England | *Wembley Track Study* | 2002 |

## Other Documents

| | | |
|---|---|---|
| Cricket Australia | *From Backyard to Baggy Green* | 2005 |
| Cricket Australia | Injury Reports | 2003–2005 |
| MCC | *A Seat In The Upper House* | 2007 |
| Cricket Reform Group | *Making English Cricket Great – For Everyone* | 2003 |
| The Sports Nexus | Report and Update | 2004 & 2005 |

Paton & Cooke *Attendance at County Cricket – An Economic Analysis* in *Journal of Sports Economics*, 2005
Dennis et al, *Bowling workload and the risk of injury in elite fast bowlers* in *Journal of Science and Medicine in Sport*, 2003.

## Interviews

David Willis, David Brook, Richard Bevan and nine senior present or recent past executives within England cricket.

## DVDs

| | |
|---|---|
| *Cricket in the '70s – The Chappell Era* | ABC |
| *Cricket in the '80s – Rookies, Rebels & Renaissance* | ABC |

# INDEX